THE CORPORATE DIVERSITY JIGSAW

Although diversity in companies is a topic of great interest, significant aspects of the issue are often left out of the debate. *The Corporate Diversity Jigsaw* connects all the dots so that steps taken to address issues of diversity in business organisations can be more effective. Akshaya Kamalnath offers a nuanced justification of exactly what types of diversity are most useful for corporations, where they should be implemented, and how best to address diversity in ways that account for recent social movements such as #MeToo and Black Lives Matter. After a critical assessment of quotas and disclosure requirements across jurisdictions, she provides a different way to solve the problem, by encouraging companies to make improvements to their culture and internal processes. This timely book offers a balanced analysis, practical solutions, and fresh perspectives on how corporate culture and social movements impact diversity efforts.

Akshaya Kamalnath is a senior lecturer at the Australian National University College of Law. She writes about diversity in companies in legal journals, popular media, and her blog, *The Hitchhiker's Guide to Corporate Governance*.

The Corporate
Diversity Jigsaw

Akshaya Kamalnath

CAMBRIDGE
UNIVERSITY PRESS

University Printing House, Cambridge CB2 8BS, United Kingdom

One Liberty Plaza, 20th Floor, New York, NY 10006, USA

477 Williamstown Road, Port Melbourne, VIC 3207, Australia

314–321, 3rd Floor, Plot 3, Splendor Forum, Jasola District Centre,
New Delhi – 110025, India

103 Penang Road, #05–06/07, Visioncrest Commercial, Singapore 238467

Cambridge University Press is part of the University of Cambridge.

It furthers the University's mission by disseminating knowledge in the pursuit of
education, learning, and research at the highest international levels of excellence.

www.cambridge.org
Information on this title: www.cambridge.org/9781316513033
DOI: 10.1017/9781009071635

First published 2023

A catalogue record for this publication is available from the British Library.

Library of Congress Cataloging-in-Publication Data
Names: Kamalnath, Akshaya, 1987– author.
Title: The corporate diversity jigsaw / Akshaya Kamalnath,
Australian National University, Canberra.
Description: Cambridge, United Kingdom ; New York, NY : Cambridge University
Press, 2023. | Includes bibliographical references and index.
Identifiers: LCCN 2022025412 | ISBN 9781316513033 (hardback)
| ISBN 9781009071635 (ebook)
Subjects: LCSH: Corporation law – Social aspects.
| Social responsibility of business – Law and legislation.
Classification: LCC K1315 .K3635 2023 | DDC 346/.0664–dc23/eng/20220924
LC record available at https://lccn.loc.gov/2022025412

ISBN 978-1-316-51303-3 Hardback
ISBN 978-1-009-06993-9 Paperback

For my parents

CONTENTS

ACKNOWLEDGEMENTS

I gratefully acknowledge The Institute for Humane Studies for providing some financial support for this project. I am thankful to the reviewers for their comments on the proposed book and to my editor at Cambridge University Press, Matt Galloway, and the rest of the team that worked on this book. A version of Chapter 3 of this book was published as an article in the *Georgetown Journal of Gender and the Law*. A version of Chapter 4 of this book will be published in the *Seattle University Law Review*.

I would like to thank Leonid Sirota for his unwavering support while I worked on this project and for reading and commenting on most of the chapters, Charles Rickett for first telling me that I 'had a book in me', Umakanth Varottil and Allan Beever for talking me through the book publishing process, Cindy Schipani and Charlotte Villiers for enthusiastic support of the project, and Sandeep Gopalan for supervising my PhD thesis on the topic of board gender diversity, which eventually led me to think more broadly about diversity in the corporation.

I am also thankful to Tony Connoly, Sally Wheeler, Will Bateman, Pauline Ridge, and Kate Ogg for their encouragement of this project since I joined ANU.

Many others generously provided feedback and comments on different chapters – Eleanor Hickman, Kim Krawiec, Iris Chiu, Lloyd Mander, Marianne Jennings, Vivienne Brand, Tom C. W. Lin, Jennifer S. Fan, and Afra Afsharipour. I am very appreciative of their help. I am also thankful to Pauline Ridge, Kate Ogg, and Will Bateman for their encouragement.

I gratefully acknowledge Aparajita Kaul, Hitoishi Sarkar, Rajat Maloo, and Devina Srivastava for providing valuable research assistance. I would also like to acknowledge Ruth Martin for her assistance with indexing.

This book was written in three different cities – Auckland, Bangalore, and Canberra – and I have used libraries, cafés, and sunny spots in each of these cities. Having to relocate so frequently in a short span of time is exhausting and I only managed to keep writing this because of the support of friends and family in all three cities.

Finally, I am grateful to all my mentors; and to my parents for supporting and encouraging me through all my unconventional choices and during the writing of this book.

INTRODUCTION

When I presented a paper on diversity in corporations (or corporate diversity as I call it in this book) at a corporate law conference a few years ago, one of the professors in the audience told me that they had already written about the topic and had thought that there isn't much more to say about it. Listening to my paper had apparently made them think otherwise. This comment gave me pause. It occurred to me that the conversation about corporate diversity was indeed largely focused on a few specific questions:

(1) How to increase the number of women on boards?
(2) Should we have mandatory quotas for this?
(3) Do women increase firm profits?
(4) How to increase racial minority representation on corporate boards? Followed by questions (2) and (3) for racial minorities.

Since then, I have started to imagine a jigsaw puzzle in which only a few pieces are located and attached while the glaring gaps are ignored. The few pieces that are affixed only show us part of the scene, and maybe even distort it. Yet, we are mostly content to ignore the gaps, perhaps because the pieces that go into them are harder to identify. But this is no excuse if ignoring them makes us react in ways that are not only inappropriate but also counter-productive. This book aims to find various other pieces of the corporate diversity jigsaw and explain how they interact with each other, so that we can have a more thorough understanding of the issues pertinent to diversity in the corporation. In doing this, the book does not shy away from weighing the costs and benefits of all the relevant issues – something that, I believe, is lacking in much of the diversity conversation at present.

The primary message of this book is that there is more to the diversity puzzle than meets the eye, and even after we find many of the missing pieces and the interactions between each of these pieces, there is no easy solution that can be introduced through the law. Instead, this book argues in favour of firm-specific solutions that involve changes to company and board culture and suggests a range of ideas that each firm can draw from and adapt to its own workforce and unique circumstances. Encouraging companies to think about the specific problems their culture and internal structures generate and solve them in innovative ways will allow firms to distinguish themselves from others on diversity measures. Ultimately, this book calls for a more compassionate and empathetic model of corporate governance.

In writing this book, I have drawn from the work of scholars from both law and other disciplines because this topic transcends disciplines. I have also drawn from biographies and other writings of business people, and from news articles, to supplement my arguments with examples and real-life stories. However, since I am a law academic, there is a significant focus on law and theories informing the law – particularly in Chapters 4 and 6.

The book consists of three parts. Part I consists of the first three chapters. Together, these chapters introduce and define the corporate diversity jigsaw, and explain and put together some significant pieces. Starting at the very beginning, the book asks in Chapter 1, what the term diversity even means and why there is such a push for diversity in corporations. It then asks what diversity should mean at each level of the corporate hierarchy – the board, management, and the workforce. Table 1.1, the diversity rubric, can also be used as a summary of Chapter 1 and a quick reference guide that tells you how this book deals with some primary issues.

Chapter 2 then zooms in on corporate governance and examines how diversity fits into the corporate governance matrix. So, the chapter is concerned with issues relevant to diversity at the board and management levels. It also discusses the currently all-important chief diversity officer role and what it will take to make this role a useful one.

Chapter 3 looks outside the corporation at social movements (specifically #MeToo and #BlackLivesMatter) and how corporations are responding to them. This chapter thus begins to discuss diversity issues vis-à-vis employees and the wider community.

In Part II, Chapter 4 reviews legal and market initiatives introduced to address the issue of diversity (or the lack of it) in corporations. Although this piece of the puzzle is one of the most discussed ones, the conversation on this presumes that mandatory quotas or disclosure requirements accompanied by investor pressure are the only two options on the table. Chapter 4 however eschews both options because of the costs they impose on both the corporations and the diverse candidates who are hired and, instead, argues in favour of firm-specific solutions that support and retain diverse employees.

Chapter 5 examines possible firm-specific solutions. It specifically discusses three other pieces of the diversity puzzle – corporate culture, board and management culture, and the role of external consultants providing board advisory, recruitment, and other services in addressing diversity issues. The discussion in this chapter is novel inasmuch as it links the much talked about idea of corporate culture to diversity and also because it draws attention to the fact that appointing diverse candidates without sorting out board and company culture is like inviting guests to a house where they are not welcome. The guests will be upset when they see how they are received and then either leave or stay on uneasily for a while. Neither outcome is desirable. After underscoring the importance of good corporate culture for diversity to flourish in a company, the chapter also discusses the role that board consultancies can play in helping firms address internal issues and in helping diverse candidates inform themselves about potential employers and if they do take on the position, to navigate difficult environments.

The third and final part of the book, consisting of Chapter 6, provides a blueprint to reconcile corporate law with diversity and other issues at the intersection of corporations and society. In doing so, it addresses an enduring question in corporate law, namely what is the purpose of the corporation. This final chapter is a response to one of the most prominent pieces of the diversity jigsaw – a piece that seems to ask whether diversity can enhance firm profits. This chapter argues that there is a strong case for diversity and other social justice issues to be addressed by corporations even if they don't promise immediate profits. Thus, Chapter 6 provides the theoretical framework through which corporations, their regulation, and specifically the regulation of corporations with respect to diversity and other social issues should be viewed. While academic convention dictates that a chapter providing the theoretical underpinnings of the topic being examined be provided at the beginning of the book, I have taken a different approach because I think that conducting an analysis of the pieces of the corporate diversity jigsaw allows us to build on the existing theoretical understandings with the insights gleaned from the earlier analysis.

The Conclusion first, briefly highlights some of the main arguments in the book and sets out avenues for further research.

This book does not claim to find and fix all pieces of the jigsaw. In addition to the future research areas that I have highlighted in the Conclusion, I am sure that I or others will discover newer issues that are relevant to the diversity discourse as we continue to work to bring diversity in corporations.

TERMINOLOGY

I use the terms corporation, company, firm, business, and organization interchangeably in this book. I also use the terms shareholders, investors, and stockholders interchangeably. When I'm referring to board members, I might sometimes also use the term directors. To refer to members of the top management team, I use C-Suite, management, or top management. When referring to both directors and executives together, I use the terms company leadership or senior leadership. Where needed, the relevant chapter will provide a quick note on specific word usage within the chapter.

WHO SHOULD READ THIS BOOK AND HOW?

If you work in a corporation in any capacity – board, management, or anywhere else in the workforce, you would have come across the idea of diversity and might be vexed, interested, or just curious about it.

Even if you don't work in a corporation, you might have come across talk of diversity in your own sector, or in the media. If you are a university student, you will be no stranger to diversity discussions. This book speaks to all of you and offers you a different perspective on the issue. If you are an academic who researches on diversity, no matter which disciplinary lens you are using, this book speaks to you. Some of you may already have formed opinions about how diversity should be addressed, if at all it should be addressed. Irrespective of what your opinion is, and especially if it is different from mine, I hope that you will read and engage with this book. In fact, I have drawn from the work of many scholars and thinkers whose proposals I disagree with and I believe that this book is stronger because of it.

Although I have written this book with a general audience in mind and in an ideal world, would like everyone to read the book in its entirety, below, I have identified chapters that might be most significant for each of you.

You have to first read Chapter 1 or at least Table 1.1 to understand how the book defines diversity at each level of the corporation. After this, if you are an executive and/or a board director, part of a board advisory firm or board consulting firm, or an employee at a corporation wanting to understand how corporate culture can help address diversity issues, Chapters 2, 3, and 5 (specifically Section 2.3) will be useful.

If you are a lawyer or legal academic looking for an analysis of legal and market initiatives introduced to address diversity issues, you will probably find Chapter 4 most useful. Of course, other chapters (especially Chapters 3 and 5) will flesh out the need for, and avenues for, firm-specific solutions. You will also find Chapter 6, which provides insights into the theories of the corporation and how corporate law can be reconciled with diversity and other ESG issues, interesting.

PART I

1 DEFINING DIVERSITY

When we think of diversity in corporations, we often think about the board of directors needing to include more women, perhaps because that is the slice of the diversity story that has been most in the news. While diversity is indeed important for the board (the corporation's governing body), it is also important at other levels of the corporation. Many countries (e.g. Norway, the United States, and the UK) have attempted to address the lack of diversity on corporate boards through various laws or softer guidelines. However, unless we are clear about what needs to be addressed and why, we cannot effectively answer the question of how this should be done. We must therefore begin the jigsaw puzzle by first defining diversity in the corporation. In so attempting a context-specific definition, we will also briefly assess why diversity is important within the corporation.

A good starting point to the task of defining diversity is to look back at how the idea took root in the corporate context. Interest in diversity on corporate boards was not originally motivated by corporate governance concerns. Instead, after the global financial crisis (GFC) brought the extent of the power wielded by company boards to the public's attention, public discussions rightly focused on why this power should not be exercised exclusively by men. However, to make the idea of board diversity attractive to companies, narrow 'business justifications' (the idea that diversity results in increased profits) started to be developed. Corporate governance benefits eventually formed a subset of these business rationales.

Despite this early sleight of hand, diversity does have the potential to enhance corporate governance, and indeed the output of various teams within the corporation, under certain conditions. But we must be careful about how we define diversity for this purpose. Moreover, even beyond corporate governance, there is an equality-based rationale for diversity. Ultimately, how we define diversity matters for both these goals: improved corporate governance and equality in the workplace. Yet as I will argue later, the more simplistic business justifications that just assume that appointing women to the corporate board will result in increased profits are not entirely reliable and might even prove harmful.

An important facet of defining diversity is the determination of what part or parts of the corporation are to be diversified. As already stated, the initial push was to diversify boards of directors, which were seen to be symbolic of corporate power. To this day, most legal mandates and the general diversity discussion tend to focus only on the board. However, diversity at the management level and all other levels in the workforce is an important issue, even if it is not given as much prominence in the general discourse. This facet of diversity is important to the 'defining diversity' piece of the puzzle because different aspects of diversity might be relevant at different levels within the corporate hierarchy. Further, clarifying what we are trying to achieve through the diversity project at various levels of the corporation (or in other words, the rationales for corporate diversity) will be important in determining how diversity should be defined at each level. Ultimately, clarifying the what and the why can help us decide how the goals of the diversity project should be achieved.

Incidentally, defining diversity in the corporate context will help address the lurking challenge that diversity measures are 'anti-merit'; more on this later.

1.1 WHAT IS DIVERSITY IN THE CORPORATE CONTEXT?

Diversity has come to mean something distinct from its dictionary meaning.[1] The *Oxford English Dictionary* defines it as 'a range of

---

[1] *See generally* Akshaya Kamalnath, *Defining 'Diversity' in Corporate Governance: A Global Survey*, 45 J. LEGIS. 1 (2018).

different things',[2] while the *Cambridge English Dictionary* provides more detail[3]:

- The fact of many different types of things or people being included in something; a range of different things or people.
- The fact that there are many different ideas or opinions about something.

While the first prong (or Prong 1) of this definition (demographic or identity-based diversity) has become well accepted, the second prong (Prong 2) (viewpoint diversity or cognitive diversity) is usually left out of the diversity agenda. If one means to talk about viewpoint diversity, one has to specify it. Simply using the term diversity is likely to just refer to the first prong given the way that the diversity debates have generally been framed, including in the corporate context.

In the United States, usage of the term 'viewpoint diversity' in the corporate diversity discourse suggests a narrower meaning, referring specifically to political viewpoints. For example, a shareholder proposal calling for viewpoint diversity on the board of Costco noted that 'there is ample evidence that the many companies operate in ideological hegemony that eschews conservative people, thoughts, and values'.[4] The second prong of the dictionary meaning of diversity is in fact wider than this understanding. It speaks more generally to ideas and opinions. The 2018 iteration of the UK Corporate Governance Code (UK Code) seems to have adopted this wider version of the second prong, stating that board appointments and succession plans 'should promote diversity of gender, social and ethnic backgrounds, cognitive and personal strengths'.[5] While 'cognitive strengths' has not been defined, we can infer that it refers to diverse skills, knowledge, and experience, which would be the basis for people to form different ideas or opinions. This formulation goes beyond a mere political ideology. Accordingly, in this

---

[2] *Diversity*, OXFORD ENGLISH LIVING DICTIONARIES, https://en.oxforddictionaries.com/definition/diversity.

[3] *Diversity*, CAMBRIDGE DICTIONARY, https://dictionary.cambridge.org/dictionary/english/diversity.

[4] *FEP Calls on Costco to Consider Viewpoint Diversity*, VALUEWALK (Jan. 21, 2020), www.valuewalk.com/2020/01/viewpoint-diversity/.

[5] UK Code, Principle J.

book, viewpoint diversity will refer to the wider dictionary meaning (rather than the narrow usage seen in the United States).

Despite the dictionary meaning, and the reference to 'cognitive strengths' in the UK Code, cognitive diversity or viewpoint diversity has not gained as much prominence in the diversity discourse. This is a mistake. In the corporate diversity discourse (particularly corporate governance), even within the first prong, the focus has almost exclusively been on gender. This has now changed in the wake of activism and regulatory intervention in the United States in this regard (discussed in more detail in Chapters 3 and 4). In the UK too, there is rising awareness about racial diversity. The Parker Review on ethnic diversity in business leadership, commissioned by the UK government and published in 2017, made recommendations to increase ethnic diversity in UK boards.[6] Further, the McGregor-Smith Review on Race in the Workplace drew attention to racial diversity in the workplace more generally and proposed measures to retain talented employees that belong to racial minorities.[7] Despite this, the main focus is usually around gender diversity. Further, numerical targets and quotas specified by law typically only focus on gender diversity and particularly on increasing the number of women, with two recent laws/rules focusing on race, ethnicity, and LGBTQ+ people.[8] Other types of diversity based on cultural backgrounds, age, nationality, and so forth are usually only referred to in passing. It is important to note here that the term 'gender' in the context of corporate diversity debates of most countries usually refers to adding women directors to the board, rather than to LGBTQ+ people. This book will also use the phrase 'gender diversity' to refer to women and men in the corporation and make specific reference to LGBTQ+ people when appropriate.

The second prong, cognitive diversity, makes it into the corporate governance discussions only in terms of gender and, occasionally, racially diverse members of boards bringing different perspectives to the table. This is probably because cognitive diversity is not outwardly observable. The different aspects of diversity within the first prong

---

[6] *See* The Parker Review Committee, A Report into the Ethnic Diversity of UK Boards (Oct. 12, 2017).

[7] *See* The McGregor-Smith Review, Race in the Workplace (Feb. 28, 2017).

[8] Specifically, the law in California and Nasdaq's diversity rule provide for this. See Chapter 4.

(consisting of facets like gender, race, age, etc.) also have the potential to provide different viewpoints. This is because these facets speak to the different experiences of the people in question. These diverse viewpoints provide value (or a 'diversity bonus') in the context of team decision-making within corporations, particularly because many decisions involve 'understanding the actions, preferences, and capabilities of diverse people', namely employees and various stakeholders.[9] Diversity facets such as skills, experience, age, and economic and geographical background are in fact even more likely to result in diverse viewpoints than gender and race diversity – particularly when the women or minority candidates for board membership went to the same universities and are part of the same elite networks as their white, male counterparts.[10]

Despite the UK Code explicitly mentioning diversity in terms of cognitive and personal strengths, the value of viewpoint diversity in various parts of the corporation still needs to be better understood. A discussion of the rationales for diversity in corporations will help tease out the value of both viewpoint diversity and demographic diversity.

1.2 WHAT ARE THE RATIONALES FOR DIVERSITY IN THE CORPORATION?

Most justifications and arguments for corporate diversity can be categorised under two broad heads: equality and business benefits. Both justifications are employed to further Prong 1 diversity, especially gender diversity, even though some of the business benefits arguments might be more suitable for Prong 2 diversity or cognitive diversity. Also, as I argue in the following text, both rationales are also pertinent for Prong 2 diversity.

---

[9] SCOTT E. PAGE, THE DIVERSITY BONUS: HOW GREAT TEAMS PAY OFF IN THE KNOWLEDGE ECONOMY 24 (Princeton University Press, 2017). Page discusses the diversity bonus in the context of teams performing complex tasks. Many ideas in his book are pertinent to decision-making at various levels of the corporation.

[10] As Page explains, identity-based diversity can provide 'diversity bonuses' because they are often linked to other types of diversity that are not outwardly visible. Using the iceberg analogy, he further explains that we may see a person's skin colour, gender, and age; hear the person's accent; but cannot see their values and beliefs, which are often influenced by life experiences beyond what is immediately visible. Page, *id.*, 138.

1.2.1 Equality

Some corporate diversity laws go to the extent of imposing mandatory gender quotas on company boards. In other laws there are less drastic requirements like disclosure of diversity data. Quotas have already been used for women members in legislatures in a few countries and have been justified with the argument that structural discrimination faced by women and other disadvantaged groups has to be accounted for.[11] Similarly, in the context of the workplace, structural barriers that women face include societal expectations that women should provide most of the housework and care (for children and the elderly) within the home. The effects of COVID-19 have also set many women further back in this regard because of childcare becoming unavailable during periods of government-mandated lockdown.[12] Businesses require long working hours, with managerial positions demanding round-the-clock availability with no place for family responsibilities.[13] Further, the ideal worker was (and in some quarters still continues to be) seen to be able to fit into the following job model where 'unfailing availability and total geographical mobility at all times is required in addition to a linear career path with no breaks'.[14] Indira Nooyi recounts in her biography that when she first joined PepsiCo in 1994, all fifteen of the top executive positions in the corporation were held by white American men who fit into this job model. To point out how similar these men were, she says[15]:

> Almost all wore blue or grey suits with white shirts and silk ties and had short hair or no hair.... Most of them golfed, fished, played

---

[11] CONSTITUTING EQUALITY: GENDER EQUALITY AND COMPARATIVE CONSTITUTIONAL LAW 59 (Susan H. Williams ed., Cambridge University Press, 2011).

[12] Amanda Taub, *Pandemic Will 'Take Our Women 10 Years Back' in the Workplace*, N.Y. TIMES (July 29, 2020), www.nytimes.com/2020/09/26/world/covid-women-childcare-equality.html; MCKINSEY & COMPANY, WOMEN IN THE WORKPLACE 2021 (Sept. 27, 2021) www.mckinsey.com/featured-insights/diversity-and-inclusion/women-in-the-workplace. [One of the findings of the study was that women were 'even more burned out now than they were a year ago (i.e., before the COVID-19 pandemic), and the gap in burnout between women and men has almost doubled'. Further, after the pandemic began 'one in three women has considered leaving the workforce or downshifting their career – a significant increase from one in four in the first few months of the pandemic'.]

[13] J. M. Hoobler, Grace Lemmon, & Sandy Wayne, *Women's Underrepresentation in Upper Management: New Insights on a Persistent Problem*, 40(3) ORGAN. DYN. 151, 152 (2011).

[14] Bernali Choudhury, *New Rationales for Women on Boards*, 34(3) OJLS 511, 540 (2014).

[15] INDIRA NOOYI, MY LIFE IN FULL: WORK, FAMILY, AND OUR FUTURE (Hachette, 2021) 135.

tennis, hiked, and jogged. Some hunted for quail together. Many
were married with children. I don't believe any of their wives
worked in paid jobs outside their homes.

She rightly explains that this was the result of a society crafted around a
family model where there was a female homemaker and a male bread-
winner.[16] Because of this division, the men could fit into the mould of
the ideal worker where they were 'available on a regular schedule with
no outside noise during set hours'. Additionally, the men would be
able to spend time outside official work hours, mingling with clients,
competitors, and friends.[17] Because of this framing of the ideal worker,
Nooyi notes that 'even the most accomplished women were milling
about in middle management'.[18] While more women may be making it
to executive positions than they had in 1994, the definition of the ideal
worker has not changed very much.

Another barrier often cited in the context of improving gender
diversity in the workplace is bias against appointing and promoting
women to management and board positions. This bias is also often
encountered by other sorts of diverse individuals (for example, racial
minorities). Managers and board members, who appoint new directors, do not always act rationally.[19] They might be influenced by conscious and unconscious bias towards candidates based on their race
and/or gender. This may also be true for hiring at the management
level and sometimes in lower levels of the corporate hierarchy as well.
Moreover, the recruitment and promotion processes at managerial
level are informed by the image of the 'stereotypically masculine'
successful manager.[20] The attributes of the dominant race also often
define the image of the successful candidate for these roles, and these
affect recruiters' perceptions of 'competence'.[21] This results in fewer
women and racial minorities being appointed to senior executive roles,
which further leads to fewer women and minority candidates in the

---

[16] *Id.*, at 136.
[17] *Id.*, at 136.
[18] *Id.*, at 135.
[19] Mike Noon, *The Fatal Flaws of Diversity and the Business Case for Ethnic Minorities*, 21(4) WORK EMPLOY. SOC. 773, 779 (2007).
[20] Joan Acker, *From Glass Ceiling to Inequality Regimes*, 51 SOCIOL. TRAV. 199, 208 (2009).
[21] *Id.*, at 209.

pool of candidates considered for board positions.[22] Qualified women or minority candidates encounter such obstacles while trying to secure a board or senior executive position. For instance, Shefaly Yogendra, current vice chair of London Metropolitan University, stated in an interview that, when she first moved to the UK from India, she ran up against people not believing her CV and asking if she was in the country legally.[23]

Another barrier that diverse candidates including women and racial minorities come up against is that elite bodies like boards tend to hire through their social networks, and social networks are invariably composed of people with similar characteristics and interests. There is an element of trust or reliability in director selections, which often arises from personal relationships. In the absence of such personal relationships, boards tend to use similarities between the candidate and themselves as a proxy for trust.[24] Thus, the manner in which board nominations are made can itself pose a barrier to women securing board positions. In the UK the Lord Davies review, titled 'Women on Boards' which specifically focused on barriers faced by women in attaining board positions, found that 'the informal networks influential in board appointments, the lack of transparency around selection criteria and the way in which executive search firms operate' were the major barriers to women reaching board positions.[25] All of these issues are pertinent to racial minorities as well.

Apart from addressing the structural barriers, the lack of women and minorities in corporate boards and executive positions, which are the most visible positions of power in the corporate sector, means that young women and people belonging to minority groups are denied role models that they can relate to. Although the situation has improved for women on boards, executive positions are still male dominated. The importance of role models comes through in many real-life examples of women or persons belonging to minority groups

---

[22] Jean du Plessis, Ingo Saenger, & Richard Foster, *Board Diversity or Gender Diversity? Perspectives from Europe, Australia and South Africa*, 17 DEAKIN L. REV. 207, 240 (2012).

[23] LaToya Harding, *'People Didn't Believe My CV', Says Board Director*, BBC NEWS (June 16, 2021), www.bbc.com/news/business-57486592.

[24] Choudhuri, *supra* note 14.

[25] LORD DAVIES, WOMEN ON BOARDS (Report, 2011), 6. (Hereinafter, 'DAVIES REPORT').

recounting what led them to their chosen profession. For example, Gwynne Shotwell, president and COO at SpaceX, recounted a visit to an event organised by the local Society of Women Engineers where she was inspired by a female engineer who was running her own business.[26] Even within a company, the lack of female or minority members in top management and the board may signal to employees (or potential employees) that it is not realistic to aim for those roles. Asako Hoshino, who is currently a top executive at Nissan Motor Co. Ltd., recounts that when she was first hired by Nissan, she 'didn't have a single female boss…, so if you ask me if my career path was visible, it was completely unclear'.[27]

While these stories highlight the importance of diversity at the top, it is also important to focus on diversity in the workforce more generally. One immediately apparent aim should be to address structural barriers so that diverse candidates can rise up the ranks and be available for top management and board positions. The issue of having to negotiate domestic care responsibilities alongside work is relevant for women, but the other barriers of coming up against conscious or unconscious bias in hiring and promotions stands in the way of most types of diverse candidates. Addressing these barriers at all levels of the workforce would allow diverse candidates to be retained and eventually rise up the corporate ladder according to their merit.

Allowing and nurturing viewpoint diversity within the workplace could also be brought under the umbrella of the equality rationale for diversity, although this has not been canvassed in the mainstream corporate diversity literature. To the extent that certain viewpoints come from demographically diverse people, it could be argued that silencing such views adds to the pre-existing structural barriers against these candidates. However, even when a white male employee espouses non-mainstream views, it could similarly be argued that shutting down such views would work as a barrier to that employee and anyone else who thinks differently. A high-profile example that many of us might recall is that of James Damore, the Google employee who was fired for

---

[26] ERIC BERGER, LIFTOFF 100 (William Collins, 2021).
[27] Kana Inagaki, *Many Thought Women Should Simply Decide a Car's Colour*, FINANCIAL TIMES (June 7, 2021), www.ft.com/content/c32665f8-da27-42a1-bf71-41a4a9b6d000.

circulating a document that criticised the company for vilifying those with differing views on the issue of gender diversity.[28] What is interesting for the present discussion is Damore's claim that 'Google's left bias has created a politically correct monoculture that maintains its hold by shaming dissenters into silence'.[29] The fact that he was fired for making this observation (and for citing some research about differences between men and women) seems to prove his point.[30] This and other similar incidents ultimately illustrate that persons with diverse viewpoints might also experience exclusion and retaliation if their counterviews are shut down.[31]

Discrimination against employees who express a different view need not just be limited to the employee's broader views on political and social issues. One could imagine similar exclusion and retaliation against an employee who reports problems regarding potential misconduct, compliance failures, etc. when the rest of the team is happy to go along with what is being practiced. In a case like that, not only does such treatment of the employee go against the broader goal of equality in the workplace, it comes in the way of detecting potential business and legal risks.

---

[28] James Damore, *Google's Ideological Echo Chamber* (July 2017), https://s3.documentcloud .org/documents/3914586/Googles-Ideological-Echo-Chamber.pdf.

[29] *Id.*

[30] Akshaya Kamalnath, *A Memo to Google – Firing Employees with Conservative Views Is Anti-diversity*, THE CONVERSATION (Aug. 11, 2017), https://theconversation.com/a-memo-to-google-firing-employees-with-conservative-views-is-anti-diversity-82318.

[31] Damore's incident is but one example of a larger phenomenon that has come to be called as 'cancel culture', that is the shutting down of some minority views. As Haidt and Lukianoff explain, the phenomenon often plays out in this way: 'employees face calls for discipline or termination for expressing non-conforming opinions, even when those opinions are expressed away from the workplace or with no hostile intent'. Haidt and Lukianoff also provides other examples of cancel culture including that of a data scientist, David Shor who was 'fired from Civis Analytics for a tweet sharing academic research indicating violent protest decreased votes for Democrats while non-violent protest increased it'. See Jonathan Haidt and Greg Lukianoff, *How to Keep Your Corporation Out of the Culture War*, PERSUASION (Dec. 3, 2021), www.persuasion.community/p/ haidt-and-lukianoff-how-to-end-corporate. For another example of an employee being fired as a result of cancel culture, this one from Apple, *see infra* Chapter 3, Section 3. See also Stefan J. Padfield, *An Introduction to Viewpoint Diversity Shareholder Proposals*, 22 TRANSACTIONS: TENN. J. BUS. L. 271 (2021). Padfield discusses how cancel culture results in discrimination based on specific viewpoints expressed by the employee in question and outlines shareholder proposals highlighting this issue.

1.2.2 Business Benefits

The business rationale is based on the functional benefits of diversity for companies. Most people making these arguments ultimately aim to show that diversity (mostly in the context of board gender diversity) would result in increased profits for the firm. This is what I call the narrow business case for diversity. Some cite other benefits like reputational benefits and improved corporate governance, or in other words, the broader business benefits rationale.

To borrow the categorisation of the Davies Report in the UK, most of the arguments under the business rationale can be classified into four categories: (i) improving performance; (ii) accessing the widest talent pool; (iii) being more responsive to the market; and (iv) improving corporate governance.[32] When we assess each of these arguments, it will be obvious that many of them are relevant to positions beyond the board and to diversity beyond gender diversity.

1.2.2.1 Firm Performance

The first claim, that diversity improves performance (measured in terms of firm profits), is perhaps the least compelling rationale for corporate diversity in general and board diversity in particular. Studies that are cited in this regard tend to focus on the effect of women directors on firm performance, mostly relying on simple correlations to prove their claims. As it happens, there is no dearth of studies making a contrary finding. However, such inconvenient studies are often ignored. As Fried rightly noted in an article, NASDAQ, while proposing diversity requirements, selectively cited favourable studies and ignored studies showing that board diversity actually impaired firm performance. Ironically, Fried notes that many of the studies that NASDAQ failed to cite were authored by female economists.[33] The studies that Fried points to provide a nuanced assessment of the impact of diversity and go much beyond simple correlations. For instance, Fried discusses a

---

[32] DAVIES REPORT, *supra* note 25, at 8.
[33] See generally Jesse M. Fried, *Will Nasdaq's Diversity Rules Harm Investors?*, European Corporate Governance Institute – Law Working Paper No. 579/2021 (Mar. 31, 2021), https://papers.ssrn.com/sol3/papers.cfm?abstract_id=3812642.

study by Adams and Ferreira which provides some benefits of board diversity (female directors result in increased attendance at board meetings), but also finds that board gender diversity leads to excessive monitoring of executives which in turn, will generally have a negative impact.[34] I will return to this study in Chapter 2, but it is interesting to note here that NASDAQ cites the aspects of the study that show positive impacts of board gender diversity while ignoring the potentially negative conclusions from the same study.[35]

Additionally, relying on studies that simply show correlations between women directors and firm profits (which does not tell us anything about whether women directors actually *cause* increased firm profits) makes what is generally referred to as the business case, flimsy. As Rhodes and Packel note, it is important to control variables that might explain such correlation and even then, results could be skewed by any extreme values in the group.[36]

Relying on this type of argument is also dangerous because it implies that women and other minorities should be hired on the corporate board only because they increase the firm profits. On that account, any studies showing a negative correlation between diverse board members and firm performance would mean that there is no valid argument for diversity on corporate boards. Ultimately, firm profits depend on many variables beyond the demographic aspects of members of the corporate board, and selectively using studies that show a positive correlation between the two factors is not only misleading but also dangerous for the diversity project.

There might, however, be certain areas within a firm which benefit from diversity and might (under certain conditions) result in increased profits in the long term. For instance, constructive disagreement within teams is likely to result in more innovative decisions.[37] Diverse teams are likely to have more views on offer, but whether the expression of

---

[34] Renee Adams & Daniel Ferreira, *Women in the Boardroom and Their Impact on Governance and Performance*, 94 J. FIN. ECON. 291 (2009).

[35] Fried, *supra* note 31.

[36] Deborah H. Rhode & Amanda K. Packel, *Diversity on Corporate Boards: How Much Difference Does Difference Make?*, 39(2) DEL. J. CORP. LAW 377, 384 (2014).

[37] Amy Gallo, *Why We Should Be Disagreeing More at Work*, HARV. BUS. REV (Jan. 3, 2018), https://hbr.org/2018/01/why-we-should-be-disagreeing-more-at-work.

dissenting views is encouraged would depend on the leadership and culture within the team and firm more generally. In this context, diversity would mainly refer to viewpoint diversity. An example of how such diverse thinking helped in an organisation is that of some engineers in NASA's Johnson Space Center realising in the 1980s that the mission control setup was outdated. Despite their concerns being disregarded by the organisation, they went on to develop new software (named pirate system) which eventually went on to win an award. The group of engineers later designed the mission control system for the International Space Station.[38] Amazon gives us another example of diverse thinking helping an organisation. The idea for Amazon Prime (which allows customers who paid an annual fee to receive their orders much faster) came from Charlie Ward, an engineer at Amazon rather than from top management. Unlike NASA however, Amazon encouraged employees to pitch ideas that might improve the business via a digital suggestion box that was available to all employees. The idea has been a massive success.[39] These two contrasting examples tell different stories. While the NASA story is of employees persisting with ideas despite concerns of being disregarded, the Amazon story is one of the management seeking out ideas. Thus, having diverse thinking within teams is not enough. To enjoy its benefits, companies should foster a culture where dissenting views are encouraged. Even demographic diversity (i.e. people of different genders, ages, races, etc.) is likely to bring different perspectives to the team because of the candidates' diverse experiences. Just like with viewpoint diversity, it is up to companies to ensure that diverse candidates feel safe and comfortable to share their ideas, if they truly want to gain returns from diversity.[40]

Even beyond those who disagree with the management view on firms, encouraging diverse views can also mean that some employees will be encouraged to make the case for innovative changes within the

---

[38] Loizos Heracleous & David Robson, *Organisations Tend to See Rebels as Troublemakers – But Suppressing These Individuals and Their Ideas Could Backfire*, BBC NEWS (June 2, 2021), www.bbc.com/worklife/article/20210528-positive-deviants-why-rebellious-workers-spark-gr-ideas.

[39] VIVEK WADHWA, ISMAIL AMLA, & ALEX SALKEVER, FROM INCREMENTAL TO EXPONENTIAL 132–33 (Harper Business, 2020).

[40] CAROL FULP, SUCCESS THROUGH DIVERSITY: WHY THE MOST INCLUSIVE COMPANIES WILL WIN 129–30 (Beacon Press, Boston, 2018).

company. A corporation that promotes diverse views and encourages such 'intrapreneurs' will be able to reap the benefits of those innovations in the long run.[41]

There are some arguments to the effect that gender automatically brings a different work ethic (for instance, women are said to be more collaborative and/or caring) and decision-making style (for instance, women are said to be more risk-averse).[42] While this may be true for some women, propagating these essentialist arguments could also reinforce stereotypes and even prove harmful for women who do not fit the mould.[43] The point that there can be a diversity of views and characteristics within a specific identity group holds for race, age, or any other type of demographic diversity.[44] Welcoming this diversity will help firms gain from each individual's experiences and ideas, irrespective of whether or not such individuals confirm within the stereotypes associated with their various identity groups (such as women, Asians, and Gen-Zers). For example, not all women have childcare responsibilities, or have an ethic of care, or are risk-averse. Having said that, being aware of some general characteristic of groups will help corporations create optimal work conditions for them. Here, an obvious example is to provide flexible work options for those with childcare responsibilities. It is a matter of striking a balance between accommodating some group characteristics while allowing for plenty of diversity within groups.

1.2.2.2 Talent Pool

The second argument, that is the talent pool rationale is that if board gender diversity measures can force boards to look beyond their closed circles and 'boys' clubs', then companies will be able to tap

---

[41] See Gerald F. Davis & Christopher J. White, *The New Face of Corporate Activism*, 13(4) STANF. SOC. INNOV. REV. 40–45 (2015).

[42] For examples of such arguments, see Neelie Kroes, European Commissioner for Competition, Speech at the Women for Europe Event (July 16, 2009), http://europa.eu/rapid/press-release_SPEECH-09-344_en.htm?locale=en.

[43] Women and men can have varying degrees of feminine and masculine traits in them. In other words, not all women are feminine and not all women are masculine. See Mark McCann & Sally Wheeler, *Gender Diversity in the FTSE 100: The Business Case Claim Explored*, 38(4) J.L. & SOC. 542, 550 (2011).

[44] Heterodox Academy, *A Conversation with John McWhorter: Viewpoint Diversity among Black Intellectuals*, YOUTUBE (Feb. 16, 2021), www.youtube.com/watch?v=-D9LZdjnxKk.

into potential candidates who would otherwise have been overlooked. Based on this logic, it is argued that since the push for diverse boards would ensure that women and racial minorities are not overlooked, the resulting board would consist of the most qualified candidates. Conversely, a low percentage of women or other types of diverse candidates on the board would imply that the company has failed to make full use of the talent pool available to it.[45] This argument can be extended to management positions and other levels in the workforce to the extent that diverse candidates come up against barriers despite being talented, although this is not the subject of as much discussion as board diversity.

1.2.2.3 *Reflecting the Market*

The third category of business benefits arguments suggests that a diverse board would be more reflective of the different stakeholders of the company, particularly the labour market and the consumer base. In the context of gender diversity, it is argued that since at least half of the labour market and consumer base currently consists of women, the board should reflect this diversity so as to ensure that better decisions are made by considering interests of the entire consumer base.[46] Of course, this argument will not apply to corporations that are not consumer-facing. Even in those corporations that directly work with consumers, operational decisions about say, marketing a product to the appropriate consumer base and customer satisfaction would be taken by the management rather than the board. Thus, this argument will be relevant to corporate diversity more broadly, and specifically to managerial positions, rather than to the board of directors. It also extends beyond gender diversity since society (where both the labour and consumer markets come from) is diverse in many ways.

A recent example of a company catering to consumer diversity is that of a beauty and personal care company, Unilever, which decided

---

[45] FINANCIAL REPORTING COUNCIL, FEEDBACK STATEMENT: GENDER DIVERSITY ON BOARDS (Oct. 2011) 4, www.frc.org.uk/getattachment/4a64f194-a39c-4fe8-8a62-ed8105724d49/Feedback-Statement-on-Boardroom-Diversity-October-2011.pdf.

[46] DAVIES REPORT, *supra* note 25, at 9. The report notes with respect to UK that women are responsible for 70% of household purchasing decisions.

to drop the word 'normal' from its products after a study showed that it made people feel excluded.[47] An example of lack of diversity in an entire industry resulting in products that did not cater to one section of society is that of virtual reality headsets. Apparently, these headsets caused four times more side effects in women than in men, and the issue had not been identified during production.[48]

1.2.2.4 Reputational Benefits

Related to the argument that board diversity should reflect stakeholders is the argument that board diversity, because of the board members being in the public eye, has reputational benefits for the company.[49] However, any reputational value gained through symbolic appointments is subjective and might also be achieved when a non-diverse but well-known director is hired.[50] It is also worth noting here that such reputational capital gained through a symbolic appointment is delicate and might easily be lost, for instance, if diversity-related problems within the company's workforce have not been addressed despite having a diverse board.

1.2.2.5 Corporate Governance Benefits

The last of the business benefits arguments is that diversity enhances corporate governance. This argument is most relevant to diversity in the board of directors, since it speaks to the role of the board within the corporation. The general idea is that a diverse group of directors will be able to bring diverse perspectives to board decision-making, and so improve it. This is particularly important because corporate boards should be wary of what is known as 'groupthink'. Irving Janis defined groupthink as follows:

'A mode of thinking that people engage in when they are deeply involved in a cohesive in-group, when the members' striving for

---

[47] Derrick Bryson Taylor, *Maker of Dove Soap Will Drop the Word 'Normal' from Beauty Products*, N.Y. TIMES (Mar. 9, 2021), www.nytimes.com/2021/03/09/business/unilever-normal-positive-beauty.html.

[48] Mary Anne Franks, *The Desert of the Unreal: Inequality in Virtual and Augmented Reality*, 51 UCD L. REV. 499, 530–31 (2017).

[49] Stephen Bear et al., *The Impact of Board Diversity and Gender Composition on Corporate Social Responsibility and Firm Reputation*, 97 J. BUS. ETHICS 207 (2010).

[50] James A. Fanto, *Justifying Board Diversity*, 89 N.C. L. REV. 901, 911 (2011).

unanimity overrides their motivation to realistically appraise alternative courses of actions.'[51]

Corporate boards are especially susceptible to groupthink. The board appointment processes often result in members belonging to the same social and professional networks, and thus becoming a cohesive group. Most decisions are made by consensus and directors belonging to the same social circles would hesitate to rock the boat. Viewpoint diversity can help counter groupthink, if members with different views are willing to voice them. Thus, all facets of diversity would be relevant inasmuch as they can foster viewpoint diversity. For gender diversity, Norwegian directors interviewed in a qualitative study by Dhir suggest that gender-diverse boards held diverse views and perspectives which provided a broader basis for decision-making.[52] One explanation for women bringing different viewpoints is that female directors typically come from outside the groups and networks male directors belong to, and this makes them 'outsiders'.[53] At the same time, a woman and/or member of a minority group might not be very diverse in terms of viewpoints if they happen to have similar educational and socio-economic background and belong to the same social and professional networks, as their white male counterparts. This is partly because they become part of the 'in group' when they understand the 'norms, values, beliefs and ways' of the elite group that board directors and management team usually belong to.[54]

Another explanation is that, since female directors must overcome many systemic barriers to attain board positions, they tend to be highly motivated and prepared for meetings and are more willing to express different perspectives than their male counterparts.[55] Both or either one of the two explanations could also be pertinent for other types of

---

[51] IRVING L. JANIS, VICTIMS OF GROUPTHINK (Houghton Mifflin Company, 1978) 78.

[52] AARON A. DHIR, CHALLENGING BOARDROOM HOMOGENEITY 280 (Cambridge University Press, 2015).

[53] NANETTE FONDAS, *Women on Boards of Directors: Gender Bias or Power Threat?*, in WOMEN ON CORPORATE BOARDS OF DIRECTORS: INTERNATIONAL CHALLENGES AND OPPORTUNITIES 172, 173 (Ronald J. Burke & Mary C. Mattis eds., Kluwer Academic Publishers, 2000).

[54] Eleanore Hickman, *The Problems with Appointing on Merit. A Human Capital Analysis*, 21(1) J. CORP. LAW STUD. 119–20 (2021).

[55] *Id.*

demographic diversity such as race, age, and experience. For instance, an academic who becomes a board director might prepare more for meetings knowing that it is new terrain, and might also belong to different social and professional networks, thus giving them a different view. This could also be true for a board member who is much younger than the others or one who has grown up in a different country or comes from a different socio-economic background.

Further, the thinking is that while members of the in-group might be hesitant to disagree with their friends, an 'outsider' director might not have the same problem. In other words, diversity could make board 'psychologically independent' of the CEO, thus acting as a check on CEO decisions, which is part of the board's broad corporate governance mandate.[56] Of course, if the board culture discourages dissent, then it may simply ignore the dissenting views of the outsider. It will then take board members who are professionally successful before taking on the position, and willing to burn bridges if needed, to be able to overcome such a culture.[57]

The value of dissent and disagreement is also pertinent in management teams, sometimes more so than in boards, because the diverse views might help generate ideas for operational matters, and because some individuals in the management team are likely to be aware of problematic practices and disagreement might help root out these problems.[58] Ultimately viewpoint diversity, even if it exists, can help a company reap dividends only when the board and the company create a culture where these diverse views are encouraged and considered.

Encouraging diverse views at various levels of the workforce might also enhance corporate governance if management and directors are willing to listen to such views via complaint mechanisms or other channels and act upon them. This could help address issues *ex ante* and prevent legal and reputational fallout. Google's James Damore incident is

---

[56] Erica Beecher-Monas, *Marrying Diversity and Independence in the Boardroom: Just How Far Have You Come, Baby?*, 86(2) Or. L. Rev. 373 (2007).

[57] Justice Kirby makes this point in the context of the judiciary. See The Hon Justice Michael Kirby, *Modes of Appointment and Training of Judges – A Common Law Perspective*, 26 Commw. L. Bull. 540, 542–43 (2000).

[58] Akshaya Kamalnath, *Corporate Governance Case for Board Gender Diversity: Evidence from Delaware Cases*, 82 Alb. L. Rev. 23, 78–80 (2018).

an example of a company having to deal with reputational fallout by not addressing issues raised by diverse employees (from a viewpoint diversity perspective). To allow for viewpoint diversity at levels below top management and harness its benefits, companies should have multiple complaint/internal reporting mechanisms, so that the senior management and board become aware of potential issues. In other words, boards and executives should have the will to listen to employee problems and put mechanisms in place that enable them do so.[59] This has begun to be discussed in the context of corporate culture but not as much in the diversity discourse. An inclusive culture is in fact essential to allow a diverse workforce to flourish. Another useful example is that of Uber where complaints regarding sexual harassment were not taken seriously and acted upon, eventually resulting in both reputational and legal consequences when an employee detailed her allegations in a blog post and subsequently initiated legal proceedings.[60] Board members and executives with diverse experiences that made them sensitive to issues of bullying, harassment, and even diverse ideologies would have been able to effectively respond to both the above situations early on.

1.3 DEFINING DIVERSITY AT DIFFERENT LEVELS IN THE CORPORATION

We can think of three levels at the corporation, for the present purpose, in order to identify the facets of diversity relevant to each.

First, the level that has garnered the most attention so far is the board of directors. Cognitive or viewpoint diversity matters most for the board if enhanced corporate governance is the aim. The board should be able to assess and, where necessary, point out the flaws in

---

[59] Adam Grant, *Who's the Boss*, WORK LIFE WITH ADAM GRANT (May 25, 2021), https://podcasts.google.com/feed/aHR0cHM6Ly9mZWVkcy5mZWVkYnVybmVyLmNvbS-S9Xb3JrbGlmZVdpdGhBZGFtR3JhbnQ.

[60] Marisa Kendall, *Uber CEO Admits Mistakes, Vows Reforms Following Sexual Harassment Claims*, THE MERCURY NEWS (Feb. 21, 2017), www.mercurynews.com/2017/02/21/uber-ceo-admits-mistakes-vows-reform-following-sexual-harassment-claims; Daisuke Wakabayashi, *Former Uber Engineer's Lawsuit Claims Sexual Harassment*, N.Y. TIMES (May 21, 2018), www.nytimes.com/2018/05/21/technology/uber-sexual-harassment-lawsuit.htm.

management proposals. Leslie has recounted that the Wright brothers' father made them argue fiercely and then swap sides in the middle of an argument. This allowed them to objectively assess the merits and weaknesses of each other's opinions without becoming wedded to one position. Ultimately, this helped them make their machine fly in 1903.[61] The Wright brothers' father might have been on to something. Years later, Oesterle recommended that a director, designated as 'devil's advocate', and having the role of arguing the opposing (possibly uncomfortable) side might help counter groupthink on boards.[62] At present, the law in most countries requires that boards of large public companies be populated with a certain percentage of independent directors (defined as those who have no material financial interest in the company[63]), who are expected to inject independent thinking into board discussions. In other words, they are expected to play some diluted version of a Devil's Advocate. Ultimately, the board will collectively benefit from diverse views being brought to the table so that all aspects of a decision might be assessed objectively.

This viewpoint diversity could come from women and racial minority candidates. As explained earlier, their outsider status might mean that they are less hesitant to ask questions of their colleagues than their male peers, who may prefer to just go along, rather than question their friends. However, women and racial minorities who do make it to board positions might themselves belong to the same networks as that of their white male peers, thus lacking full outsider status. Despite this, their background and experience unique to their identity group might promote diverse thinking. Finally, gender and race diversity (irrespective of whether they also bring a diversity of viewpoints) would matter most if the aim is to signal a commitment to equality.

The second level is the top management or the C-suite, which makes operational decisions within the company and would benefit

---

[61] IAN LESLIE, CONFLICTED: WHY ARGUMENTS ARE TEARING US APART AND HOW THEY CAN BRING US TOGETHER (Harper Collins, 2021).

[62] Dale A. Oesterle, *Should Courts Do Behavioural Analysis of Boardroom Conduct*, 9 J. BUS. & TECH. L. 51 (2014).

[63] Although this definition is slightly different across jurisdictions, it mostly centres around financial independence rather than on psychological independence.

from diverse views concerning management decisions. Here, view-point diversity would be most relevant to ensure that well-informed decisions are made. At the same time, certain types of demographic diversity amongst top executives (like gender and race) might facilitate addressing issues of harassment, diversity, and inclusion. However, such an expectation from diverse board members and executives will mean that they are unfairly burdened. This will be discussed in detail later. In smaller companies where boards are more involved in these sorts of issues, similar arguments can be made for board directors as well.

The third level is the workforce in general, which could include employees at various levels in the corporate hierarchy. Here, both prongs of diversity matter. On the one hand, it is important to have gender and race diversity in the workforce and ensure that there are policies to ensure that there is no discrimination. This will ensure that talented individuals belonging to underrepresented groups are retained in the firm and eventually make it to leadership positions. On the other hand, the story of the group of engineers who at NASA whose views were initially not heard, but who went on to develop the successful software, suggests that viewpoint diversity is also very important in the workforce if the company wants to identify promising ideas and con-cerns early on. However, for viewpoint diversity within the workforce to matter, there should be channels through which employees at vari-ous levels may communicate their dissentient view, or identification of what they see as a problem, all the way up to the board. Additionally, the board and top management should have the will to sift through these diverse views (whether they are complaints or suggestions) and decide which ones need addressing.

The analysis of the type of diversity that is important at each level and the reasons for their importance are also captured in Table 1.1 provided at the end of this chapter. As this analysis shows, there can be no formula for diversity. The type of diversity that is most important can differ at the board, top management, and work force level. It will also depend on what is most suitable for each type of company. How a company's systems are able to harness the benefits of diversity will also matter.

Table 1.1 Diversity rubric

Type of diversity	Board	Management	Company's workforce	Does it need other factors to provide value?
Prong 1 – Identity diversity (race, sex, age, ethnicity, nationality, etc.)	Useful for signalling commitment to equality. May be useful if it also provides cognitive diversity.	May be useful if it also provides cognitive diversity.	Very useful to prevent discrimination and promote retain talent.	Yes. An inclusive work culture is important to get value from Prong 1 diversity.
Prong 2 Cognitive/ viewpoint diversity (Experiential background and qualifications can be two indicators of this.)	Very useful	Most useful	Very useful to capture ideas and concerns from the company's workforce.	Yes. A culture that encourages and embraces diverse views is important to get value from Prong 2 diversity.

1.4 DIVERSITY AND MERIT

As a consequence of understanding diversity and the relevance of its various facets at the three levels of the corporation (board, management, and everything below management), we should now be able to understand and respond to the most common anti-diversity argument – that it goes against merit. Usually, these anti-merit arguments are made against mandatory quotas for diverse candidates. As I will explain in Chapter 4, there are many problems with mandatory quotas and the anti-merit argument might sometimes be true in that context. However, they are sometimes also made against less rigid diversity-related laws or policies and hence worth addressing.

In response to this merit-based opposition to diversity, it has been argued that merit is not a neutral concept.[64] As we have already seen, even talented diverse candidates come up against structural barriers, namely care responsibilities and biased hiring and promotion metrics and processes. The idea of merit becomes further diluted because hiring and promotion decisions are often influenced by the candidate's ability to flatter, defer to, and confirm the opinion of the CEO (or other person making the hiring decision).[65] To add to this, it is argued that merit itself is a fluid concept for many elite positions and may even be redefined to fit the qualifications of favoured applicants.[66] This is particularly likely in board and management positions, where directors and the CEO are known to hire their friends or as they put it, people who are a good 'fit' for the organisation.[67] If law, policy, or

---

[64] Rainbow Murray, *Merit vs Equality? The Argument That Gender Quotas Violate Meritocracy Is Based on Fallacies*, LSE BPP (Dec. 7, 2017), https://blogs.lse.ac.uk/politicsandpolicy/merit-vs-equality-argument/.

[65] Hickman, *supra* note 52, at 119.

[66] *Id.*, at 123.

[67] A study of members of the C-suite in the FTSE 100 companies between 2016 and 2017 found that twenty-one of the companies had directors who had studied in the same university. See Eleanor Hickman, *Diversity, Merit and Power in the C-suite of the FTSE100*, 213 (2019), www.ucl.ac.uk/judicial-institute/sites/judicial_institute/files/eleanore_hickman_post_viva_thesis_0.pdf. ['Whilst frequently the common university was Oxford or Cambridge, other connections of note include the CEO and CFO of AstraZeneca both attending HEC Paris, the CEO and Chairman of Land Securities both attending the University of Reading and the CFO and Chairman of Rentokil Initial both alumni of the University of Manchester.']

even company-level executives designing diversity programs are able to clarify the facets of diversity that need to be focused on at various levels, then the conscious focus will actually add to our understanding of what 'merit' means at each level of the corporation, and accordingly change recruitment practices.

1.5 EQUITY AND INCLUSION

The corporations and diversity discourse has now begun to use the words equity and inclusion in conjunction with diversity, and the three words together form the acronym DEI which has also become commonplace. While 'diversity' refers to different types of people (in terms of demographics and viewpoints), equity refers to treating the diverse members of the corporation fairly and sometimes also to equal outcomes. As I will explain in Chapter 4, while equal opportunity and equal treatment of people in the workplace is desirable, equality of outcomes will not help us bring systemic change. Thus, for the purposes of this book, the term 'diversity' will also convey equal or fair treatment of diverse employees but not equal outcomes.

The second term that is often found complementing 'diversity' is 'inclusion'. This term refers to diverse members often not feeling included in their team within the corporation even after being hired. This issue is real and even prevalent at the highest levels of the corporation. In one study, women directors said that they were not treated as full members of the group and that 'many male directors seem unaware that they may create hostile board cultures, fail to listen to female directors or accept them as equals, and require them to continually re-establish their credentials'.[68] Carol Fulp, a black woman who has held board positions, shares her own experience in her book, saying that a point she made was ignored; but later, the same point was considered meritorious when a white male colleague made it. She also recounts another incident in which an older white male colleague expressed surprise when she, a new board member at the time, had

---

[68] Boris Groysberg & Deborah Bell, *Dysfunction in the Boardroom*, HARV. BUS. REV. (2013), https://hbr.org/2013/06/dysfunction-in-the-boardroom.

said something perceived to be smart.[69] Fulp says that her colleagues assumed that they were being equitable and fair-minded, rather than trying to insult her. The main issue they were facing was that they were more attuned to having people who looked like them as colleagues on corporate boards.[70] They now had to navigate their unconscious bias to make their diverse colleagues feel included. From the diverse member's point of view, she had the burden of navigating these issues diplomatically and working to have their views heard. Corporations would do well to address these sorts of issues through process changes and other support mechanisms rather than leaving the diverse candidates to fend for themselves. Having diverse board members' views dismissed also means that the corporation is losing out on the benefits of diversity in board decision-making. Such issues exist across all levels of the corporation and carry costs for both the corporation and the diverse members. This book will address the issue of inclusion, where relevant, within the diversity discussion. Thus, it will assume that the term 'diversity' also implies inclusion.

1.6 CONCLUSION

The idea of diversity in the corporation is more complicated than meets the eye and the facets of diversity that are relevant in particular cases should depend on the position in question and the goals of diversity at that level of the corporation. It is also important to be clear about what we mean by diversity at the outset in any discussion on corporate diversity, so as to be able to address issues like viewpoint diversity and employees with complaints or concerns, which are usually left out of the diversity discourse. This nuanced understanding of diversity in corporations is also useful while assessing how corporate law should address diversity, if at all.

[69] FULP, *supra* note 40, at 70.
[70] *Id.*

2 DIVERSITY AND CORPORATE GOVERNANCE

The main cast of characters in the corporate diversity world are: the corporation, its board of directors, its management, its shareholders including large institutional investors, and its stakeholders broadly construed.

The board of directors is the centre of corporate governance with corporations being managed 'by and under the direction of' the board of directors.[1] The term 'corporate governance' has been defined as the system by which companies are governed and controlled.[2] So while the board is responsible for governance of the corporation, in large corporations, management performs the day-to-day operations. For the diversity debate, diversity officers who are now becoming part of the C–Suite are becoming important characters within the firm.

While individual shareholders may buy or sell their shares, cast their votes on certain important decisions, they lack a strong voice because they are dispersed and are unable to act collectively. However, there is a growing rise of individual investors (called retail investors) coordinating on online forums and working together. Despite not being focused on governance issues like diversity at the moment, they certainly have the potential. On the other hand, institutional investors have begun to dominate the market. They are

---

[1] JONATHAN R. MACEY, CORPORATE GOVERNANCE: PROMISES KEPT, PROMISES BROKEN 51 (Princeton University Press, 2008). Most countries' corporate legislation now has similar language about the corporations being managed 'by and under the direction of' the board of directors.

[2] ADRIAN CADBURY, REPORT OF THE COMMITTEE ON THE FINANCIAL ASPECTS OF CORPORATE GOVERNANCE, at 2.5, 3.4 (Gee & Co. Ltd. 1992).

using their powerful voice to argue in favour of diversity, specifically gender and racial diversity on the board.

The term 'stakeholders' is broadly construed here to include society in general including individuals who are not connected to the corporation. In a globalised world with Internet and social media, every individual has a voice and many of these individuals are using their voice in corporate law and governance debates including the diversity debate.

On the outside, there are some other characters influencing the corporate diversity world. First, government and policy makers in various countries that are introducing diversity via legislation or corporate governance codes. Second, the stock exchanges are another source of regulation in this regard. Third, executive search firms and consulting firms that provide board services including consulting on board culture and hiring of directors and executives. These characters are beginning to play a significant role in the progress of corporate diversity and will likely continue to do so in future.

This chapter is concerned with the board of directors and management. The board of directors, the decision-making 'brain' of the corporation, is coming under pressure from both institutional investors and stakeholders (whose voices have become amplified by social media and the Internet) to pursue diversity. As the most visible power centre of the corporation, the board of directors is the bastion that is being stormed and diversified. Corporate law and corporate governance codes, in various jurisdictions, has introduced provisions that force diversification of the board either through mandatory quotas or through softer measures like disclosures and targets.[3] Most such laws only focus on gender diversity and some (like a California law, the UK Code, and Nasdaq's listing rule) have begun to mention race and ethnicity. As discussed in Chapter 1, the UK Code also mentions cognitive diversity. The focus on demographic facets of diversity in most other countries' laws suggests that the goal sought to be achieved is equality and signalling to society although most arguments made by governments, institutional

---

[3] However, most law (including corporate governance codes and stock exchange rules) only apply to large firms. Similarly, voluntary efforts are also usually only seen in large companies. It then follows that the gender diversity statistics are much higher for larger companies.

investors and even some stakeholders are framed in terms of the business benefits for the corporation. To further complicate matters, there is not as much emphasis on diversifying management positions. It is often argued that diversifying the board will have a 'trickle-down effect' meaning that a diverse board will eventually ensure that management will also be diversified. As I discuss in Chapter 4, this argument does not hold. Ultimately, as Dhir has said, the focus on legal reform to diversify the board, particularly non-executive directors, is probably attributable to the fact that 'it may be politically difficult to generate support for comprehensive change throughout the upper levels of the corporation, and a strategy to accomplish such objectives might prove unmanageable'.[4] In other words, it will not be an easy fix.

Thus, board diversity is emphasised over and above diversity in management and certain facets of diversity are being favoured over others in the efforts to diversify the board. This chapter argues that diversity in a corporation's senior management (also referred to as C-Suite, top management team, or top executives) is just as important as board diversity, if not more; and that the diversity focus in both the board and in senior management should go beyond gender. I will get to the issue of how this should be done in Chapters 4 and 5.

2.1 DIVERSITY AND THE BOARD OF DIRECTORS

There are two reasons to look at board diversity. The first and more obvious reason is that the law and policy developments on diversifying corporations have largely been in this space. The second and more important reason is that boards are at the apex of the corporation and have an important role to play not just within the corporation but also in determining how their corporation interacts with the broader society. Further, the role of the corporate board is not fixed. In fact, it has changed over the years and will continue to evolve. Even within a certain time period, the role of the board may be different in different firms based on the firm size, the phase of its life cycle that

---

[4] AARON A. DHIR, CHALLENGING BOARDROOM HOMOGENEITY 29–30 (Cambridge University Press, 2015).

it is currently in, and the culture of the country that the corporation is based in. Below, I will examine the value that diversity can add for board functions based on three narratives of the role of the board – monitoring role, strategy-setting role, and relational role.

2.1.1 Diversity and the Monitoring Role of the Board

The historic role of directors was to 'manage'. The board was seen as a part of the managerial structure of the corporation and consisted of mostly executive directors. Under this model, the main duties of the board included providing advice to the CEO, strategic planning, and the review of significant corporate transactions.[5] Under this conception, it was more important for the board to have corporate executives who were familiar with the company's business and strategies than independent or outside directors.[6] Boards today continue to be involved in strategic planning, even if some other functions have taken on a bigger part of its duties. While strategy usually involves planning for the near and long term, it could also involve an immediate response to crises. The type of crisis could range from a hostile takeover bid being made on the corporation to something more global like the coronavirus pandemic. While normal or foreseeable risks are typically addressed through risk management frameworks, something as big as the pandemic (or even the global financial crisis of 2008), required boards to respond on short notice. This too is part of the board's strategic role.

In normal times however, the board's role has evolved to emphasise active oversight or monitoring of management. This evolution coincided with corporations becoming larger and their shareholders becoming more dispersed.[7] Oversight broadly involves the hiring and firing, supervision, and compensation of officers. Day-to-day management shifted to officers (i.e. executives or top management teams) appointed with the specific task of management.[8] This still allowed the

---

[5] Jill E. Fisch, *Corporate Governance: Taking Boards Seriously*, 19 CARDOZO LAW REV. 272 (1997).

[6] *Id.*, at 274.

[7] JOHN FARRAR, CORPORATE GOVERNANCE: THEORIES, PRINCIPLES AND PRACTICE 92 (Oxford University Press, 2008).

[8] *Id.*

board to engage with questions of strategy and also to act as a sounding board for the CEO and other senior management.[9]

The theoretical basis for the monitoring role of the board is provided by agency theory, which is premised on the idea that there would be costs (known as agency costs) involved in ensuring that the agents (in this case managers) acted in the principals' (here, shareholders) best interests.[10] The idea that the board of directors should exercise oversight over management provides one mechanism through which agency costs are mitigated.[11]

The emphasis on the monitoring role of the board can be traced back to Professor Eisenberg's model for reform in 1976.[12] His proposal came in the wake of opposition, in the 1970s, with respect to corporate practices relating to the Vietnam War, environmental protection, occupational safety, and equal employment. A number of corporate collapses had also put the spotlight on corporate boards, and many studies had concluded that the board was no longer able to check CEO power.[13] In fact, some of the concerns identified by these studies are still issues that are considered problematic today. For one thing, they found that outside directors had not been effective monitors since they were usually chosen from the same networks as top executives and since they were likely to be sitting with them on boards of other companies. This familiarity would make it unlikely that the so-called outside directors would challenge the decisions of top executives.[14] These are commonly heard complaints today and diversity tends to be one of the answers offered up. As discussed in Chapter 1, it is hoped that diversity brings psychological independence to the board.

---

[9] DONALD C. LANGEVOORT, *The Human Nature of Corporate Boards: Law, Norms and the Unintended Consequences of Independence and Accountability*, in CORPORATE GOVERNANCE: THEORY AND POLICY 338, 339 (Thomas W. Joo ed., Carolina Academic Press, 2004).

[10] Michael C. Jensen & William H. Meckling, *Theory of the Firm: Managerial Behaviour, Agency Costs and Ownership Structure*, 3 J. FIN. ECON. 308 (1976).

[11] *Id.*, at 65.

[12] MELVIN A. EISENBERG, THE STRUCTURE OF THE CORPORATION: A LEGAL ANALYSIS (Little Brown & Co., 1976).

[13] Dalia Tsuk Mitchell, *The Import of History to Corporate Law*, 59 ST. LOUIS U. L.J. 688–89 (2015). See also Roberta S. Karmel, *The Independent Corporate Board: A Means to What End?*, 52 GEO. WASH. L. REV. 534, 542 (1984).

[14] Karmel, *Id.*

Further, in a landmark study conducted in 1971 by Mace, a majority of the interviewees said that the prestige of the directors was the main criteria on which selection of outside directors was based.[15] Another reason for the lack of effective monitoring was found to be that directors simply did not meet often enough and that relevant information was often not sent to the board before board meetings.[16] Again, these issues have been highlighted in current times with diversity served up as an answer to both breaking the clubby nature of boards and lack of seriousness with which the board processes are followed when all directors belong to the same social networks as the CEO and fail to question one another or the management.

To provide some context to Mace's study, in the 1970s, the corporations statutes in each state in the United States and most other countries provided that the role of the board was to manage the corporation. However, Eisenberg, in his famous book, 'The Structure of the Corporation', explained the difference between what was provided for in law and the reality. At the time, corporations had become such large entities that in practice, the board of directors could not manage the day-to-day operations, especially when the board largely comprised of non-executive directors. It was instead the executives who were involved in management and also in initiating policy decisions. The board's role seemed to be limited to 'receipt and consideration of after-the-fact reports'.[17]

He therefore proposed that the board should primarily have a monitoring function where it supervises, monitors, and selects executive management. He went on to propose that the laws should ensure the effective performance of these functions by the board by making the board independent of the executives whose performance they monitor, and by ensuring that the board receives adequate and objective information to enable it to execute its monitoring function.[18] Based on Eisenberg's and other similar recommendations,[19] the American Law Institute (ALI) in its 1984 proposal sought to enhance the monitoring

---

[15] MILES M. MACE, DIRECTORS: MYTH AND REALITY (Harvard University Press, 1971).
[16] Id.
[17] Supra note 11, at 68, 40, and 141.
[18] Id.
[19] Supra note 12, at 69 and 690.

(or oversight) function of the board.[20] Ultimately, this translated into a focus on increasing the number of independent directors on the board.[21]

Similar changes took place in the UK as well, which is reflected in the Cadbury Report, published in 1992, emphasising the need for non-executive directors to perform a monitoring role. It states that the board of directors is responsible for the governance of the companies. This job of 'governance' is then explained by detailing the board's responsibilities to include 'setting the company's strategic aims, providing the leadership to put them into effect, supervising the management of the business and reporting to shareholders on their stewardship'.[22] The report also noted the different roles of executive and non-executive directors. While executive directors would have greater knowledge of the business, non-executive directors would bring a broader view to the company's activities.[23] Non-executive directors would be responsible for reviewing the performance of the board and of the management; and for taking the lead when potential conflicts of interest arose.[24] The report stresses the need for non-executive directors, in line with their duty of reviewing the work of the board and of the management, to make their views known to the chairman.[25] The Cadbury Report also goes on to recommend that non-executive directors should be of such 'calibre and number' that 'their views will carry significant weight in the board's decisions'.[26] Thus, the monitoring function seems to rely on the ability of non-executive directors to bring diverse views to the board, their willingness to voice them, and their numbers being large enough to make a difference to the board's decision-making. Again, similar arguments have been made in the context of diversity, even when only talking about women directors, although this can be extended to other types of diverse directors as well.

---

[20] American Law Institute, Principles of Corporate Governance: Analysis and Recommendations (Tentative draft No. 2, 1984) § 3.04.

[21] Jeffrey N. Gordon, *The Rise of Independent Directors in the United States, 1950–2005*, 59(6) STANFORD LAW REV. 1465 (2010).

[22] Cadbury Report, *supra* note 2, at 2.5.

[23] *Id.*, at 4.1.

[24] *Id.*, at 4.4.5, 4.6.

[25] *Id.*, at 4.5.

[26] *Id.*, at 4.11.

To reflect the emphasis on the monitoring function of the board of directors, the legislation regulating corporations in most countries currently states that the business of the company is to be managed by or under the direction of the directors.[27] The phrase 'under the direction of' was a later addition in most of these legislations to reflect the shift in the understanding of the board's role. In the agency costs language, independent directors monitoring management serve as an important mechanism to minimise the agency costs between managers and shareholders.

What follows from this premise is the assumption that boards with a majority of independent directors would result in increased firm performance because of reduced agency costs. However, the empirical studies on this issue are contradictory and hence far from unequivocal.[28] Scholars have rightly explained these contradictory results with the logic that one size does not fit all and that not all companies might need a board full of independent directors.[29] Bhagat and Black suggest that a moderate number of insiders in the board might add value although they add a caveat that their results on this might not be robust.[30] It could also be argued that firm performance is dependent on a number of factors and not merely on the board of directors. If there has been no robust empirical evidence of the value of independent directors to firm performance, we should carry those lessons into the diversity realm and do away with the argument that board diversity should be pursued because it will surely result in better form performance. Rather, many other factors are at play, just like in the context of independent directors. The more relevant business benefits argument for board diversity should be that it has the potential to improve the board's monitoring role.

The collapse of Enron, WorldCom, and other companies in and after 2008 reopened the debate about board effectiveness. Many of

---

[27] For instance, Corporations Act, 2001 (Australia), § 198(A)(1) of the provides that 'The business of a company is to be managed by or under the direction of the directors'.

[28] See generally Sanjai Bhagat & Bernard Black, *The Uncertain Relationship between Board Composition and Firm Performance*, 54 BUS. LAWYER 921 (1999), which is a meta-analysis of the many studies on the issue.

[29] STEPHEN M. BAINBRIDGE, THE NEW CORPORATE GOVERNANCE IN THEORY AND PRACTICE 198 (Oxford University Press, 2008).

[30] Bhagat and Black, *supra* note xxviii, at 954, 955.

the companies that collapsed around this time had complied with relevant stock exchange rules which required the board to have a majority of independent directors. Despite this, the boards had failed to perform their monitoring role.[31] While the response after the financial crisis mostly involved tightening the requirements of 'independence', board gender diversity also began gaining traction as a possible way to strengthen board effectiveness.

Some empirical studies, including one conducted by Adams and Ferreira find that board gender diversity may indeed enhance the board's monitoring role. However, the optimal level of monitoring is dependent on other firm-specific factors and so not all firms benefit from the increased monitoring.[32] A qualitative study by Dhir interviewed directors in Norway which found that women on boards ask more questions.[33] This is a sign of an active board and hence supports the 'gender diversity leads to enhanced board monitoring' thesis. Consistent with this, Brown, Brown, and Anastasopoulos found that the main governance practices that are affected by the presence of women are those associated with more active and independent boards of directors.[34] They argue that outer diversity is a proxy for inner diversity (i.e. diversity of views which leads to a constructive debate) and find that boards with more women surpass all-male boards in their attention to audit and risk oversight and control.[35] While this is

---

[31] Marlene A. O'Connor, *The Enron Board: The Perils of Groupthink*, 71 U. CIN. L. REV. 1233 (2003); Erica Beecher-Monas, *Marrying Diversity and Independence in the Boardroom: Just How Far Have You Come*, Baby?, 86(2) OR. L. REV. 373 (2007).

[32] Adams and Ferreira, studying data from the United States, made the link between women directors and monitoring and, in turn, the effect of women directors on firm performance in 2009. They found that although the correlation between gender diversity on boards and firm value or operating performance appears to be positive, this correlation disappears once reverse causality and omitted variables are accounted for. This means that firms would perform worse when there are more women directors on the board. It was found that this could be explained by the effect of gender diverse boards on monitoring. Since the authors find aspects of firm monitoring to have improved when boards are gender diverse, they conclude that too much monitoring would decrease shareholder value. Rene'e B. Adams & Daniel Ferreira, *Women in the Boardroom and Their Impact on Governance and Performance*, 94 J. FINANC. ECON. 291 (2009).

[33] Dhir, *supra* note 4, at 29–30.

[34] David A. H. Brown, Debra L. Brown, & Vanessa Anastasopoulos, The Conference Board of Canada, Ottawa, *Women on Boards: Not Just the Right Thing … But the 'Bright' Thing Report* (2002) 341.

[35] *Id.*, at 5.

consistent with Beecher-Monas' argument that board diversity might help make boards more (psychologically) independent, it is important to remember that outer diversity does not always correspond to inner (viewpoint diversity).

Indeed, a study conducted by Guest and published in 2019 found that ethnic board diversity is not associated with improved monitoring outcomes (CEO compensation, accounting misstatements, CEO turnover–performance sensitivity, and acquisition performance).[36] Guest provides two explanations for this result that seems to defy the theoretical expectation. For one thing, the recruitment process might select in favour of those minority candidates that hold similar perspectives to the existing board members and management team. Another factor could be that minority directors could face pressure to confirm and not behave differently from the group.[37] Both explanations are valid. As anecdotal evidence of the former point, Dambisa Moyo, a black woman who is from Africa and has held many board positions, says that she got rejected multiple times and continues to do so for board positions because she has not held executive positions.[38] Focusing only on candidates from C-suite backgrounds, irrespective of their demographic diversity, would mean that they have no diversity of experience. Ultimately on both this point and on the point discussed earlier (facing pressure to confirm),it would depend on the will of the CEO and board chair to be more open while hiring; and to enable diverse members to function effectively. In recent times, it is not uncommon for large companies to hire consultants to improve board culture so as to address these issues.[39]

The issue of diverse directors facing pressure to confirm has been addressed by proposals to have a critical mass (a minimum of three directors or 30% of the board) of diverse directors.[40] Only then can

---

[36] Paul M. Guest, *Does Board Ethnic Diversity Impact Board Monitoring Outcomes?*, 30 BR. J. MANAG. 53 (2019).

[37] *Id.*, at 54.

[38] *IoD Online: How Boards Can Work Better in a Chaotic World – In Conversation with Dr Dambisa Moyo*, YOUTUBE (May 17, 2021), www.youtube.com/watch?v=yrOevysNFPE&t=131s.

[39] George Anderson, Michael Vad, & Enzo De Angelis, *In a New Era for Boards, Culture Is Key*, SpencerStuart (April 2018), www.spencerstuart.com/research-and-insight/in-a-new-era-for-boards-culture-is-key.

[40] Lissa Lamkin Broome, John M. Conley, & Kimberly D. Krawiec, *Does Critical Mass Matter? Views from the Boardroom*, 34 SEATTLE U. L. REV. 1060 (2011).

their contributions to have an impact, according to some scholars. In a study by Broome, Conley, and Kraweic, some interviewees said that they felt special pressure to do well because as the first and only woman director (or minority director), they were more visible and closely scrutinised.[41] As an example of being made to feel 'different', one of the interviewees in the study said that, at the end of her first board meeting in the company, the board chair told her: '*You were wonderful to be here. We didn't even realise you were a woman.*'[42] However, other interviewees had a positive spin on being the only woman on the board. They considered themselves 'path-breakers' as the only woman/minority member on the board. Further, they exhibited pride in their 'outsider' status and were of the opinion that they were highly qualified and did not need additional members similar to themselves (in terms of gender or race) to support them.[43] Kantor, whose research on the issue is well regarded, also agrees that being a token could at times be an advantage because the lone women director is viewed as 'different' and becomes highly visible; and that this is good in a system where becoming known is a factor in becoming successful.[44]

The critical mass theory was further tested in the Norwegian context in 2011 by Torchia, Calabro, and Huse who conducted a study by analysing the effect of boards with one, two, or at least three women directors on organisational innovation. They found that once the number of women directors increased 'from a few tokens (one woman, two women) to a consistent minority ("at least three women"), they are able to effectively influence the level of organisational innovation'.[45] Although the latter study is not strictly about the board's impact on monitoring, the impact of a critical mass of diverse directors is relevant.

However, since it might not always be possible or even efficient to have three (or 30%) of any diverse category, there needs to be other

---

[41] *Id.*

[42] *Id.*, at 1070.

[43] *Id.*, at 1051.

[44] Rosabeth Moss Kantor, Men and Women of the Corporation 207 (Basic Books, 1977).

[45] Mariateresa Torchia, Andrew Calabro, & Morten Huse, *Women Directors on Corporate Boards: From Tokenism to Critical Mass*, 102 J. Bus. Ethics 299, 308 (2011).

ways to ensure that diverse candidates are able to function. Fostering a board culture that encourages different perspectives, even dissentient views, on the board is important. While companies have begun to hire consultants to help with board processes and diversity management, it is ultimately the will of the CEO and board chair that can bring about real change in board culture. The UK Corporate Governance Code has addressed this while setting out the role of the board chair who 'leads the board and is responsible for its overall effectiveness in directing the company'.[46] Principle F states that the chair should 'demonstrate objective judgement throughout their tenure and promote a culture of openness and debate'.[47] It further goes on to stipulate that 'the chair facilitates constructive board relations and the effective contribution of all non-executive directors, and ensures that directors receive accurate, timely and clear information'. This latter point pushes past facilitating effective board discussions and speaks to the point about requiring management to provide the information needed. In the United States, where the board chair and CEO is often the same person, a lead independent director often takes on the role of the board chair.

One example of innovation in this regard is the model followed by Netflix, although it is not specifically aimed at board diversity. This model includes a practice that some other companies might claim to have, although it is not common, is to do with board culture. One board member describes the culture as follows:

> Reed [The CEO] has always been masterful at hiring really good people, pushing decision making to those people, and not micromanaging. Letting decisions roll up and be debated rather than micromanaged. That style, that kind of management philosophy rolls up into the board meetings where any one of the members of Reed's staff can comment or disagree, or take questions from any of us around the table and answer them openly.[48]

Another board member says that 'the overall tone Reed has set, really from early days, is around transparency. ... There is no editorializing.

There's no censorship.'[49] Although the directors talk about the quality of board members, the striking point about culture is that both board members and the management staff are free to disagree, ask questions, and voice their own ideas. This also underlines the important role a CEO plays in setting the tone and culture for board directors.

Thus, to ensure that the benefits of board diversity are not lost due to outsiders not being able to contribute, either both or one of two conditions should prevail – (i) a critical mass of diverse directors and (ii) a board culture that welcomes and nurtures diversity. However, since both hiring of board members and fostering an effective board culture highlight the role of the CEO (along with that of the board chair) and perhaps other members of the top management team, management commitment to both diversity and making diversity work is essential when we think of board diversity.

2.1.2 Diversity and Strategy-Setting Role of the Board

Having diverse boards might have benefits beyond merely enhancing the monitoring role of the board. Diverse boards may bring diverse perspectives to matters of strategy if management works collaboratively with them. The Netflix model seems to be taking boards in this direction by encouraging managerial inputs from the board. Beyond board culture, the Netflix model has two novel practices. The first practice is that directors regularly attend monthly and quarterly senior management meetings; albeit in an observing capacity. The second practice is that board communications are 'structured as approximately 30-page online memos in narrative form' with links to supporting analysis. Board members may then ask clarifying questions to the author of the memo. This memo is written by and shared with the top ninety executives as well as the board.[50] Such practices involve the board more closely in ensuring that strategies are being implemented and even providing inputs on such implementation. While this

---

[49] David F. Larcker & Brian Tayan, *Diversity in the C-Suite – The Dismal State of Diversity among Fortune 100 Senior Executives*, STANFORD CLOSER LOOK SERIES (Apr. 1, 2021) 4, www.gsb.stanford.edu/sites/default/files/publication-pdf/cgri-closer-look-82-diversity-among-f100.pdf.

[50] *Id.*, at 1.

model may not be suitable for larger corporations, big events like the coronavirus pandemic meant that the board and management had to respond to a novel situation. Diversity in the board and management team could have greatly enhanced such responses. Louise Pentland, an executive at PayPal, and a non-executive director at Hitachi, said that the pandemic had pushed boards to 'empathy and the humanitarian element of leadership'.[51] Diversity of experiences and backgrounds on the board and management teams would have helped set responses that were sensitive to both employees and customers who depended on the corporation if that was the case.

2.1.3 Diversity and the Relational Role of the Board

Beyond monitoring and guiding management, the board also provides access to networks or contacts that the corporation might find beneficial.[52] This role of the board helps the corporation gain access to needed resources, that is information, advice, and contacts.[53] Indeed certain types of diverse members allow companies to access certain resources, for example an American company might appoint a director from Germany before undertaking investment into Germany. Such a director might, on the one hand, have useful networks in Germany which helps the company, and, on the other hand, their presence on the board might assure the German parties doing business with the American company. Companies generally recognise these needs while recruiting directors. For instance, Moyo (referred to earlier), who is from Zambia and an economist, says that many of the boards she initially served on had emerging markets footprints because of her background and expertise.[54] Interestingly, despite its importance, geographical diversity gets very little attention in the diversity discourse.

---

[51] Andrew Hill, *What Coronavirus Tells Company Boards about the Next Crisis*, FINANCIAL TIMES (May 26, 2021), www.ft.com/content/3369fbc0-8b07-11ea-a109-483c62d17528.
[52] Lynne L. Dallas, *Two Models of Corporate Governance*, 22 U. MICH. J.L. REFORM 19 (1988).
[53] Lynne L. Dallas, *The Relational Board: Three Theories of Corporate Boards of Directors*, 22 J. CORP. L. 1, 10 (1996).
[54] DAMBISA MOYO, HOW BOARDS WORK: AND HOW THEY CAN WORK BETTER XIII (The Bridge Street Press, 2021).

Although this has not been emphasised as much in the policy justifications for board diversity, in practice, racial and gender diversity on
the board have been leveraged by companies seeking to mend relationships with both internal and external stakeholders. As Barker and Chiu
observe, such types of diversity on the board can improve social and
stakeholder legitimacy and engagement.[55] Many companies do recognise this. For instance, in response to the Black Lives Matter movement, Reddit appointed a black director to their board.[56] However,
this does not always work. In any case, while such board appointments
speak to diversity issues within the corporation by signalling from the
top, it is ultimately up to management to effect change within the corporation, and also to seek out these board members for their views
and involvement in pertinent management issues as seen in the Netflix
model. Top management teams thus seem to be crucial in ensuring
that the company harnesses the benefits of board diversity. One way to
ensure a commitment to diversity from top management teams might
be to ensure that these teams are themselves diverse.

2.2 DIVERSITY AND TOP MANAGEMENT TEAMS

As the discussion above shows, diversity in top management teams
is just as important, and perhaps even more so, than board diversity.
In reality, management possesses much power in the corporation and
simply focusing on board diversity will mean that management functions and decisions will not be able to benefit from diversity. Even
though the board has to approve important decisions, management
is in charge of day-to-day operations, conduct negotiations with
external parties, and oversee the workforce, just to name a few functions. Further, in majority of the companies, the board is dependent

---

[55] Roger M. Barker & Iris H.-Y. Chiu, *Corporate Governance and Firm Innovation: Are Conventional Corporate Governance Standards a Hindrance*, 9 GEO. MASON J. INT'L COM. L. 143 (2018).

[56] Isabel Togoh, *Michael Seibel Becomes Reddit's First Black Board Member after Alexis Ohanian's Resignation*, FORBES (June 10, 2020), www.forbes.com/sites/isabel-togoh/2020/06/10/michael-seibel-becomes-reddits-first-black-board-member-after-alexis-ohanians-resignation/#5e551498430a.

on management to be able to glean information about the company. Thus, as Dhir says, for diversity's 'full value to governance to be realized, it cannot exist at the board level alone'. Instead, it should 'be sought at all governance levels, in the boardroom and in the senior management suite, which is itself an essential part of the "pipeline" to the boardroom'.[57] Not only this, diverse top management teams will be also able to bring more diversity at lower levels of the work force. One study, based on surveys of senior executives in nineteen Australian organizations, where women constituted 30% of the top three levels of executive leadership, found that gender diversity in management teams helped change both the culture and decision-making methods.[58] One male interviewee explained that more women in management has meant that male networks (or 'male clubbing' as he puts it) have given way to more transparent practices.[59] One can assume that transparency then helps ensure that meritorious candidates, which will include diverse candidates, are hired rather than just candidates that are friends of or similar to the management group being hired.

Apart from hiring, diverse members of management teams will bring different perspectives to decision-making based on their life experiences. To provide a concrete example, let us consider remote work that has become an important discussion point as countries begin to recover from the COVID-19 pandemic and consequently begin to ease restrictions. CEOs are in the news for deciding whether to require employees to start going back to the office.[60] The backlash against companies requiring employees to go back to the previous model of in-person work with no flexibility allowed suggests that employees want flexible and hybrid arrangements even outside of the pandemic. Thus, even if top management in many firms failed to learn from the

---

[57] Dhir, *supra* note 33, at 29.
[58] Colleen Chesterman, Anne Ross-Smith, & Margaret Peters, *The Gendered Impact on Organisations of a Critical Mass of Women in Senior Management*, 24(4) POLICY SOC'Y 69 (2017).
[59] *Id.*, at 72.
[60] See, e.g., Tracy Moor, *A Seismic Standoff over Remote Work Is Building*, THE WASHINGTON POST (May 22, 2021), www.washingtonpost.com/opinions/2021/05/21/i-dont-want-go-back-office-im-not-alone/; Andrew Hill, *Bagpipes and Barbecues: Incentives Abound to Lure Staff Back to the Office*, FINANCIAL TIMES (July 21, 2021), www.ft.com/content/5d5597fc-a4c8-4496-9905-04554854f376

pandemic and accept that remote working was possible, they will have to pay attention to employee concerns. Those corporations that do so will be able to attract and retain talent better than others. Perhaps diverse management teams would have been better able to understand the benefits of normalising working remotely when required and thus would have avoided the negative backlash from employees.

Women, and sometimes men with childcare responsibilities, would stand to gain in the long run, from these arrangements. Indira Nooyi, former Chair and CEO of PepsiCo, who initially joined PepsiCo as Senior Vice President of corporate strategy and planning constantly talks about the all-consuming nature of work in the corporate sector, in her book.[61] Advocating for the corporate sector to accommodate flexible work for people who need it she says that 'job flexibility and remote work ... will give families the chance to take care of home life obligations during the workday without feeling loaded with emotional consequences'.[62] Nooyi was able to continue working despite having two children only because, by her own admission, she had an effective support system from her husband, her parents, and her husband's parents.[63] Since the pandemic has brought both technological innovation and practical experience of working remotely, corporate leaders only need a change in mindset to allow for this long term. Providing the option of remote work will allow 'families the chance to take care of home life obligations during the workday without feeling loaded with emotional consequences'.[64] While Nooyi, a woman who had to juggle work alongside familial responsibilities, is keenly advocating the issue of remote work, a male executive who had a non-working spouse, or a female executive with no children, may not be sensitive to the advantages that remote work can provide. Being aware of and addressing problems that diverse candidates, in this case women, face will help retain those employees who might have opted to leave the company because they are unable to juggle multiple responsibilities in the absence of work flexibility.

---

[61] See generally INDIRA NOOYI, MY LIFE IN FULL: WORK, FAMILY, AND OUR FUTURE (Hachette, 2021).
[62] *Id.*, at 156.
[63] See generally Nooyi, *supra* note 61.
[64] *Id.*, at 156–57.

So, diverse management teams might be able to ensure that the issues faced by diverse members of the workforce face are addressed. This need not be limited to gender and race. To draw again from Nooyi's biography, she recounts that when she first joined PepsiCo, she noticed that the team that she took on lacked international diversity. This was relevant to the company because it was investing in international markets, and they had to provide talent to those markets. So, she asked the company's internal recruiter to send more diverse members in the next team.[65] Perhaps this obvious issue was apparent to Nooyi who was herself originally from India but had not been apparent to those previously in her role. Similarly, a member of the management team that had expertise in a particular area, say technology, might see the value of hiring some employees with a technological background if that was relevant to the firm in question. The same could work with other types of diversity such as age and educational background.

Unfortunately, most diversity statistics that are available are only in terms of gender and race. Of course, it is much harder to collect data about and measure other types of diversity. As it stands, management teams are even less diverse than corporate boards even in terms of race and gender. As of 2020, only 7% of the CEOs in Fortune 500 companies were women and 9% were ethnically diverse persons.[66] Comparing them to aristocrats of old, the Economist says that they are mostly white and male.[67] Even beyond the CEO position, there is very little diversity in the top management (or senior leadership) positions that report directly to the CEO according to a Stanford University study.[68] Looking at data from Fortune 100 companies, the study found that women in the C-suite mostly hold positions that are less likely to lead to CEO appointments (general counsel, human resources, chief risk officer, etc). A much smaller percentage held positions that would lead to CEO appointments (CEO, CFO, and those with Profit & Loss responsibilities). Racial diversity in the

---

[65] *Id.*, at 143.
[66] Larcker & Tayan, *supra* note 49.
[67] *Bartleby: The New Aristocrats of Power*, THE ECONOMIST (February 23, 2019), www .economist.com/business/2019/02/21/the-new-aristocrats-of-power.
[68] Larcker & Tayan, *supra* note 49.

C-suite is similarly skewed towards positions with lower potential to lead to a promotion to the CEO job.[69]

There are various reasons for this lack of diversity including the fact that women and ethnically diverse people may simply not fit the typical image of a corporate leader, because there have not been many precedents. Even though Nooyi was later appointed as the CEO of PepsiCo, she recounts how there were some who were not convinced. She says that one such person wrote to the former CEO that they were 'furious that the board had elevated someone so different from past CEOs'.[70] It could also be a result of these positions being awarded to people who are part of the existing networks of the CEO and other influential executives and board members. In many cases, the nomination committee will only look at a non-traditional candidate when there has been a crisis. This takes us to the issue of glass cliff appointments.

2.2.1 Glass Cliffs

Even those in positions that could lead to the top job are not sure to be appointed as CEOs. For instance, Mary O'Connor who was appointed as the interim CEO of KPMG UK after its former CEO, Bill Michael, stepped down following his controversial comments on a staff call, was not appointed as the firm's permanent CEO.[71] Instead, Jon Holt, KPMG's then head of audit was put forward as the only candidate for the partners to vote on. O'Connor subsequently left KPMG.[72] The story is significant not only because a woman qualified enough to be the interim CEO was passed over for a more permanent position but also because her interim appointment seems to be an attempt to soothe stakeholders. The previous CEO, Michael, had told consultants in KPMG to 'stop moaning' about the impact of COVID-19 and subsequent lockdown and to stop 'playing the victim card' in an online

---

[69] *Id.*

[70] Nooyi, *supra* note 61, at 198.

[71] Michael O'Dwyer, *KPMG's Mary O'Connor Quits after Being Passed over for Top UK Jȷb*, FINANCIAL TIMES (Apr. 29, 2021), www.ft.com/content/d0acea9c-3468-4efb-a2de-3daf1aec7b13.

[72] *Id.*

meeting with 500 staff members.[73] When this video became public, both staff concerns and reputational impacts had to be addressed. The fact that a woman was then appointed as an interim CEO speaks to what is known as the glass cliff phenomenon, whereby women and minority candidates are appointed to leadership roles in precarious situations.[74] The phenomenon is backed up empirically. One example is a study by Cook and Glass, which found, based on a study of Fortune 500 firms over a period of 15 years, that women and people of colour were likelier than white men to be promoted to CEO of weakly performing firms.[75]

One reason for glass cliffs is that women and minorities accept these positions despite the dangers because they feel like it could be their only opportunity while men (usually white men) could decline these roles.[76] Another reason, as in O'Connor's case could be to enhance the organization's reputation after backlash over a male leader's actions (or lack of appropriate action) in a crisis, particularly one that has a gender or race dimension to it. This latter reason also animates some appointments of women and minority candidates on company boards (as seen with Huffington's appointment to the board of Uber after the sexual harassment allegations became public). Apart from being unfair to women and minority candidates, the class cliff phenomenon also indicates that corporations are missing the benefits of diverse candidates in top management teams. Only a crisis seems to push them to look for unconventional candidates, and in many cases, only in the short term.

2.2.2 Mergers and Acquisitions

The benefits of diverse candidates in top management positions go beyond reputational gains. These executives, especially the CEO, play

---

[73] *KPMG Boss Bill Michael Quits after 'Stop Moaning' Row*, BBC NEWS (Feb. 12, 2021), www.bbc.com/news/business-56038215.

[74] Michelle Ryan & Alexander Haslam, *The Glass Cliff: Exploring the Dynamics Surrounding the Appointment of Women to Precarious Leadership Positions*, 32(2) ACAD. MANAG. REV. 549 (2007).

[75] Alison Cook & Christy Glass, *Above the Glass Ceiling: When Are Women and Racial/Ethnic Minorities Promoted to CEO?*, 35(7) STRATEG. MANAG. J. 1080 (2013).

[76] Emily Stewart, *Why Struggling Companies Promote Women: The Glass Cliff, Explained*, VOX (Oct. 31, 2018), www.vox.com/2018/10/31/17960156/what-is-the-glass-cliff-women-ceos.

a substantial role in mergers and acquisitions (M&A), which are significant events in a corporation's life.

Referring to behavioural bias and identity literature, Afsharipour suggests that managers' traits play a role in decision-making in the context of M&A.[77] While there are some studies suggesting that male executives are more overconfident, and seek to 'empire build', thus resulting in more value destroying acquisitions, evidence on the role of women in top management positions is scarce.[78] Considering the low number of women in these positions, perhaps this lack of evidence is not so surprising. Similarly, there are very few studies on racial diversity in top management teams and their impact on M&A.

On the other hand, studies tend to focus on the impact of women directors on M&A. For instance, Levi et al. studied decision-making in the context of M&A (using data for S&P 1500 firms during 1997–2009) and found that women are less inclined to pursue risky deals and tend to demand more for the company's money.[79] Particularly focusing on the bidder corporation's board (rather than the target corporation being acquired), they found that women were less acquisitive than men.[80] Perhaps the results of these studies might be extended to make inferences about women executives. I should add the caveat here that even if we draw some general inferences about the value of diversity in executive positions through these studies, we should always remember that not every woman will fit this mould. An incidental point that comes from these studies is that there are more studies looking at board gender diversity rather than on diversity in management, in the M&A context which is perhaps a product of two factors. The first and more obvious factor is the high percentage of women directors as compared to women CEOs (and even senior managers). The other factor is that law and policy on corporate diversity, particularly gender diversity, has tended to focus on the board of directors, which have

---

[77] Afra Afsharipour, *Bias, Identity and M&A*, 2020 Wis. L. Rev. 471 (2020).

[78] Jiekun Huang & Darren J. Kisgen, *Gender and Corporate Finance: Are Male Executives Overconfident Relative to Female Executives?*, 108 J. Financ. Econ. 822 (2013).

[79] Maurice Levi, Kai Li, & Feng Zhang, *Men Are from Mars, Women Are from Venus: Gender and Mergers and Acquisitions* (Mar. 15, 2011), https://papers.ssrn.com/sol3/papers .cfm?abstract_id=1785812.

[80] *Id.*

given rise to a number of such studies attempting to provide insights into the impact of women director on various firm activities. More research on diversity (even beyond gender diversity) in the management context will be useful to understand the impact of diverse teams on this important firm event.

2.2.3 Preventing Misconduct and Corporate Culture

While the dominant role of the board is to monitor management including setting risk management frameworks, management has the job to effect these strategies and frameworks. Thus, diversity on management teams can also enhance governance outcomes just like board diversity.

When I was a doctoral researcher, I was motivated by the law and policy developments around board diversity, and specifically board gender diversity. I therefore set out to conduct a qualitative study to understand the impact of gender on board functioning which I published in 2018.[81] However, I ended up making inferences on management team diversity as well. The study was a qualitative content analysis of judgements in cases (from Delaware where most corporations in the United States are incorporated) where violations of directors' legal duties were at issue. The idea was to look at cases where things had gone wrong and then check the composition of the board, what the board members had done to avoid problems, and finally match those failings with the purported benefits of board gender diversity (based on a review of various studies). One of the surprise findings of the study was that diversity on top management teams mattered just as much, if not more, than on the board of directors. The study also found that other forms of diversity were perhaps more important on board and management teams. This too was a surprise because my aim was to focus the study specifically on gender diversity.

Before getting into the details of the study's findings, let me give you a quick tour of the data set and methodology. The study mined the text of the judicial decisions in the data set for factual information

---

[81] Akshaya Kamalnath, *The Corporate Governance Case for Board Gender Diversity – Evidence from Delaware Cases*, 82 (1) ALB. L. REV. 23 (2018–19).

about board functioning within the circumstances of each case. The data set consisted of six cases and was selected by narrowing the results of an initial search for Delaware Chancery Court cases dealing with directors' duties. Some results were excluded where the company in question was not a public company, or if the case was dismissed on procedural grounds or where the case simply did not have enough factual material to analyse.[82]

Some of the themes from the study's findings and conclusions is most relevant to the current discussion, and so I have briefly summarised it here. In one of the cases in the data set (AIG[83]), the CEO also held the position of board chair. This was possibly one reason for the board's inability to monitor CEO excesses. Further, the fact that the CEO and his 'inner circle' functioned as a 'criminal organisation' suggested that if gender diversity has ethical benefits to offer, then management might benefit from it since it is in a position to control and (mis)manage many aspects of the company. A study by Adhikari et al. finds that companies with women in top executive positions are subject to fewer litigations.[84] Whether this is because of women being more ethical or simply more risk-averse is unclear. Relatedly, in another case in the data set (Massey[85]), the CEO was willing to risk non-compliance with safety regulations because he was of the opinion that he knew better. The studies relating to women being less over confident (in the context of M&A) seem to support this.

Additionally, groupthink might also be a problem in the management context. Dominant CEOs like the ones in AIG and Massey were not questioned by other executives, and it became easy for them to conceal or misrepresent information to the board. Thus, it might be necessary to rethink the exclusive focus of the diversity efforts on company boards and to complement this with similar efforts in the management context. To counter groupthink, it is not just gender or race

---

[82] *Id.*

[83] In re American International Group, Inc. 965 A.2d 763 (2009).

[84] Adhikari, Binay K., Anup Agrawal, & James Malm. *Do Women Managers Keep Firms out of Trouble? Evidence from Corporate Litigation and Policies* 67(1) J. ACCOUNT. ECON. 202 (2019). The study finds that increased representation of women in top management had the effect of reducing lawsuits overall, particularly lawsuits relating to product liability, environment, medical liability, labour, and contracts.

[85] In re Massey Energy Company. A.3d (2011) (Unreported).

diversity, but also cognitive diversity that will be useful. Further, as the study by Guest showed, such diverse members should ideally also come from different backgrounds and networks, in order to counter groupthink. Ultimately, it is up to the CEO to seek out diverse opinions from the inner circle, rather than mere 'yes men' (or 'yes women'). For instance, while recounting how she put her team in place after becoming CEO, Nooyi says this about the CFO she chose: 'he was respected, meticulous, and fearless in giving his opinions'. About the chief HR officer that she chose, Nooyi says that she 'had great ideas, which she frequently expressed at board meetings' and that that was why Nooyi 'needed her around'.[86] The takeaway then is that diversity on top management teams might help ensure that corporations are able to identify and assess risks effectively, provided that the CEO seeks out ideas and opinions from the team.

There are examples pointing to this conclusion even beyond the cases in my study. Volkswagen AG and its infamous emissions scandal, where the company admitted to installing devices to defeat emission detectors used by the US Environment Protection Agency, and thus got away with emitting forty times more pollutants with what was allowed in the United States, might also have some lessons in this regard.[87] It was later found that the problem went beyond the United States – Volkswagen cars' emission results in the UK, Italy, France, South Korea, Canada, and, Volkswagen's home jurisdiction, Germany were also investigated. Although the corporation has tried to maintain that the problems were the result of the actions of 'a few engineers', this hardly seemed credible.[88] Volkswagen commissioned an internal investigation by law firm Jones Day, and the interim findings of the investigation, as reported in late 2015 by the then Chairman of Volkswagen was that it was 'not a one-off error, but an unbroken chain of mistakes'.[89] The then CEO Matthias Müller went as far as to

---

[86] Nooyi, *supra* note 61, at 196.
[87] For more details on the emissions scandal or 'diesel dupe' or 'diesel gate', see Russell Hotten, *Volkswagen: The Scandal Explained*, BBC NEWS (Dec. 10, 2015), www.bbc.com/news/business-34324772.
[88] *Id.*
[89] Chris Cottrell & Peter Dahl, *VW Releases Internal Probe Findings*, DW (Dec. 10, 2015), www.dw.com/en/vw-releases-internal-probe-findings/a-18909535.

say that the problems could be attributed to individual misconduct, flawed processes, and a 'willingness in some departments to ignore the rules'.[90] Despite Volkswagen's official line that it was caused by a few rogue engineers, Müller's statement seems more likely. As commentators have argued, since the wrongdoing was so large scale and spanned seven years, it was plausible that senior management was aware of the scheme or had seen red flags suggesting that something was wrong.[91] Sure enough, in March 2021, Volkswagen accused former CEO Martin Winterkorn, and former head of group brand Audi, Rupert Stadler, of breaching their legal duties (specifically, the duty of care).[92] Winterkorn was accused of having knowledge of possible use of cheat devices a few months before the scandal was uncovered, despite not being actively involved.[93] He was also accused of failing to take proper action after the red flags were identified.[94]

Armour has suggested that personal liability for managers who themselves engage in misconduct or who fail to engage in adequate risk management might be one way to counteract the incentives that gave rise to such misconduct.[95] These recommendations for legal reform are definitely worth considering. However, the Volkswagen scandal, and the cases in the study discussed earlier (AIG and Massey), should put us on notice about harmful corporate culture that makes people willing to ignore the rules, as Müller had said about some departments in Volkswagen. The concern should go beyond expecting senior

---

[90] *Id.*

[91] See John Armour, *Volkswagen's Emissions Scandal: Lessons for Corporate Governance? (Part 1)*, OXFORD BUSINESS LAW BLOG (May 17, 2016), www.law.ox.ac.uk/ business-law-blog/blog/2016/05/volkswagen%E2%80%99s-emissions-scandal-lessons-corporate-governance-part-1; Josephine Sandler Nelson, *Fumigating the Criminal Bug: New Research on the Insulation of Volkswagen's Middle Management*, OXFORD BUSINESS LAW BLOG (May 5, 2021), www.law.ox.ac.uk/business-law-blog/blog/2016/05/ fumigating-criminal-bug-new-research-insulation-volkswagen%E2%80%99s-middle.

[92] Volkswagen investor relations communication, *Joint Report of the Supervisory Board and Board of Management of VOLKSWAGEN AG on Agenda Items 10 and 11*, VOLKSWAGEN AG (Sept., 2018), www.volkswagenag.com/presence/investorrelation/publications/ sonstrechtlangelegentheiten/2021/Preliminary%20report.pdf.

[93] *Id.*, at 6.

[94] *Id.*, at 6–7.

[95] See John Armour, *Volkswagen's Emissions Scandal: Lessons for Corporate Governance? (Part 2)*, OXFORD BUSINESS LAW BLOG (May 18, 2016), www.law.ox.ac.uk/business-law-blog/blog/2016/05/volkswagen%E2%80%99s-emissions-scandal-lessons-corporate-governance-part-2.

management to take appropriate action after finding red flags about wrongdoing, and focus on actively engaging the workforce to incentivise ethical conduct. Diversity is just one step in this direction.

Indeed, the focus on corporate culture has begun to gain ground, not in the wake of corporate misconduct seen in cases like Volkswagen but rather in the wake of the #MeToo movement which brought to light many instances of workplace sexual harassment.[96] BlackRock, one of the biggest institutional investors, identified human capital management (HCM) in corporations as one of its core engagement priorities since 2018.[97] In its 2019 investor stewardship annual report, it highlights the creation of a 'positive culture' and prevention of 'unwanted behaviours' to prevent HCM risks.[98] It further highlights the level of reporting the board receives from management, so that it is capable of assessing how policy on these issues is being implemented.[99]

While these are helpful pointers in the context of sexual harassment, these metrics are also useful when thinking about the development of corporate culture that is able to prevent misconduct even beyond sexual harassment. In fact, the term HCM itself is capable of being read more broadly to include the well-being of the workforce. This is discussed in more detail in Chapter 5. Getting rid of incentives to engage in misconduct or conversely setting incentives to act ethically can be one way to promote employee well-being. However, the benefit of a sound corporate culture goes beyond employee well-being if it is able to prevent scandals like dieselgate at Volkswagen. The UK Code might be leaning towards this more expansive view when it tasks the board with assessing and monitoring culture.[100] It further says that where the board is 'not satisfied that policy, practices or behaviour throughout the business are aligned with the company's purpose, values and strategy, it should seek assurance that management has taken corrective action'.[101] So, there seems to be a somewhat

---

[96] See generally Amelia Miazad, *Sex, Power, and Corporate Governance*, 54(4) U.C. Davis L. Rev. 1913 (2021).

[97] Blackrock, Investment Stewardship Annual Report, BLACKROCK (2019) 20, www .blackrock.com/corporate/literature/publication/blk-annual-stewardshipreport-2019.pdf.

[98] *Id.*

[99] *Id.*

[100] UK Code, 2018, provision 2.

[101] *Id.*

implicit emphasis on the interdependence with board and management roles and communication, albeit with a focus on what the board should seek from management.

As the discussion here has shown, management teams, their composition and interaction with each other, including the ability to disagree and question the CEO and other members of the senior management is significant for risk management. Further, as the discussion earlier in this chapter has shown, the role of senior management, particularly the CEO is also important, alongside that of the board chair, to ensure that the board is able to harness the benefits of diversity amongst its directors. A similar commitment will be required from both the CEO and board chair to ensure that management teams are themselves diverse and that the culture in management teams and on the board is able to foster this diversity. Since hiring and firing executives is amongst the board's most important roles, the board should be able to prioritise the right attributes in a CEO and also be able to decide when a CEO's actions or lack of action is not in line with the broad policy objectives it sets, including that of corporate culture. Corporate culture will be discussed in more detail in Chapter 5, but it is important to remember that diversity on board and management teams can be effective only if it is supported by a culture that allows executives and board members to question each other, thus overcoming groupthink. Further, a corporate culture that encourages reporting of problems through multiple channels will help the board and management address issues early on and prevent large scale misconduct.

2.2.4 Chief Diversity Officers

With the growing importance of diversity in corporations, it has become common practice for large organizations to create a C-suite position, the chief diversity officer (CDO). This move from diversity being managed by the HR manager to a C-suite executive might indicate that that diversity has taken on significance for both shareholders and stakeholders. It also shows that a more central executive, with direct access to the CEO, is at the helm of diversity efforts. However, this has not always been very effective. Why?

An explanation may be found by a study in the university context, which found that executive level diversity officers or CDOs did not have a significant impact on the hiring of diverse faculty. This is interesting since, as the authors of the study say, the hiring of such a CDO often signifies the university's commitment to diversity. The study is quantitative and does not explain why CDOs are unable to have an impact although it says at the outset that 'in a university with shared governance, it is not immediately clear how much influence an executive level CDO can exert upon faculty hiring decisions made by individual departments'.[102] Despite the study's university context, it seems to resonate with the views of some CDOs in the corporate sector. They have been quoted in a news article saying that the lack of resources available to them is often the greatest impediment for them. One CDO has cited two important resources namely a direct reporting line to the CEO and access to human resources data. Both these issues, particularly the former, speak to the basic issue of whether the company management is genuinely interested in diversity or is merely signalling interest in diversity by hiring a CDO.[103] Not only should the CDO have a direct reporting line to the CEO, they should also have the authority to audit the business so that they can figure out all the pain points for diversity to flourish. Hiring, performance evaluations, access to opportunities, and compensation are some of the usual pain points for diversity in corporations.[104] After identifying the issues, the CDO should then be given authority to address them by ensuring that the firm sets the right incentives for managers, middle managers, and the broader workforce to fall into line with the CDO's initiatives.[105] The point is for the CDO to be able to effect a cultural shift within the company, and this cannot happen without the support of the CEO.

---

[102] See generally Steven W. Bradley, James R. Garven, Wilson W. Law, & James E. West, *The Impact of Chief Diversity Officers on Diverse Faculty Hiring* (2018), www.nber.org/papers/w24969.

[103] Taylor Nicole Rogers, *Black Lives Matter Ushers in New Era for Diversity Officer*, FINANCIAL TIMES (Jan. 27, 2021), www.ft.com/content/0147a2af-3c3d-4e05-9463-8b91d221e9be.

[104] JOAN C. WILLIAMS, BIAS INTERRUPTED: CREATING INCLUSION FOR REAL AND FOR GOOD, 12 (Harvard Business Review Press, 2021) 151.

[105] *Id.*, at163.

To sum up, it seems that the commitment of the CEO to diversity is crucial for the CDO to ensure that there is no discrimination in the firm and to take on meaningful programs that have an impact in terms of both the type of employees hired and addressing problems stemming from diversity being mismanaged.

2.3 CONCLUSION

This chapter has argued that diversity efforts should go beyond the board of directors and reach into the C-suite, if its effects on corporate governance are to be gained. The current focus on the board is because this is easier to legislate on for governments and institutional investors actually have a right to vote on that appointment of board directors. However, BlackRock's HCM efforts, and also efforts of other institutional investors, indicate that the focus might be slowly starting to shift. This chapter has also re-iterated the message from Chapter 1 that diversity should not be limited to gender, in the board, and in top management positions. It has further argued that the HCM effort, focused as it is on the entire workforce, is broad enough to be read as covering other types of diversity. Last but not least, this chapter has pointed out that the CDO position will be worthwhile only if it is adequately empowered.

A running theme in this chapter that emerged, both with respect to the board and management, is the importance of culture – on the board, within top management teams, and between board and management interactions. The culture of the corporation more generally will be set by how the board and management work and through efforts of top management including the CDO. There will be more discussion of culture in Chapters 3 and 5.

3 SOCIAL MOVEMENTS, DIVERSITY, AND CORPORATE SHORT-TERMISM

Social movements like #MeToo and #BlackLivesMatter (BLM), powered by social media, have given rise to heightened corporate activism on social issues. This chapter argues that although the focus on such social issues is desirable and indeed necessary, myopic responses to social media pressures can be counterproductive. Instead, it proposes that corporate decisions and actions regarding diversity should be geared towards addressing issues that help the companies' and their stakeholders, particularly employees, in the long term. The chapter also notes that companies can create a niche for themselves via social justice innovations that solve diversity issues within the firm.

While the book has taken the view that diversity includes both factors based on identity and demography (namely race, sex, and age) and cognitive or viewpoint diversity, this chapter will mostly focus on diversity of sex and race because the two movements discussed in this chapter are focused on these two aspects of diversity. However, some solutions proposed here could also help address issues of viewpoint diversity being suppressed. Ultimately, the proposals in this chapter, while addressing concerns of the workforce, will provide the means for corporate boards to detect and fix problems *ex ante*. The range of solutions proposed in this chapter rely on technological tools and behavioural shifts that can create a more compassionate corporate culture.

Employees, customers, suppliers, and creditors are usually considered the stakeholders of a corporation. However, society more generally may also be considered a stakeholder because of the overall significance of corporations, particularly bigger ones. When members of society come together 'on the basis of shared collective identities' and beliefs to 'engage in political or cultural conflicts' via 'networks of informal interactions', we have a social movement.[1] In recent times, we have had social movements regarding race (#BlackLivesMatter or BLM) and gender (#MeToo[2]), both of which were amplified by social media as indicated by the hashtags prefixing the two terms. These two movements have sounded off corporations in the United States (where each of these movements originated) and elsewhere[3] about the importance of sexual misconduct, racial equality, and ancillary social justice issues. These movements are, amongst other things, powered by millennial and Gen Z users who are (or at least a section of them are[4]) both comfortable sharing views and experiences on social media, and who place a premium on social issues.[5] Whether as consumers, investors, employees, or simply individuals with opinions, these generations are making themselves heard on what is known in the corporate governance world as environment, social, and governance (ESG) issues. A survey conducted in 2013 noted that 66% of US millennials believed that it was their responsibility to communicate views publicly after a negative experience with a brand.[6] A 2018 survey asked American consumers about what attracted them to a brand. Some of the major factors listed in the survey are: transparency about how the business treats it employees and where it sources its materials from (66% of respondents), following through on its promises (66% of respondents), and standing up for societal

---

[1] Definition adapted from Mario Diani, *The Concept of Social Movement*, 40(1) SOCIOL. REV. (1992).

[2] An associated movement is #TimesUp. This article will simply refer to #MeToo as the bigger umbrella movement.

[3] See, e.g., Nassim Khadem, AMP's 'MeToo' Moment Raises Bigger Questions for Corporate Australia about Sexual Harassment, ABC News (Aug. 25, 2020, 4:41 AM), www.abc.net .au/news/2020-08-25/amp-sexual-harassment-metoo-corporate-culture/12589602.

[4] *See infra* notes 131–33.

[5] See Sandeep Gopalan & Akshaya Kamalnath, *Mandatory Corporate Social Responsibility as a Vehicle for Reducing Inequality: An Indian Solution for Piketty and the Millennials*, 10 NW J. L. & SOC. POL'Y 34, 109–20 (2015), for a discussion on the rise of millennials and a discussion on their preferences. See Sergio Alberto Gramitto Ricci & Christina M. Sautter, *Corporate Governance Gaming: The Power of Retail Investors*, 22 NEV. L. J. 51 (2021), for a discussion of both millennials and Gen Zers. See generally Michal Barzuza, Quinn Curtis, & David H. Webber, *Shareholder Value(s): Index Fund ESG Activism and the New Millennial Corporate Governance*, 93(6) S. CAL. L. REV. 1243 (2020).

[6] *Engaging Tomorrow's Consumers*, ACCENTURE (2013), www.accenture.com/SiteCollection Documents/PDF/Accenture-EngagingConsumers-Infographic.pdf.

and cultural issues (50% of the respondents).[7] Even beyond modifying their choices as consumers, millennials and Gen Zers are using social media to express their opinions about these issues and directly target corporations. COVID-19 and the consequent lockdowns around the world have further increased the use of online communication channels, including about and against corporations.[8] This online activism has impacted corporate behaviour with many large corporations viewing the need to engage with social activism as a cost of doing business.[9]

To be clear, activism and social movements aimed at corporations are not a new phenomenon brought on by social media. Corporations have been aware of the importance of stakeholders, and some firms have supported social issues (equal opportunity for racial minorities in the 1960s and 70s and LGBTQ rights in the 1980s and 90s) in the past.[10] In most cases, the support from corporations was a result of social movements targeting corporations on these issues.[11] This seemingly curious phenomenon of large corporations supporting social movements is easily explained when one considers that although a small baker may refuse to sell to some customers, big corporations cannot survive by only catering to one type of customer.[12] At this point in time, a much

---

[7] *From Me to We: The Rise of the Purpose-Led Brand,* ACCENTURE (Dec. 5, 2018), www .accenture.com/us-en/insights/strategy/brandpurpose?c=strat_competitiveagilnovalue_1 0437227&n=mrl_1118.

[8] SALLY WHEELER, *What Have We Learned about the Corporate Sector in Covid-19?,* in PANDEMIC LEGALITIES: LEGAL RESPONSES TO COVID-19 – JUSTICE AND SOCIAL RESPONSIBILITY 155, 168 (Dave Cowan & Ann Mumford eds., Bristol University Press, 2021). Noting that collective action might become more prevalent 'during a time of limited movement', that is the government mandated lockdowns in the wake of COVID-19.

[9] Michael Peregrine, *How Companies Engage with Social Activism,* FORBES (Apr. 6, 2021, 7:00 AM, www.forbes.com/sites/michaelperegrine/2021/04/06/corporate-leadership-faces-ever-evolving-social-justice-concerns/?sh=754fcfa57c4d. See also Tom C. W. Lin, *Incorporating Social Activism,* 98(6) *B.U. L. Rev.* 1535, 1546 (2018) ('The broad reach and deep impact of social activism powered by new information technology means that businesses are frequently engaged in social issues whether they want to be or not.').

[10] See generally CARLOS A. BALL, THE QUEERING OF CORPORATE AMERICA: HOW BIG BUSINESS WENT FROM LGBTQ ADVERSARY TO ALLY (Beacon Press, 2019); Lin, *id.,* at 1540–44. Both Ball and Lin describe how corporations have played both the role of antagonists to social movements in which case, they were the targets of social activism, and the role of supporters of social movements.

[11] Ball, *id.*

[12] TYLER COWEN, BIG BUSINESS – A LOVE LETTER TO AN AMERICAN ANTI-HERO 5–6 (St. Martin's Press, 2019).

larger percentage of corporations are responding to social movements because of the traction these movements have gathered as a result of younger generations' preferences and their ability to use social media.

In fact, corporations are not only responding to these movements but also trying to proactively engage in speech or conduct indicating their support of these and even of older movements like LGBTQ+ rights. In many cases, responses do not go beyond supportive public statements. However, some companies have taken more concrete steps. Others have attempted to become part of the social movements themselves, for example by firing employees who became the target of activists' complaints. Thus, corporations today feel compelled to respond hastily to social movements.

This chapter argues that corporations ought to take steps to address issues that help the companies' stakeholders, particularly employees (who are most affected by these issues), in the long term, rather than make hasty decisions just to appease the social media outcry in question. To do so, it will first discuss the implications of #MeToo and propose solutions that might help companies make sustained change. It will then discuss BLM and transpose some of the solutions discussed for #MeToo into this context. Finally, the chapter addresses the issue of corporate short-termism in response to social movements and proposes instead that companies should take measures that aim to create sustained and meaningful change. These measures can be tailored to a firm's individual circumstances, thus allowing for firm-specific innovation that can in turn lead to competition with peers, thus incentivising social justice innovations.

3.1 #METOO

Although the term was originally coined by Tarana Burke in 2006, the social media version of the movement started as a reaction to sexual harassment in the entertainment industry in 2017 with the news about Harvey Weinstein being published.[13] From there, the movement had

---

[13] Sandra E. Garcia, *The Woman Who Created #MeToo Long before Hashtags*, N.Y. TIMES (Oct. 20, 2017), www.nytimes.com/2017/10/20/us/me-too-movement-tarana-burke.html.

ripple effects across industries, with victims of harassment sharing their experiences. It took companies out of a compliance mindset, where the goal was simply to avoid liability, to one where the reputational fallout of such incidents, irrespective of legal liability, had to be factored in.[14] Again, social media has a role to play in empowering women to speak up and thus increasing the reputational costs of stakeholder dissatisfaction.[15] Even before #MeToo, social media had incentivized businesses to act honestly, or alternatively render an apology when some misconduct is uncovered, rather than face reputational penalties.[16] With #MeToo gaining steam, it was not going to be enough to simply apologize. So, #MeToo resulted in a number of executives getting fired or demoted, and representations being included in merger agreements to provide recourse to bidder firms in the event that sexual misconduct was discovered after the deal was closed.[17] Another consequence of the movement has been that corporations have started including a #MeToo termination option in CEO employment contracts. This includes conduct relating to sexual harassment, discrimination, and violations of company policies.[18] Further, Delaware courts might be becoming more sympathetic to sexual harassment claims.[19]

The movement has also fed investor views. A study conducted by Billings, Klein, and Shi to test the market reaction to the #MeToo movement finds that firms received abnormal positive returns if they

---

[14] See generally Amelia Miazad, *Sex, Power, and Corporate Governance*, 54 UC Davis L. Rev. 1913 (2021).

[15] See Terry Morehead Dworkin & Cindy A. Schipani, *The Role of Gender Diversity in Corporate Governance*, 21 U. Pa. J. Bus. L. 105, 126–27 (2018).

[16] Cowen, *supra* note 15, at 39.

[17] See generally Miazad, *supra* note 17.

[18] James Hicks, Rachel Arnow-Richman, & Steven Davidoff Solomon, *Anticipating Harassment: MeToo and the Changing Norms of Executive Contracts* (Working Paper, 2021), https://papers.ssrn.com/sol3/papers.cfm?abstract_id=3787232.

[19] Ann Lipton, *Capital Discrimination*, Houston L. Rev. (Forthcoming), https://papers.ssrn.com/sol3/papers.cfm?abstract_id=3882274 (citing Marchand v. Barnhill, 212 A.3d 805 (2019). Additionally, Lipton notes that Delaware has recently begun to look more favourably on claims that boards ignored or encouraged illegal conduct. She cites *In re* Clovis Oncology Deriv. Litig., 2019 WL 4850188 (Del. Ch. Oct. 1, 2019) as an example). See also Roy Shapira, *A New Caremark Era: Causes and Consequences*, 98 Wash. L. Rev. 1855 (2021), https://privpapers.ssrn.com/sol3/papers.cfm?abstract_id=3732838.

have what the authors term inclusive cultures[20] (meaning that they hired women directors in the period preceding the #MeToo movement and even the earlier push from institutional investors to hire women directors). These same firms did not receive abnormal positive returns during 'placebo dates', that is time periods that did not coincide with major events of the #MeToo movement.[21] The authors of the study infer, based on their results, that as a consequence of the #MeToo movement, firms with all-male boards are deemed by the market to be more exposed to the risk of sexual misconduct revelations than those with a critical mass of women on the board. While a critical mass of women on boards might not necessarily prevent sexual misconduct with the firm, the converse might be true. Firms with cultures that prevent sexual misconduct and other forms of misconduct are able to attract and retain women in positions of power including on the board of directors.

The role of firm culture in preventing and even addressing issues of sexual harassment and also other forms of workforce issues (racial discrimination, bullying, etc.) is important. While Billings and co-authors used firms that hired women directors in the absence of pressure to do so as an indicator of an inclusive culture, it is useful to think about the specific steps corporations may take to build such a culture. How can a firm prevent the risk of sexual harassment or other forms of workforce issues (bullying, racial discrimination, etc.)? A rich source of ideas on this question is the report containing recommendations of Eric Holder, who had been appointed by Uber to investigate an employee's sexual harassment claims (Ms. Susan Fowler had made these claims via a blog post).[22] Holder's brief from Uber was to deal with three issues: the company's workplace environment as it related to the employee's allegations of discrimination, harassment, and retaliation; its policies and practices in this regard; and steps Uber could take to uphold its commitment to a diverse and inclusive workplace.[23]

---

[20] Mary Billings, April Klein & Crystal (Yanting) Shi, *Investors' Response to the #MeToo Movement: Does Corporate Culture Matter?* (NYU STERN SCHOOL OF BUSINESS, Finance Working Paper No. 764/2021, 2021), https://papers.ssrn.com/sol3/papers .cfm?abstract_id=3466326.

[21] *Id.*

[22] However, I should note here that I do not agree with all the recommendations in the report.

[23] COVINGTON RECOMMENDATIONS, https://drive.google.com/file/d/0B1s08BdVqCgrUVM 4UHBpTGROLXM/view [hereinafter *The Holder Report*]. See also Polina Marinova,

Holder's report states at the outset that 'diversity is generally viewed as focusing on the presence of diverse employees based on religion, race, age, sexual orientation, gender, and culture'.[24] Thus, the Report echoes the popular understanding of diversity as being limited to demographics. While I don't endorse this limited view of diversity, the Report is useful insofar as issues relating to prong 2 diversity (as defined in Chapter 1 and Table 1.1), that is demographic diversity is concerned. The Report also highlights the importance of inclusion and retention policies to complement diversity efforts. Some aspects of the Report are helpful when trying to design best practices for organizations that want to deal with issues impeding demographic diversity from flourishing. These, along with some newer proposals, are critically assessed below under the following three categories: (i) harassment, discrimination, and employee relations; (ii) board oversight; and (iii) training.

3.1.1 Harassment, Discrimination, and Employee Relations

On the issue of harassment and discrimination, the Report said that Uber should adopt a zero-tolerance policy for substantiated complaints of harassment and discrimination against employees, even for high-performing ones.[25] Further, it recommends that all policies must be applied evenly and that no special treatment should be given based on level, tenure, and past performance of the employee.[26] This is consistent with Netflix' famous statement of company culture which says that 'brilliant jerks' will not be tolerated in the company.[27]

---

10 Things You Need to Know about Eric Holder's Uber Report, FORTUNE (June 14, 2017, 11.39 PM), http://fortune.com/2017/06/13/uber-internal-investigation-results-public/; Oliver Staley, *The Official Recommendations for Reforming Uber Describe the Perfect Modern Company*, QUARTZ (June 14, 2017), https://qz.com/1005316/eric-holders-recommendations-for-uber-describe-the-perfect-modern-company/. For a more detailed discussion of these recommendations, see Akshaya Kamalnath, *Corporate Diversity 2.0: Lessons from Silicon Valley's Missteps*, 20 OR. REV. INT'L L. 113 (2018).

[24] The Holder Report, *supra* note 23.

[25] *Id.*, at VIII.A.

[26] *Id.*, at VIII.I.

[27] *Netflix Culture*, NETFLIX JOBS, https://jobs.netflix.com/culture (last visited Aug. 8, 2021) ('Our view is that brilliant people are also capable of decent human interactions, and we insist upon that. When highly capable people work together in a collaborative context, they inspire each other to be more creative, more productive and ultimately more successful as a team than they could be as a collection of individuals.').

The Holder Report further recommends that barriers for employees to transfer to another team within the company must be removed and must not be tied to performance.[28] The Report goes on to specify that a human resources person review transfer requests and decisions in order to evaluate if such requests are a result of hostile or divisive environments and if they are being blocked for improper reasons.[29] The report also suggests tracking both harassment complaints and transfer requests to identify patterns and underlying problems.[30]

Even beyond harassment at the hands of 'brilliant jerks', there could be trouble-makers who get away with bad behaviour because they belong to an 'in-group' within the firm. A study titled the Good Finance Framework published in 2021, based on interviews of forty-four women working in financial and professional services, is informative in this regard.[31] A number of interviewees mentioned office politics as the barrier to getting ahead, particularly as they moved up the ladder.[32] Channels to report such behaviour, complemented with tracking such reports to identify patterns, as suggested in the Holder report, can even be helpful in such cases. Some market solutions already exist for employees or potential employees to be able to track issues like company culture. Glassdoor, a company set up on the premise that workplace transparency has value, has been providing useful information about firms based on employee feedback.[33] For corporations to be able to address these issues internally, similar anonymous forums and surveys could help the board and management learn about internal work culture issues and fix them. Chapter 5 discusses these and other issues on firm culture in more detail. The next broad issue considered in the Holder Report that is relevant to the discussion here is board oversight.

---

[28] *The Holder Report, supra* note 25, at VIII.D.

[29] *Id.*

[30] *Id.*

[31] Grace Lordan, *The Good Finance Framework*, Women in Banking & Finance, The Inclusion Initiative at London School of Economics, The Wisdom Council (June 2021), www.wibf.org.uk/images/uploads/documents/WIBF_ACT_Good_Finance_Framework_Report.pdf.

[32] *Id.*

[33] A recent example is a survey about the top CEOs in 2021 based on employees' feedback. *Glassdoor Reveals Employees' Choice Awards for the Top CEOs In 2021* (June 15, 2021), www.glassdoor.com/about-us/top-ceos-in-2021/.

3.1.2 Board Oversight

The Holder Report stressed the need to involve the board and senior management in issues of workforce diversity. It recommended that the board create an 'ethics and culture committee' to oversee issues pertaining to diversity and ethical business practices.[34] This committee would oversee senior management responsible for ethics, compliance, human resources, and risk.[35] Further, the committee could introduce metrics to establish and monitor compliance with Uber's values regarding diversity and inclusion.[36] The Report also recommended that a member of the senior management team should be responsible for giving effect to this committee's recommendations.[37] Many companies do create 'diversity committees' to address diversity issues. However, as Williams notes, for such a committee to be effective, it should include people who are powerful and influential, the committee work should be part of the performance evaluations of committee members, and serving on the committee should be 'a plum assignment' rather than 'one more thing to do'. Further, she notes that the committee should include white men, not only because they tend to be have more influence but also because this challenging work should not become an additional burden on diverse candidates.[38] So the message for firms is that they will not solve diversity problems by merely creating a diversity or ethics and culture committee. They should also ensure that the committee has the means to be effective.

The Holder Report also recommended that Uber's audit committee oversee the compliance efforts of the company to ensure that significant compliance and harassment issues could be brought to the committee without going through the CEO.[39] Where necessary, the audit committee could also oversee the response to such issues, including any potential investigations.[40] This is a significant recommendation

---

[34] The Holder Report, *supra* note 25, at II.C.
[35] *Id.*
[36] *Id.*
[37] *Id.*, at II.E.
[38] JOAN C. WILLIAMS, BIAS INTERRUPTED: CREATING INCLUSION FOR REAL AND FOR GOOD 12 (Harvard Business Review Press, 2021) 152–53.
[39] *Id.*, at III.A.
[40] *Id.*

because it brings harassment issues under the purview of the audit committee, which is responsible for overseeing the financial reporting process, risk management, internal controls, and compliance with laws and regulations. The media coverage of harassment claims against powerful people in the #MeToo climate has made this a high priority issue, and it is therefore pertinent to make the audit committee ultimately responsible for such matters. Since the #MeToo movement has shown the reputational and financial consequences of corporations not acting to address issues of harassment and discrimination, companies should be looking to adopt such best practices whether or not they are required to by law.

However, the practical concern is that harassment issues might never reach the board and audit committee. Stevelman and Haan have suggested that modern technology can be deployed to ensure that board committees are able to access relevant information directly.[41] This sits nicely with the Holder Report's recommendation that patterns of complaints against a person or within a team should be tracked. Setting up technological systems that the relevant committee members of the board have direct access to can be useful. In the same vein, Brand notes that 'whistleblowing bots' or technologically enabled systems that alert board members of certain issues might be a possibility.[42] These suggestions are not as futuristic as they sound. Simply setting up a reporting system that relevant board committee members have access to is achievable with the kind of technological capabilities that exists today. In fact, Vault has recently developed an app that allows employees to report workplace incidents. It also provides the option of anonymous reporting. However, the truly innovative feature is what they call 'go together' which allows employees to check if others have had problems with the same colleague.[43] So in a way, it is allowing employees themselves to check for patterns, and this sort of technology is something that boards should be interested in.

---

[41] See generally Faith Stevelman & Sarah C. Haan, Boards in Information Governance, 23 U. PA. J. BUS. L. 179 (2020).

[42] Vivienne Brand, Corporate Whistleblowing, Smart Regulation and RegTech: The Coming of the Whistlebot?, 43 U.N.S.W.L.J. 801 (2020).

[43] Ed Butler, Can Apps Move the #MeToo Movement Forward?, BBC NEWS (Sept. 1, 2021), www.bbc.com/news/business-58260533.

Although boards are time poor, an app that alerts them about repeated complaints against the same employee should be an efficient way of staying informed. Further, the fact that specific board committees are able to access these reports will likely act as a check against human resources personnel and senior management from concealing complaints. It will be in the interest of corporations to develop these sorts of solutions and take preventive action. If not, the negative information will eventually percolate out through employee surveys (conducted by companies like Glassdoor) or in extreme cases, a public social media post.[44] There could also be legal implications. Directors' duties, as prescribed by Delaware law, require them to set up robust risk management systems that enable them to pay attention to 'red flags'.[45] Some version of this exists in other jurisdictions as well. In light of this, Stevelman and Haan rightly argue that ensuring effective informational flow to the board becomes crucial.[46] Thus, using innovative technologies will be important for directors to be able to fulfil at least one part of their legal duties. Further, as #MeToo has shown, the reputational costs of social media movements could be as damaging (if not more) as lawsuits and that should act as an incentive for firms to strengthen internal reporting systems.

3.1.3 Training

The Holder Report recommended training for leadership, management, human resources, and other employees with respect to conducting interviews and handling of complaints regarding harassment, discrimination, and retaliation.[47] This is a useful recommendation that could also be adopted for complaints regarding any other workforce issues.

---

[44] Companies that sought to restrain employees from doing this via concealment clauses in the employment contract might have to rethink their strategy in the wake of investor pressure. See Patrick Temple-West 'Investors challenge concealment clauses at large tech groups' FINANCIAL TIMES (Dec. 15, 2021), www.ft.com/content/61dead66-65cb-4e07-a12a-c079ff406aa1.

[45] *See* In re Caremark Int'l Inc. Derivative Litig., 698 A.2d 959, 968 (Del. Ch. 1996) and subsequent cases that reinforce this requirement. See also sources cited *supra* note 173.

[46] Stevelman & Haan, *supra* note 41, at 270.

[47] The Holder Report, *supra* note 25, at V.A.

The Holder Report explained that the management training was meant to ensure inclusive leadership, combat implicit bias, and encourage a culture of openness where employees feel comfortable proposing different ideas.[48] The latter part of this statement encourages viewpoint diversity. In this regard, I would also argue that employees who express opinions that go against the accepted wisdom of the team and senior employees should be protected. However, the efficacy of training as a tool to address implicit bias and to promote inclusive leadership is questionable. Research suggests that mandatory diversity training can backfire and cause defensiveness.[49] Thus, diversity training, if at all used, should be voluntary and designed carefully to avoid any negative effects. Ultimately, diversity training is not a silver bullet. If it was, we would have got rid of diversity issues caused by bias a long time ago, considering the widespread adoption of diversity training by various organizations. Instead, implicit bias can be addressed in other ways. Kramer and Harris, in a book published in 2019, suggest that executives making important decisions about hiring, promotion, compensation, etc. should be required to make them only after explaining them to another person. This will introduce some deliberation into the decision as against instinctual decisions that tend to be more biased. Alternatively, they say that 'career-affecting decisions should be made on a comparative basis', meaning that these decisions should only be made after comparing the candidate with two other viable candidates and then articulating the reasons for choosing the candidate over others. This, say Kramer and Harris, will force the executives in question to make decisions based on objective criteria. Another suggestion they provide is that executives making these decisions should be told that their decisions will be reviewed by an independent person and group. Simply knowing that such a review exists will force the executives

---

[48] *Id.*

[49] Frank Dobbin and Alexandra Kalev, *Why Diversity Programs Fail* (July–August 2016, Harvard Business Review), https://hbr.org/2016/07/why-diversity-programs-fail. Referring to mandatory diversity training in many companies, Dobbin and Kalev write that 'laboratory studies show that this kind of force-feeding can activate bias rather than stamp it out' because 'as social scientists have found, people often rebel against rules to assert their autonomy'. Instead, they find that 'it's more effective to engage managers in solving the problem, increase their on-the-job contact with female and minority workers, and promote social accountability – the desire to look fair-minded'.

in question to think slowly and carefully about the decision. This is because they would 'want to appear fair, careful, and objective'.[50] Now that the CDO role is becoming prominent, these and other ideas along these lines should be something that the CDO introduces and implements. Of course, as already mentioned in Chapter 2, for any of this to be possible, the CEO and the board should empower and support the CDO adequately.

Human Resources personnel, being the first point of contact along the reporting line for harassment complaints, also need to be adequately trained to handle complaints. The Holder Report recommends that such training should include proper investigation of complaints regarding harassment, discrimination and/or retaliation, and appropriate documentation of such complaints and resulting investigations.[51] Most importantly, the Report recommends that personnel should be trained to identify when incidents should be escalated and brought to the notice of the company's legal team.[52] Here again, I will add that it is important that human rights personnel are alert to various types of issues faced by diverse employees. While the usual narrative is that a senior person might create problems for underlings, research shows that diverse employees across sectors also face issues with administrative staff. In many cases, it could be diverse administrative staff that are unhelpful and hostile to diverse employees. Williams based on her multi-industry study on this issue notes that 'women lawyers were twice as likely than white men to say that they did not get the same level of admin support as their colleagues (despite the fact that most admins are women)'. People of colour in architecture have similarly reported lack of administrative support even though many of the admin staff in the companies were people of colour. Williams reasons that this phenomenon is probably a result of a system where white men are most influential, leading admin staff (especially women and people of colour) to conclude that 'it makes more sense to hitch their future to a white man'.[53] Irrespective of the reasons, lack of support from admin

[50] ANDREA S. KRAMER & ALTON B. HARRIS, IT'S NOT YOU, IT'S THE WORKPLACE 194–95 (Nicholas Brealey Publishing, 2021).
[51] The Holder Report, *supra* note 25, at 5.B.
[52] *Id.*
[53] Williams, *supra* note 38, at 142–44.

staff is something that should be taken seriously and remedied, either by providing access to different admin staff for the diverse employees in question or by ensuring that the admin staff is made to understand that such behaviour will not be tolerated. It may also be the case that a diverse employee notices disparities in their pay or some other perk with that of others and reports this to Human Resources. Such a report should prompt Human Resources to investigate the claim and either remedy it at their end or escalate the matter if this is not possible.[54] These are just examples. The key message here is that human resources personnel should be aware of various issues facing diverse employees, so that they are able to take necessary action including escalating the complains where necessary.

The reporting process itself could be strengthened by creating multiple avenues for complaints, to give employees alternative options in case they fear retaliation through any one avenue.[55] Examples could be reporting to the immediate manager and to human resources. Again, the Holder Report recommends that protocols for escalating and tracking complaints are set for both human resources personnel and managers.[56] As discussed earlier, tech-based complaint mechanisms and alert systems could also supplement the measures discussed here.

3.1.4 Fault Lines after #MeToo and Potential Solutions

The solutions discussed above have largely focused on providing multiple reporting channels to facilitate the handling of workforce issues within the board's risk management framework and on information regarding employee issues and complaints being shared with the board when problematic patterns emerge. They also have a theme of pivoting the culture of the company to one where wrongdoing of any sort will not be tolerated, and where employees can have their concerns heard and addressed. In 2018, a memorandum of the law firm Wachtell,

---

[54] Indra Nooyi notes that 'it was always an uphill battle' while asking human resources personnel about pay disparities. As she says, human resources 'should have been flagging these issues and systematically addressing them'. Indira Nooyi, My Life in Full: Work, Family, and Our Future 172 (Hachette, 2021).

[55] *The Holder Report, supra* note 23, at VI.C.

[56] *Id.,* at VI.D.

Lipton, Rosen, and Katz suggested that many corporate boards had indeed started to focus on issues of sexual harassment, corporate culture, and gender diversity. Institutional investors had also begun to become active on these issues by 2018.[57] The activism has only grown and expanded since 2018. However, changing a company's culture is not a quick and easy task and each corporation has to tailor changes to its business and circumstances. Even beyond introducing the programs and mechanisms discussed above, it is important for the board and senior executives to actively commit to these issues (set the right tone at the top[58]) to reassure employees about the genuineness of such programs.

Further, while #MeToo has brought about changes to the extent that corporate leadership takes discrimination and harassment seriously, it has not addressed the issue of implicit bias. Men have traditionally been seen to possess leadership qualities, while women tend to be perceived as more nurturing.[59] Researchers have noted that mentoring and networking tend to help women overcome barriers created by such implicit bias and gain leadership positions.[60] For instance, at the recruitment level, doubts about the suitability of a candidate for a board or C-suite role might be countered by a recommendation from a male mentor or champion who belongs to the similar demographic group and/or social circles as the people of the hiring team. For instance, Nooyi said about PepsiCo's then CEO, Roger Enrico, that he mentored her and that showed others that she 'was destined for

---

[57] David A. Katz & Laura A. McIntosh, *Corporate Governance Update: Shareholder Activism Is the Next Phase of #MeToo*, HARVARD LAW SCHOOL FORUM ON CORPORATE GOVERNANCE (Sept. 28, 2018), https://corpgov.law.harvard.edu/2018/09/28/corporate-governance-update-shareholder-activism-is-the-next-phase-of-metoo/.

[58] Julie Walsh, *Setting the Tone at the Top*, 29 LAW NOW 27 (2005) ('Organizations whose management and board espouse a culture of integrity, high ethical standards and compliance help to create a well governed company, with a strong and positive tone at the top.'). See also Alfredo Contreras, Aiyesha Dey, & Claire Hill, *Tone at the Top and the Communication of Corporate Values: Lost in Translation*, 43 Seattle U. L. REV. 497 (2020).

[59] Cindy A. Schipani, Terry Morehead Dworkin, & Devin Abney, *Overcoming Gender Discrimination in Business: Reconsidering Mentoring in the Post #Me-Too and COVID-19 Eras*, 23 U. PA. J. BUS. L. 1072 (2021).

[60] Cindy A. Schipani, Terry M. Dworkin, Angel Kwolek-Folland, & Virginia G. Maurer, *Pathways for Women to Obtain Positions of Organizational Leadership: The Significance of Mentoring and Networking*, 16 DUKE J. GENDER L. & POL'y 89 (2009).

bigger things'.[61] He also publicly gave her credit and 'celebrated her as part of the inner circle and crucial to PepsiCo's future' while making a presentation about an important acquisition.[62] Clearly, an incidental but important function of a mentor seems to be signalling the value of the mentee, which might be necessary to convince people who are used to the old idea of the 'ideal worker'.

From the perspective of women who are qualified but might hesitate to put their hands up for leadership positions, mentors, and champions play a significant role. Take the example of Margaret Keane, the first CEO of Synchrony, who has shared that as a middle manager at General Electric Co. in 1996, she had felt nervous about presenting to the then CEO of the company. However, she credits her then immediate boss Mike Neal's encouragement and championship for being able to take on the CEO role at Synchrony Financial just before it began separating from General Electric.[63] She also mentions others who helped deal with issues like 'work blunders' and 'uncooperative colleagues'. One such helpful colleague, Rick Hartnack, former non-executive board chairman of Synchrony Financial, tutored her about how to get the most out of fellow board members. Such informal advice is just as important as championing a woman to get the leadership position.[64] Ms. Keane says that she was the only woman in the room in most of her leadership positions.[65] Since there is a dearth of women in senior executive and board positions, the role of male mentors and helpful male colleagues is especially important.

Unfortunately, #MeToo has resulted in men becoming fearful of taking on mentoring roles for women or even simply interacting with women. While some level of discomfort always existed, this has now become more pronounced after #MeToo. A 2018 survey reported that 60% of male managers in the United States were uncomfortable

---

[61] Nooyi, *supra* note 54, at 165.

[62] *Id.*, at 163.

[63] Joann S. Lublin, *Synchrony's Margaret Keane Credits These Advisers with Helping Her Reach the Top* (Aug. 14, 2021) WALL ST. J., www.wsj.com/articles/synchrony-margaret-keane-personal-board-11628885375?mod=searchresults_pos2&page=1.

[64] *Id.*

[65] *Id.*

participating in a common work activity with a woman, such as mentoring, working alone, or socializing together.[66] This was a 32% jump from statistics reported a year ago.[67] Similarly, in the UK, a 2019 survey found that 40% of male managers were uncomfortable participating in a common work activity with a woman, such as mentoring, working alone, or socialising together.[68] That was a 33% jump from how they felt before the media reports of sexual harassment.[69] In practical terms, this means that men would prefer to hire men and women would prefer to hire women.[70] This would disproportionately disadvantage women because there are less women in hiring positions.

Even beyond hiring preferences, #MeToo, and responses to the movement have resulted in a heightened awareness regarding one's identity group, and consequentially, a bias in favour of members of their own group. This is concerning because the type of mentorship and championing that lead to Ms Keane (referred to above) being appointed to leadership positions and having access to guidance even after securing these positions might not happen in this environment. More generally, equality within corporations will not be possible unless those who currently hold power (men and/or members of dominant racial groups) join the effort.[71] Not only this, women sometimes do not support other women in their firm whether it is to challenge discrimination or to simply champion another woman.[72] Thus, mentorship across identity groups is significant and should not be allowed to fall away. If #MeToo has alienated the dominant group that holds power, we need to find ways to build bridges again.

---

[66] See Key Findings, LEAN IN, https://leanin.org/sexual-harassment-backlash-survey-results#key-finding-1.

[67] *Id.*

[68] See Key Findings, LEAN IN, https://leanin.org/working-relationships-survey-results-uk.

[69] *Id.*

[70] Schipani, Dworkin, & Abney, *supra* note 59.

[71] Debora L. Spar, *Good Fellows: Men's Role & Reason in the Fight for Gender Equality*, 149 DAEDALUS 222 (2020).

[72] People have termed this 'the Queen Bee syndrome' but as Williams notes, this term has a negative connotation against women. Instead, Williams explains that women sometimes align against each other in an environment of gender bias as a survival mechanism. Ambitious professionals might decide that this is the best way to prove their value to their work groups. See Williams, *supra* note 38, at 140–42.

Solutions on the lines of formal mentoring programs being instituted, scheduling meetings in public places, etc. have been suggested.[73] However, the underlying problem of distrust and fear that seems to have been an unintended consequence of #MeToo ought to be addressed.[74] As a longer term solution, Schipani, Dworkin, and Abney have proposed that junior men should be mentored by senior women.[75] They suggest (although acknowledging a lack of research in this regard) that senior women will not fear that there will be a perception of impropriety while interacting with junior men.[76] This will encourage interactions across the groups and hopefully erase the fault lines in the longer term. This proposal also avoids the problems of diversity training which engenders defensiveness and feelings of being targeted in men (or members of the dominant group to put it more generally) as discussed earlier. Rather, it will serve to normalise interactions between men and women and even help the junior men confront their implicit biases in an informal setting.[77] Research suggests that interacting with individuals from a group helps reduce stereotyping all people from that group, on the basis of on group identity.[78] In the long term, as these junior men go on to hold more senior positions, their decision-making will be less biased against women. It will ultimately be up to each firm to find innovative ways to overcome these fault lines and encourage informal interactions across different groups.

In conjunction with the 'women mentors' proposal, Schipani, Dworkin, and Abney suggest including women in both hiring and promotion committees. The mentoring relationships will help the committee promote the right kind of individuals.[79] Such a system could prevent 'brilliant jerks', discussed earlier, from being

---

[73] Cindy A. Schipani & Terry Morehead Dworkin, *The Need for Mentors in Promoting Gender Diverse Leadership in the #MeToo Era*, 87 GEO. WASH. L. REV. 1272, 1295, 1296 (2019).

[74] *Id.*

[75] Schipani, Dworkin, & Abney, *supra* note 59, at 24.

[76] *Id.*

[77] *Id.*

[78] Zaid Jilani, *How to Beat Stereotypes by Seeing People as Individuals*, GREATER GOOD MAGAZINE (Aug. 28, 2019) https://greatergood.berkeley.edu/article/item/how_to_beat_stereotypes_by_seeing_people_as_individuals.

[79] Schipani, Dworkin, & Abney, *supra* note 59, at 28.

promoted since the more senior women will not fear the repercussions of reporting bad behaviour on the part of junior men. Carr and Dudley have suggested (in a book written for investment management firms) that a data-based approach where firms periodically review the percentage of women hired/promoted versus that of men to examine whether the processes reflected implicit bias.[80] This suggestion can be adopted by other organizations as well although the numbers alone will not provide the full picture. Another aspect that goes to implicit bias seems to be the terminology used in advertising positions. Kjerstin Braathen, the chief executive of DNB in Norway, has noted that some phrasing in job advertisements might appeal to men rather than to women.[81] Similarly, Vodafone was reportedly able to hire more women as a result of removing 'macho jargon' from job adverts.[82]

Not all the ideas discussed above will be relevant for every company. However, firms that genuinely aim to create inclusive cultures that not only eliminate overt discrimination and harassment but also implicit bias and the resulting barriers created for women will try to think of innovative solutions like these. These measures will bear dividends in the long term, if not immediately.

3.2 #BLACKLIVESMATTER

After the #MeToo movement had decelerated a little, 2020 saw the BLM become a prominent corporate governance movement. Despite the BLM having been formed in 2013,[83] it only caught corporate attention in the aftermath of the deaths of George Floyd and Breonna Taylor and the protests that followed.

---

[80] ELLEN CARR & KATRINA DUDLEY, UNDIVERSIFIED: THE BIG GENDER SHORT IN INVESTMENT MANAGEMENT 2851 (Kindle Location) (Columbia University Press 2021).

[81] Richard Milne, *Why Banks Must 'Own' Their Diversity Agenda*, FINANCIAL TIMES (Nov. 18, 2020), www.ft.com/content/d1190611-5989-4eef-ba11-157deb988772.

[82] Jane Bird, *How the Tech Industry Is Attracting More Women*, FINANCIAL TIMES (Mar. 9, 2018), www.ft.com/content/d5d6035a-f63e-11e7-a4c9-bbdefa4f210b.

[83] *Herstory*, BLACK LIVES MATTER, https://blacklivesmatter.com/herstory/#:~:text=In%20 2013%2C%20three%20radical%20Black,Trayvon%20Martin's%20murderer%2C%20 George%20Zimmerman (last visited Aug. 8, 2021).

To give some context to corporate responses to BLM in 2020, it is worth mentioning that the business community had already been steered in the direction of social justice issues by the Business Roundtable (which consists of nearly 200 CEOs of America's largest corporations) and other market actors in 2019. The Business Roundtable had issued a statement on the purpose of the corporation in 2019.[84] By then, in 2019, Larry Fink, the head of Blackrock, one of the largest institutional investors, had written an open letter to the CEOs of companies in which Blackrock invests.[85] After describing current global problems like stagnant wages and excessive nationalism, the danger of losing jobs to technology, etc., Fink asked CEOs to move away from the pursuit of short-term shareholder returns and run their businesses with a 'purpose'. This purpose, according to Fink, should be what drives businesses to create value for stakeholders other than shareholders. For instance, he said[86]:

> …companies must embrace a greater responsibility to help workers navigate retirement, lending their expertise and capacity for innovation to solve this immense global challenge. In doing so, companies will create not just a more stable and engaged workforce, but also a more economically secure population in the places where they operate.

Then came the 2019 statement by the Business Roundtable on corporate purpose that despite beginning by reinforcing a belief in the free market system, went on to make 'a fundamental commitment to all stakeholders'.[87] This was then further elaborated on by stressing on commitment to customers, employees, suppliers, communities, and finally, 'long-term value' for shareholders.[88] (More details on this topic are discussed in Chapter 6.) It is against this backdrop of having articulated a commitment to stakeholders and activism

---

[84] THE BUSINESS ROUNDTABLE STATEMENT, STATEMENT ON THE PURPOSE OF A CORPORATION, https://opportunity.businessroundtable.org/wp-content/uploads/2019/09/BRT-Statement-on-the-Purpose-of-a-Corporation-with-Signatures.pdf (last visited Aug. 8, 2021).

[85] Larry Fink, *Purpose & Profit*, BLACKROCK (2021), www.blackrock.com/corporate/investor-relations/larry-fink-ceo-letter.

[86] *Id.*

[87] *Id.*

[88] *Id.*

from institutional investors on stakeholder issues that corporate America's reaction to the BLM after the events in 2020 should be viewed.

The BLM movement, having initially re-started in 2020 in the form of protests aimed at addressing racism in the criminal justice system, eventually moved on to other areas, including corporations. Since this came in the context of #MeToo, institutional investor activism regarding the importance of stakeholders, and a reiteration of this focus on stakeholders by the Business Roundtable, corporations were quick to signal their support for BLM by making public statements. However, there were other, more tangible, responses too. Yet even amongst these, not all promise long-term solutions for the problem of racism within the corporation. I examine corporate responses aimed at engaging various stakeholders, and measures aimed to address employee concerns below. I then outline how companies should prepare to overcome the fault lines that might emerge as an unintended consequence of BLM, just like with #MeToo.

3.2.1 Engaging Stakeholders

As an immediate reaction, a number of corporations made public statements in support of BLM. This was met with snarky comments like 'open your purse' on social media.[89] Eventually firms did so and made donations to organizations like National Association for the Advancement of Coloured People and the Black Lives Matter Foundation.[90]

Some corporations took specific measures with a view to addressing concerns of the consumer base. For instance, Walmart, Walgreens, and CVS announced that they would stop placing African-American beauty products in anti-theft cases, similar to other beauty products

---

[89] Terry Nguyen, *Consumers Don't Care about Corporate Solidarity. They Want Donations*, Vox (June 3, 2020), www.vox.com/the-goods/2020/6/3/21279292/blackouttuesday-brands-solidarity-donations (the phrase was coined by a TikTok user and later went viral).

[90] For instance, Amazon donated $10 million to the NAACP and other groups supporting justice and equity. See Levi Sumagaysay, *Companies Declared 'Black Lives Matter' Last Year, and Now They're Being Asked to Prove It*, Market Watch (Mar. 6, 2021, 4:34 PM), www.marketwatch.com/story/companies-declared-black-lives-matter-last-year-and-now-theyre-being-asked-to-prove-it-11614972986.

that are not given the same protections.[91] Other corporations have attempted to engage black suppliers. For instance, Sephora committed to devoting 15% of its shelf space to products from black-owned businesses.[92] An example that addresses both customers and suppliers is that of Netflix adding a BLM genre to its service, to showcase the work of black creators and black history.[93]

Advertisements that channelled the BLM movement were also used by a number of companies to engage with both consumers and society more generally. For example, Procter and Gamble released an advertisement called 'The Choice', calling on white Americans to become allies, advocates and activists in ending racial inequality.[94] Another company, Papa John's, released an advertisement, 'Making a Difference', which ended with a quick mention of the brand's charitable contributions towards fighting racial injustice (among other causes).[95] Reactions to such advertisements or to public statements from companies about their support for BLM have been mixed.

While some ads were well received, in other cases, social media users criticized companies for making these statements and adverts without effecting change within their own companies. In some cases, the criticism was not particularly well informed. Take the example of Saatchi and Saatchi whose BLM statement on Instagram received a comment about the ad firm's lack of diversity despite its global head, Magnus Djaba, being black.[96] However, there was also some informed criticism

[91] *Walmart, CVS, and More to Stop Locking UP Beauty Products for Black People*, Dazed Beauty (June 15, 2020), www.dazeddigital.com/beauty/head/article/49521/1/walmart-cvs-and-more-to-stop-locking-up-beauty-products-for-black-people.

[92] Jemima McEvoy, *Sephora First to Accept '15% Pledge', Dedicating Shelf-Space to Black-Owned Businesses*, Forbes (June 10, 2020), www.forbes.com/sites/jemimamcevoy/2020/06/10/sephora-first-to-accept-15-pledge-dedicating-shelf-space-to-black-owned-businesses/?sh=606292574b02.

[93] Todd Spangler, *Netflix Launches 'Black Lives Matter' Collection of Movies, TV Shows and Documentaries*, Variety (June 10, 2020, 6:20 AM), https://variety.com/2020/digital/news/netflix-black-lives-matter-collection-1234630160/.

[94] Simon Gwynn, *Ad Industry Says Brands Should Speak Out about Black Lives Matter*, Campaign US (June 12, 2020), www.campaignlive.com/article/ad-industry-says-brands-speak-black-lives-matter/1686233.

[95] Ace Metrix, *Black Lives Matter Themed Ads See Success*, Ace Metrix: An iSpot.tv Company (July 14, 2020), www.acemetrix.com/insights/blog/black-lives-matter-themed-ads-see-success/.

[96] Tom Braithwaite, *How Companies Decided That Black Lives Matter*, Financial Times (June 5, 2020), www.ft.com/content/6bd46c48-ee90-42b8-af70-78d949025c1d.

from media commentators, scholars, and most importantly, employees calling for corporations to clean house before making public statements. An article in the Harvard Business Review rightly noted that many employees were experiencing 'statement fatigue', referring to companies that made statements without taking action.[97] The article quoted an employee of a tech company saying that it was 'ironic that senior leadership prioritized their public image when internally they dismissed or ignored the very Black voices that they claimed to care about'.[98]

It is true that both statements and tangible actions – whether in the form of donations, or advertisements, or working with black suppliers – do not address issues of diversity within the corporation. Despite this, a relevant point to note here is that the firm's commitment to black customers or suppliers can have a positive impact on a diverse workforce, particularly black employees, to the extent that it signals a commitment to fight racism. However, it will not have any impact, and sometimes even negative impact as the quote from the tech employee mentioned above shows, if companies do not follow up such actions with internal measures.

3.2.2 Engaging Employees

In terms of issues relevant to workforce diversity, some companies pledged to appoint black directors while others announced mechanisms to diversify the workforce more broadly. Reddit is notable in that one of its board members (and co-founder) Alexis Ohanian resigned from the board and asked to be replaced by a black person. The company then announced that Michael Seibel, Y Combinator's CEO, would take Ohanian's place on the board.[99] While this resulted in one black person being appointed to Reddit's board, it does not seem like a long-term solution to the issue of appointing and then

---

[97] Erin Dowell & Marlette Jackson, *'Woke-Washing' Your Company Won't Cut It*, HARVARD BUSINESS REVIEW (July 27, 2020), https://hbr.org/2020/07/woke-washing-your-company-wont-cut-it.

[98] *Id.*

[99] Nick Statt, *Reddit Names Y Combinator CEO Michael Seibel as Alexis Ohanian's Replacement*, THE VERGE (June 10, 2020, 5:00 AM), www.theverge.com/2020/6/10/21285835/reddit-board-replacement-alexis-ohanian-michael-seibel-y-combinator.

retaining diverse employees. Unless Reddit follows this up with specific mechanisms targeted at the workforce, this will just be a one-off reaction to the BLM movement.

A number of companies came together in September 2020 to launch 'The Board Challenge' which calls on companies to 'pledge' to appoint at least one black director within the next year.[100] Again, while this may be a good start, simply pledging to appoint one black director does not indicate a concrete or sustained plan for diversifying the entire workforce (which is just as important as diversifying the board).

Some companies have committed to diversifying leadership positions. Uber aims to double the number of black employees in leadership positions by 2025.[101] Another example is PepsiCo, which declared its goal to increase black managerial representation by 30% and more than double business with black-owned suppliers.[102] What measures will be taken to achieve these goals is not clear from the announcements. Still, it is encouraging to see companies thinking of diversifying positions below the board level.

Other corporations have looked deeper and sought to improve their workforce diversity. An example is Adidas (which also owns Reebok) announcing that it would fill at least 30% of all new positions in the United States at Adidas and Reebok with black and Latinx people. The company also noted that it would be announcing a target aimed at increasing representation of black and Latinx people within its workforce in North America.[103] In June 2021, the company reported on its progress in this regard, noting that about 30% of all positions had

---

[100] THE BOARD CHALLENGE, ABOUT US, https://theboardchallenge.org/about-us/ (last visited Aug. 8, 2021).

[101] Lizette Chapman & Bloomberg, *Uber Pledges to Double Company's Black Leadership by 2025*, FORTUNE (July 17, 2020), https://fortune.com/2020/07/17/uber-double-black-leadership-2025/#:~:text=Uber%20Technologies%20Inc.,a%20blog%20post%20on%20Friday.

[102] Richard Feloni & Yusuf George, *These are the Corporate Responses to the George Floyd Protests That Stand Out*, JUST CAPITAL (June 30, 2020), https://justcapital.com/news/notable-corporate-responses-to-the-george-floyd-protests/; PEPSICO, PEPSICO'S RACIAL EQUALITY JOURNEY – BLACK INITIATIVE, www.pepsico.com/about/diversity-and-engagement/racial-equality-journey-black-initiative.

[103] Adidas, MESSAGE FROM THE ADIDAS BOARD: CREATING LASTING CHANGE NOW (June 9, 2020), www.adidas-group.com/en/media/news-archive/press-releases/2020/message-adidas-board-creating-lasting-change-now/.

indeed been filled by black or Latinx people. It also announced that
its new target was that at least 50% of new hires for all open positions
was to be diverse candidates (in terms of gender, sexual orientation,
disability, veteran, etc.). Further, it said that the company was targeting 20–23% black and Latinx employee representation in corporate
roles by 2025, and 12% in leadership positions in the United States by
that time.[104] While this seems like a sustained hiring effort, it obviously
needs to be followed up with measures to retain diverse employees in
the company. These measures will have to tackle implicit bias by putting in place the type of mechanisms discussed earlier in the context
of #MeToo.

Companies like Salesforce and Snap Inc have, apart from
announcing similar diversity targets for their respective workforces,
made their diversity data available to the public.[105] Indeed, releasing
such data makes it possible for institutional investors to engage more
substantially with corporations on the issue of diversity as Martinez
and Fletcher have argued.[106] However, numerical disclosures are not
the most effective tool to effect serious change. In fact, since disclosures open companies up to criticism, they incentivise manipulation.
Even corporations that are not dishonest might not address systemic
issues holding their employees back from rising up the ladder because
their diversity resources have been expended on measuring, disclosing, and then responding to investor pressure to increase numerical
representation.[107]

While hiring more black employees may be a more pertinent
response for companies that do not have a diverse workforce, and setting targets to have more diverse candidates in leadership positions

---

[104] Adidas, Fact Sheet: Progress on Creating Lasting Change Now (June 2, 2021),
www.adidas-group.com/en/media/news-archive/factsheet/2021/fact-sheet-progress-
creating-lasting-change-now/.

[105] See Sales Force, We Believe in Equality for All, www.salesforce.com/company/
equality/ (Aug. 9, 2021); Sarah Frier & Bloomberg, *Snap Unveils Diversity Numbers,
Plans to Double Women and Minorities on Staff*, Fortune (July 30, 2020), https://fortune
.com/2020/07/29/snap-diversity-numbers-double-women-minorities/.

[106] Veronica Root Martinez & Gina-Gail S. Fletcher, *Equality Metrics*, The Yale Law
Journal Forum 869 (2021).

[107] Alison Taylor, *More Disclosure Is Not the Answer to Corporate Diversity Shortfalls*,
Quartz at Work (June 30, 2021), https://qz.com/work/2027020/disclosure-is-not-
the-answer-to-corporate-diversity-shortfalls/?utm_term=mucp.

could be the next step, a mere focus on numbers is usually unhelpful. To achieve true diversity, it is important to ensure that there is
an inclusive culture, as discussed earlier in the context of #MeToo,
to ensure that black members of the workforce are able to contribute
without barriers. The Holder Report's recommendations on employee
relations, board oversight of issues pertinent to the well-being of
diverse employees, and training of HR and managerial staff to ensure
that appropriate matters are escalated and addressed; alongside other
solutions discussed earlier in this chapter, are a useful framework for
companies to adopt in the context of black employees as well. These
practices are time- and resource-intensive, which probably explains
why very few companies have gone down this path. More innovative solutions (as discussed in the context of #MeToo) like appointing
mentors who are senior women, or in this context, senior employees
of colour to junior members of the dominant group – men or in this
context white employees will be helpful in addressing implicit bias,
albeit in the long term.

A small number of companies have indeed taken steps that might
suggest an interest in more long-term measures. DoorDash announced
that it was creating a 'Dashers of Color Council', a formal group to
advise the company on issues facing the black community in the
organisation. It also stated that it would collaborate with experts to
identify ways to combat bias on its platform.[108] This was in addition to
other steps including a partnership with Kiva to match up to $150,000
in crowdsourced loans for black business owners. It also launched a
'black-owned' tag for restaurants participating on DoorDash, offering
USD 0 delivery fees from those establishments, as well as zero commission fees for 30 days for new black-owned restaurants that sign
up for its platforms.[109] While this seems well intentioned, marking
out black businesses in this way might not be wise. Pricewaterhouse

---

[108] Tony Xu, *Standing Together for Justice*, DoorDash (June 3, 2020), https://blog.door-dash.com/standing-together-for-justice-dc98cf164b7b.

[109] *Introducing New Initiatives to Support Black-Owned Businesses on DoorDash and Caviar*, DoorDash (July 8, 2020), https://blog.doordash.com/introducing-new-initiatives-to-support-black-owned-businesses-on-doordash-and-caviar-6b2b7cb4586c; Tatum Hunter, *These Companies Took Action in Support of #BlackLivesMatter*, BUILT IN BETA (June 2, 2021), https://builtin.com/diversity-inclusion/companies-that-support-black-lives-matter-social-justice.

Coopers (PwC) created a Diversity and Inclusion (D&I) Partner Advisory Council and announced that it would also be creating a D&I Staff Advisory Council.[110] Even prior to BLM, PwC had deliberately focused on diversity over the past three years and tripled hires from Historically Black Colleges and Universities.[111] Another example is General Motors which created an Inclusion Advisory Board, consisting of eleven internal and external leaders to guide the company in improving inclusion and diversity.[112] While the constitution of such diversity bodies would suggest that the companies are keen to reduce barriers for black and other diverse employees, it is not yet clear what sorts of measures they will take or how sustained the efforts will be.

Hiring of diversity officers and related positions also increased by 50% in response to BLM. Interestingly, such jobs had been slashed in the wake of the COVID-19 pandemic, which had begun a few months before the BLM protests in the United States. The sudden uptick in postings indicates that companies were responding to the backlash to their public support of BLM. In one glaring example, Thumbtack, which had laid off its diversity and inclusion leader due to the impact of the pandemic, sought to hire a new leader just two months later.[113] However, as discussed in Chapter 2, hiring a diversity officer is not a solution unless the person appointed to this role is given both authority and resources to effect change.

3.2.3 Preparing for Fault Lines after BLM

Even beyond the statements of support about BLM, donations, BLM-related ads, and measures like working with black suppliers and

---

[110] PWC, What PWC is Doing to Stand Up Against Racism (Aug. 9, 2021), www .pwc.com/us/en/press-releases/what-pwc-is-doing-to-stand-up-against-racism.html.

[111] Nicholas Wyman, *How Cisco and PwC Turned Their Diversity Efforts into Measurable Results*, HR Morning (Aug. 4, 2020), www.hrmorning.com/articles/improving-diversity/.

[112] GM, Inclusion Advisory Board, www.gm.com/our-company/leadership/inclusion-advisory-board.html (Aug. 9, 2021); Kalea Hall, *GM Names Members of New Inclusion Advisory Board*, The Detroit News (June 22, 2020), www.detroitnews.com/ story/business/autos/general-motors/2020/06/22/gm-names-members-newly-formed-inclusion-advisory-board/3236091001/.

[113] Jenna McGregor, *Diversity Job Openings Fell Nearly 60% after the Coronavirus. Then Came the Black Lives Matter Protests*, The Washington Post (July 15, 2020), www.washingtonpost .com/business/2020/07/15/diversity-jobs-coronavirus-george-floyd-protests/.

diversifying the workforce, companies have come to realise that millennials and Gen Zers expect them to take a public stand on political issues. (Such corporate political activism has come to be known as woke capitalism.[114]) However, there are also suggestions that BLM and the subsequent corporate activism might have increased racial tensions (just like #MeToo seems to have created fault lines between men and women) in the workplace.[115] Again the concern in this context is that racial minorities should not lose out on mentoring and networking opportunities, similar to the concerns with regard to the unintended effects of #MeToo. Companies will have to find innovative solutions to ensure that there is a culture where employees help one another, irrespective of what group they belong to. At the moment, unfortunately firms seem to be unsuccessful in thinking about these issues with a long-term focus and this has led to decisions that might alienate a section of the workforce as I explain below.

3.3 CORPORATE ACTIVISM AND SHORT-TERMISM

Corporate activism (or woke capitalism, to use the phrase that is in vogue) on political issues might indeed have a positive impact. However, increased pressure via social media by members of society seems to be pushing companies to take hasty decisions aimed at calming the social media backlash without consideration of long-term consequences.

First, let us consider the positive implications. Corporate activism in response to social media pressure could result in ethical conduct and support for social justice issues because, as the examples

---

[114] This phrase has gained usage from both sides of the political spectrum. See Stefan J. Padfield, *Corporate Governance and the Omnipresent Specter of Political Bias*, 104 MARQ. L. REV. 47, 77 (2020). Padfield says that the term 'woke' has found a broad application. Although Sharfman and Moore have argued that the phrase 'woke capitalism' should be retired because it is meaningless, its wide adoption means that the phrase is here to stay. See Bernard Sharfman & Marc Moore, *The Corrupting Influence of the Term 'Woke Capitalism'*, REAL CLEAR MARKETS (July 14, 2021), www.realclearmarkets.com/articles/2021/07/14/the_corrupting_influence_of_the_term_woke_capitalism_785334.html.

[115] Robert Booth, *Black Lives Matter Has Increased Racial Tension*, 55% say in UK poll, THE GUARDIAN, www.theguardian.com/world/2020/nov/27/black-lives-matter-has-increased-racial-tension-55-say-in-uk-poll.

discussed above indicate, mere signalling without supporting actions will be called out. Insincere corporations will be publicly shamed, after which they will respond with corrective behaviour. As we saw with #MeToo, this phenomenon brought tangible benefits with regard to addressing sexual harassment issues. Further, social movements can benefit from corporate resources. In turn, corporations could be rewarded with enhanced value both by investors and consumers that see the corporation's actions align with their views.[116]

However, a closer examination might reveal possible negative consequences. It is not certain that corporate hypocrisy with respect to social justice issues will be identified and called out. The social media users are not necessarily investigating individual corporations in detail. Tweets or posts that go viral are not always the most informed ones. In fact, the nature of social media is such that the identity of the author is immaterial. Sometimes, the post may be factually incorrect, as was the case with the Instagram comment about Saatchi and Saatchi's lack of diverse leadership. Millennials and Gen Zers distrust corporations and financial institutions, and this might taint some of their assessments of corporate actions.[117] Even assuming that corporate hypocrisy is appropriately identified and results in social media pressure for course correction, in most cases, the response is only aimed at quelling the backlash in the short term without long-term measures. The short-term measures may even cause employees to limit their interactions to their own identity-based groups and develop a bias against those belonging to other groups.

One example of a knee-jerk reaction is that of Apple firing Antonio Garcia-Martinez, who had been hired as an advertising technology engineer just a month earlier, because of what it termed as 'discriminatory

---

[116] See Lin, *supra* note 9, at 1574–82.
[117] *The Deloitte Global 2021 Millennial and Gen Z Survey*, DELOITTE (2021), www2.deloitte .com/global/en/pages/about-deloitte/articles/millennialsurvey.html (less than half of millennials and Gen Zers surveyed see business as a source of good in society. This negative view of business is largely influenced by the financial crisis). See Tunku Varadarajan, *Can Vivek Ramaswamy Put Wokeism Out of Business?*, WALL STREET JOURNAL OPINION (June 25, 2021, 3:33 PM), www.wsj.com/articles/can-vivek-ramaswamy-put-wokeism-out-of-business-11624649588?mod=searchresults_pos8&page=1 ('By the end of the crisis, Americans "were actually pretty jaded with respect to capitalism. Corporations were the bad guys. The old left wanted to take money from corporations and give it to poor people".').

behaviour' on his part.[118] According to Garcia-Martinez, there was no discriminatory behaviour. Instead, his firing was the result of an outcry over a passage in his non-fiction book which I have reproduced below[119]:

> Most women in the Bay Area are soft and weak, cosseted and naive despite their claims of worldliness, and generally full of shit. They have their self-regarding entitlement feminism, and ceaselessly vaunt their independence, but the reality is, come the epidemic plague or foreign invasion, they'd become precisely the sort of useless baggage you'd trade for a box of shotgun shells or a jerry can of diesel.

Apparently, 2,000 Apple employees signed an internal petition criticizing his hiring based on this passage. Many employees had also criticised the hire on social media.[120] For his part, Garcia-Martinez has been contrite. The Wall Street Journal has reported that Garcia-Martinez said the book 'is not me now, it wasn't even me then' and that he 'was trying to create a style in my naive, first-time book writer sort of way, which in retrospect, I think was a mistake and I regret much of it'.[121] So not only was there no workplace misconduct as was implied in Apple's statement, but Garcia-Martinez had also expressed contrition for that passage. Further, Apple sought Garcia-Martinez out, rather than the latter applying for the job, and knew of Garcia-Martinez' book when he was hired as is evident from the fact that they questioned his referees about it.[122] Since Apple chose to hire him well aware of the book, what his firing implies is that the company was now merely trying to prevent social media outrage. The incident could

[118] Tim Higgins, *Former Apple Engineer Accuses Company of Defamatory Statements Over Dismissal*, WALL ST. J. (May 14, 2021, 10:06 PM), www.wsj.com/articles/former-apple-engineer-accuses-company-of-defamatory-statements-over-dismissal-11621044377.

[119] Matt Taibbi, *On the Hypocrites at Apple Who Fired Antonio Garcia-Martinez*, TK NEWS BY MATT TAIBBI (May 14, 2021), https://taibbi.substack.com/p/on-the-hypocrites-at-apple-who-canceled?fbclid=IwAR2EvNdCVrCyIvfEI-mY436ESGSnFL3VkH9 C14eFbbFHvGDUu9zdkomIdaE.

[120] Tyler Sonnemaker, *Apple Engineer Leaves Company after Employees Speak out about His 'Misogynistic' Past Comments*, BUSINESS INSIDER AUSTRALIA (May 13, 2021), www.businessinsider.com.au/apple-employees-speak-publicly-about-misogynistic-hire-2021-5?r=US&IR=T.

[121] Higgins, *supra* note 107.

[122] Jemima Kelly, *What Happens When Virtue-Signalling Enters Corporate life* FINANCIAL TIMES (May 20, 2021), www.ft.com/content/a01eed6c-966d-4e99-9700-f15d4c022617.

have been used as a chance to have internal discussions about why that statement was problematic and how such generalizations can be harmful.[123] Instead, by firing the employee for a past action, Apple seems to have simply reacted to pressure. The action is even more ironical because Garcia-Martinez, a Cuban-American is in his own words, one of the few people of colour who has risen to a senior level.[124] One columnist has assessed that the move seems to be an effort to protect Apple's 'brand and bottom line' rather than to protect its employees.[125] I will qualify that assessment and add that Apple's brand and bottom line *in the near-term* was being prioritised. The incident is likely to further mark out the fault lines between men and women in the workplace, which, as discussed above in the context of #MeToo, is not good for equality in the firm.

The Apple incident is not an isolated one in terms of firms coming under pressure to make a quick decision, without a view to long-term improvements. Firms that started disclosing diversity metrics after BLM might also fall under this category if they did not complement such disclosures with a more sustained focus on creating a firm culture that values diversity. This pattern is reminiscent of the kind of myopic decision-making that has been criticised in the context of investor activism. The conventional narrative in that context is that activist investors (typically, institutional investors like hedge funds) pressure management to maximise profits in the short-term goals and prevent the corporation from pursuing long-term goals that benefit all stakeholders.[126] This view of investor activism is also expressed in the context of allowing founders of innovative companies to have higher voting rights attached to their shares, so that they are able to realise their vision of the company, free from investor pressure to maximise

---

[123] Akshaya Kamalnath, *Apple and Diversity*, The Hitchhiker's Guide to Corporate Governance (May 16, 2021), https://corporatelawacademic.wordpress.com/2021/05/16/apple-diversity/.

[124] Kelly, *supra* note 122.

[125] *Id.*

[126] Mark R. DesJardine & Rodolphe Durand, *Disentangling the Effects of Hedge Fund Activism on Firm Financial and Social Performance*, 41(6) Strateg. Manag. J. 1054–82 (2020). The article finds that the benefits of hedge fund activism are shareholder centric and short-lived. These benefits however come at 'a mid- to long-term cost to other stakeholders, captured by decreases in operating cash flow, investment spending, and social performance'.

short-term returns.[127] Similarly, when companies play to the gallery and make decisions to address social media criticism in the moment, they might make temporary reputational gains, but open themselves up to future, more serious issues.

In some cases, even the temporary gains do not materialise, because the issues may be divisive enough to result in a backlash no matter which side the company takes.[128] Further, social media trends do not always accurately reflect society's preferences. Social influence or peer influence on social media tends to cause 'herding', that is the tendency to follow others.[129] A few 'influencers' on these networks are responsible for starting trends and these influencers are not necessarily well informed or objectively evaluating issues.[130]

It is also important to note here that people who do not agree with the popular view tend to censor themselves.[131] According to a recent study, urbanites and well-educated individuals are more inclined to self-censor.[132] This would imply that the most well-informed and studied views are not part of the social media outrage. Further, a survey

---

[127] See, e.g., Zohar Goshen & Assaf Hamdani, *Corporate Control and Idiosyncratic Vision*, 125 YALE L.J. 560, 590 (2016).

[128] Marianne M. Jennings, *The Social Responsibility of Business Is Not Social Responsibility: Assume That There Are No Angels and Allow the Free Market's Touch of Heaven*, 16(2) BERKELEY BUS. L. J. 325, 404–5 (2019).

[129] SINAN ARAL, THE HYPE MACHINE: HOW SOCIAL MEDIA DISRUPTS OUR ELECTIONS, OUR ECONOMY, AND OUR HEALTH AND HOW WE MUST ADAPT 225–30 (Harper Collins Publishers, 2020). See also DANIEL KAHNEMAN, OLIVIER SIBONY, & CASS SUNSTEIN, NOISE 102 (William Collins, 2021) [Noting that social pressure is one of the factors affecting group decisions. 'People think that they know what is right or probably right, but they nonetheless go along with the apparent consensus of the group, or the group's early speakers, to stay in the group's good graces.'].

[130] Aral, *id.*, at 250–53.

[131] Eileen Brown, *Here's Why More US Employees Self-Censor Social Media Posts*, ZD NET (Oct. 11, 2019), www.zdnet.com/article/heres-why-more-us-employees-self-censor-social-media-posts/ (the article notes that 36% of the employees surveyed said that they avoided posting about political feelings on social media). See also James Vincent, *The 'Spiral of Silence': How Social Media Encourages Self-Censorship Online*, INDEPENDENT (Aug. 27, 2014), www.independent.co.uk/life-style/gadgets-and-tech/spiral-silence-how-social-media-encourages-self-censorship-online-9693044.html?; Alexis C. Madrigal, *71% of Facebook Users Engage in 'Self-Censorship'*, THE ATLANTIC (Apr. 16, 2013), www.theatlantic.com/technology/archive/2013/04/71-of-facebook-users-engage-in-self-censorship/274982/.

[132] James L. Gibson & Joseph L. Sutherland, *Keeping Your Mouth Shut: Spiraling Self-Censorship in the United States* (2020), https://papers.ssrn.com/sol3/papers.cfm?abstract_id=3647099.

conducted by Cato Institute found that over 50% of the respondents (people across all age groups) said that the political climate prevented them from saying what they believed because others might find them offensive.[133] Not only do people remain silent, some individuals may also falsify their preferences in public (including on social media) so as to fit in with what they see as the dominant view of the day.[134] This would indicate that the social media activism is in fact not indicative of even a majority of the millennials and Gen Zers. Not only this, the fact that dissentient views are not expressed because of self-censorship means that those that do agree with the popular view and say so can drive the overall conversation to a more extreme version. This is known as group polarization.[135] To add to these problems, the online crowd's numbers are sometimes inflated by the use of bots, and companies making decisions regarding responses to social media controversies usually do not have time to verify this or other risks involved.[136]

Considering the above problems, how should companies deal with social media crises of the sort discussed above? Law firm, Skadden, Arps, Slate, Meagher, and Flom LLP put together a memo on how companies should handle social media crises particularly when a 'senior executive is accused of wrongdoing —— sexual misconduct, bullying, financial fraud, a conflict of interest or other conduct posing a compliance or integrity concern'.[137] One important piece of advice for companies in that memo is as follows:

> Be wary of leaping to premature conclusions. Do not be afraid to say, 'We don't know yet, but these are our priorities and values, and here's what we're doing'.

---

[133] Cato Institute, *Cato Institute Summer 2020 National Survey* (2020), www.cato.org/sites/cato.org/files/2020-07/Crosstabs_Political%20Climate_0.pdf.

[134] See generally TIMUR KURAN, PRIVATE TRUTHS, PUBLIC LIES: THE SOCIAL CONSEQUENCES OF PREFERENCE FALSIFICATION (HUP, 1997).

[135] Kahneman et al., *supra* note 129, at 103–04.

[136] Jennings, *supra* note 128, at 407. Jennings argues that social media outrage may not necessarily be the 'work of angels' in light of how bots may be used on social media to run up numbers on an issue.

[137] Katherine D. (Kady) Ashley, Ryan D. Junck, Bora P. Rawcliffe, & Vanessa K. McGoldrick, *Skadden Discusses Crisis in the C-Suite: A 10-Step Plan*, CLS BLUE SKY BLOG (Oct. 27, 2021), https://clsbluesky.law.columbia.edu/2021/10/27/skadden-discusses-crisis-in-the-c-suite-a-10-step-plan/.

On similar lines, Haidt and Lukianoff rightly caution, on the issue of whether an executive or employee should be fired in response to a social media firestorm that seems to be demanding it, that there should be 'a process in place that slows things down and allows time for careful investigation and due process'.[138] Because social media storms abate quickly, they explain that 'even having just a mandatory two-week cooling off period' can be enough to ride out the storm. Further, they offer that companies should not make firing the target of the social media activism, the preferred course of action. Instead, they say that 'someone has shown extremely poor judgment but has otherwise been an exemplary employee' something short of firing should be considered and that 'as a society we should revive the virtue of forgiveness, and learn to accept apologies again'. While I am largely in agreement with this advice, as my discussion of the Garcia-Martinez incident above would show, I will add the caveat that the advice should not hold for someone who has repeatedly engaged in the conduct in question. In any case, Haidt and Lukianoff's warning to trigger happy companies should give us pause[139]:

> If you have an employee who other employees want terminated, and you do terminate them, you have set a precedent for what counts as a fireable offense. Over time, that line tends to shift in one direction only. Eventually, you may be left only with employees who share a narrow ideology and a punitive orientation toward all but the most doctrinaire speech.

On the whole, it would be prudent for firms to assess decisions with the goal of achieving sustained change, rather than simply aiming to assuage social media outrage. Since social media reactions will often involve a number of individuals without a real stake in the firm, for matters of diversity, it may be more useful to primarily focus on addressing employee concerns, in a manner that considers the interests of all employees. A company that simply takes a virtuous stand in public without solving internal issues will further alienate employees. This

---

[138] Jonathan Haidt & Greg Lukianoff, *How to Keep Your Corporation Out of the Culture War*, PERSUASION (Dec. 3, 2021), www.persuasion.community/p/haidt-and-lukianoff-how-to-end-corporate.
[139] *Id.*

is not to say that other stakeholders, like suppliers, are not important. Companies like Netflix and Sephora that are aiming to promote black suppliers (or content creators in the case of Netflix) might indeed help empower black artists and entrepreneurs.[140] The concern is when the corporate decision is aimed at signalling virtue to the online crowd without changing how the company works with stakeholders on a daily basis. Even when genuine efforts are made, this should go beyond simply increasing representation of women or racial minorities in the firm. Measures to counteract implicit bias promote a culture where harassment and discrimination is not tolerated and improve informal help (via mentoring and networking) received by women and minorities will ensure long-term change. This chapter has discussed a number of possible solutions, in the context of #MeToo and reiterated their relevance in the context of BLM as well. Ultimately, each company's needs are different and management should not only look to these suggestions but also aim to introduce innovative solutions tailored to their specific context.

The forces behind these social movements – generational preferences and social media – are here to stay,[141] and corporations should learn how to positively engage with them while at the same time, not succumbing to ill-considered responses. While #MeToo seems to have resulted in important improvements like specific representations in merger agreements and in termination clauses of employment agreements, a cultural shift can be brought about only by incorporating long-term measures of the sort outlined in this article. Many of these measures will address issues for other diverse individuals, whether it is racial minorities or people with different views, or any other facet of diversity. Such measures will bear rewards over a period of time by

---

[140] See CAROL FULP, SUCCESS THROUGH DIVERSITY: WHY THE MOST INCLUSIVE COMPANIES WILL WIN 142–60 (Beacon Press, Boston 2018). Fulp discusses the importance of engaging with diverse suppliers.

[141] But see Zaid Jilani, *The End of 'Cancel Culture'?* PERSUASION (July 23, 2021), www .persuasion.community/p/the-end-of-cancel-culture. A poll by Morning Consult found that cancel culture (publicly shaming people with different views) was unpopular amongst a majority of all the generations. Based on this, Jilani wonders if cancel culture might have already peaked. I don't agree with this inference from the poll results because a small but vocal minority seems to be enough to be driving social media movements and one unfortunate consequence of these movements is cancel culture.

ensuring that misconduct of any sort can be addressed *ex ante* and by retaining and promoting talented employees.

Beyond working on improving firm culture, boards and management should be prepared for social media activism on various issues. While these external pressures cannot be controlled, what companies can control is their own conduct. Clearly stating an ethical compass and acting accordingly will be important in an environment where corporate actions are susceptible to online criticism that can prove costly.[142] Such statement of what social issues the corporation will prioritise and address will be firm-specific, thus allowing companies to distinguish themselves from their competitors in this regard. This kind of competition in the social justice sphere amongst corporations could even lead to innovative solutions to social problems. Fulp proposes that the Company Code and Mission Statement could be useful means of communicating firm priorities.[143] This may still not prevent antagonising some individuals who are not well informed and whose views may be coloured by their distrust of corporations. However, in the long run, those stakeholders that are regularly interacting with the corporation, employees, and suppliers will spread positive information about the company. For example, surveys conducted by companies like Glassdoor reflect views of employees.

From the perspective of social movements, it is more helpful to their broader causes if corporations genuinely work towards the goals sought to be achieved, rather than simply bowing to social media pressure. Insincere corporate initiatives on social justice issues are not uncommon and have come to be known as woke-washing (similar to greenwashing in the context of environmental action).[144] Fan argues

---

[142] SALLY WHEELER, CORPORATIONS AND THE THIRD WAY 85 (Bloomsbury Publishing, 2002). Wheeler, drawing from Aristotle's virtue ethics principles, proposes that corporations should set their own standards for contributions to society against the backdrop of accumulated choices of other individuals in the community. In her conception, corporations are treated as individuals while superimposing the virtue ethics model on corporate behaviour.

[143] FULP, *supra* note 124, at 168–74 (Fulp proposes doing this by means of the Company Code and Mission Statement). See also Lin, *supra* note 9, at 1601 (Lin proposes that companies establish protocols for how they should respond to pressing social activism in a manner that will 'enhance firm value while minimizing bad publicity, reputational damage, and economic harm to the company'.).

[144] Erin Dowell & Marlette Jackson, '*Woke-Washing' Your Company Won't Cut It*, HARV. BUS. REV. (July 27, 2020), https://hbr.org/2020/07/woke-washing-your-company-wont-cut-it. A particularly ridiculous example of an insincere attempt to take a pro-social

that corporations, like social movements, can play a role in reorienting the law to address evolving social understandings.[145] This seems to be true when one considers some of the changes brought by #MeToo. However, if companies do not undertake sustained efforts to retain and promote diverse candidates, the gains of the movement (like #MeToo representations) could eventually fall away.[146]

3.4 CONCLUSION

The social movements discussed above signify, to a certain extent, a shift in power from institutional investors to members of the general public, in terms of being able to push corporations on ESG issues, and particularly diversity. It also points to a new age where stakeholders (including members of society who might never have directly interacted with the company) are able to communicate, cooperate, and coordinate with each other on specific issues via social media. In other words, they are able to overcome the classic collective action problem.[147] Because of these forces, corporations have been forced to countenance significant social justice issues including diversity. This

---

stand is that of a company (Lululemon) promoting anti-capitalist workshops. After some social media outrage over the incongruity of a company that sold pricy clothing hosting events with 'anti-capitalism' themes, Lululemon deleted the posts in question. The episode is another example of corporations attempting to play to the gallery (on social media) without putting much thought into possible negative impacts on the company. See Melissa Lopez-Martinez, *Lululemon Faces Backlash for Promoting Workshop to 'Resist Capitalism'*, CTV News (Sept. 12, 2020, 1.14 PM), www.ctvnews.ca/lifestyle/lululemon-faces-backlash-for-promoting-workshop-to-resist-capitalism-1.5102303.

[145] Jennifer S. Fan, *Woke Capital: The Role of Corporations in Social Movements*, 9(2) Harvard Bus. L. Rev. 441, 451 (2019).

[146] *Id.*, at 488, 489. Fan speculates, in the context of corporate activism against the Muslim ban (referring to former US President, Donald Trump's Executive Order No. 13769 'Protecting the Nation from Foreign Terrorist Entry into the United States'), the support of tech companies waned as the movement continued either because of decreasing public interest or because of the companies' moving on to other pressing matters. See also Darren Rosenblum, *California Dreaming*, 99 B.U. L. Rev. 1435, 1450 (2019). ('Voluntary measures and the activists that propel them—whether within institutional shareholders or among nongovernmental organizations – ebb and flow as new controversies grab shareholder attention.')

[147] Aral *supra* note 129, at 260–67 discussing how social media helps overcome the classic collective action problem in various contexts.

chapter has described corporate responses meant to appease the online crowd rather than to initiate real change and argued instead that long-term change should be prioritised. It has proposed some solutions (some of which are aided by technology) that ultimately require corporate leadership to aim for sustained and long-term cultural change. It has also cautioned against allowing the group identity-based fault lines to grow. Some of these ideas will be discussed further in Chapter 5.

The social movements described here might also have contributed to legislation requiring diversity on corporate boards, and to shareholder activism on the issue as the next chapter will discuss.

PART II

4 LEGAL AND MARKET INITIATIVES

Snowballs, Sunlight, and Better Sunlight

A snowball started to roll in 2002 in Norway. The conditions were conducive to the formation of the snowball ... The snowball is now rolling with increasing speed and size to the rest of the world, and many countries have followed Norway's example.

Morten Huse[1]

The snowball that Huse is referring to is that of legal reforms in the form of quotas (minimum number of positions allocated to a group) aimed at diversifying the boardroom in terms of gender alone. While Norway was indeed the first country to introduce legislation on board gender diversity, and this slowly spread to other countries, the broader board diversity discussion (which included race) in the United States preceded the discussion in Norway.[2] There were already calls for women directors in as early as the 1940s.[3] By the 90s, leading commentators had linked the discussion of board independence to that of diversity of race and gender. Following the financial crisis, board

---

[1] MORTEN HUSE, *Concluding Remarks on Part I*, in GETTING WOMEN ON TO CORPORATE BOARDS: A SNOWBALL STARTING IN NORWAY 24 (Silke Machold, Katrin Hansen, & Marina Brogi eds., Edward Elgar, 2013).

[2] In the United States, the Conference Board (an organisation consisting of senior executives from all industries, aiming to explore ideas of business policy and practice) had published a study to show that board diversity could increase shareholder value in 1999. See also Jill Fisch, *Reform: Are There Too Many Cooks in the Corporate Kitchen?*, 2 FORDHAM FIN. SEC. TAX L. F. 67, 82 (1997).

[3] See Sarah C. Haan, *Corporate Governance and the Feminization of Capital* (2020), https://papers.ssrn.com/sol3/papers.cfm?abstract_id=3740608. These calls for diversity are tied to more women becoming stockholders during this time.

diversity gained more attention internationally, and the US Securities Exchange Commission (SEC) introduced some amendments to the pre-existing disclosure requirements in 2010.[4] It is not clear whether the developments in Norway and other European countries that imposed mandatory gender quotas on corporate boards had any bearing on the initial SEC requirement. However, it is likely that these international developments were more influential in the aftermath of #MeToo when the SEC disclosure requirements were amended and California introduced board quotas to improve diversity.[5] Internationally, some countries like the UK and Australia have used disclosure requirements rather than quotas. As I explain later, these disclosure rules, together with external pressure, serve as aspirational quotas. Market players like institutional investors and stock exchanges have also jumped into the fray with diversity requirements for company boards.

This chapter will critically examine these measures with the aim of assessing their effectiveness. It will also examine the curious issue of industry voices publicly supporting these types of laws and regulations while their actions suggest otherwise. The main argument I make here is that both quotas and quantitative disclosures do not provide the right incentives for corporations to make genuine efforts to improve diversity. The alternative that I propose is not to simply leave matters as is, but rather for all those involved in the diversity project to steer the discourse towards long term and sustained change, taking all the pieces of the diversity jigsaw into consideration. One way to push corporations in this direction is to encourage qualitative disclosures that will incentivise innovative and firm-specific solutions.

4.1 QUOTA LAWS: COSTS OUTWEIGH BENEFITS

Quotas are a blunt tool because they essentially require all corporations of a certain type or size (depending on the legislation in question) to appoint a certain number of diverse people. This section studies the

---

[4] Securities Exchange Commission, *Proxy Disclosure Enhancements*, www.sec.gov/rules/final/2009/33-9089.pdf.
[5] Darren Rosenblum, *California Dreaming* (2019) 99(3) B.U. L. REV. 1435.

experience of some European countries and that of California and concludes that the costs of such rigid measures outweighs their benefits.

4.1.1 European Experiences with Gender Quotas

Norway was the trailblazer in setting up gender quotas for company boards. Its law requires a representation of at least 40% for each gender on boards of public limited companies.[6] This requirement was introduced in a phased manner with an initial window of two years being allowed for voluntary compliance by companies.[7] After this two-year period, companies that failed to comply with the requirement could be dissolved by the court after having been given sufficient notice.[8] A hard quota like this is bound to ensure that the number of women on corporate boards will drastically improve. And it did. However, when we look deeper, the story is more complicated and might offer valuable lessons for other countries seeking to take this path.

Apparently, firms complied with the law by appointing the same set of women who had made it to leadership positions resulting in what has become known in Norway as the 'golden skirts' in reference to the few women who are hired by multiple boards.[9] Thus, the quota did not result in ensuring that more women were able to overcome the barriers to reaching board positions. Rather, it merely resulted in the same few women being appointed to many boards. This is despite the fact that the Norwegian government set up a database of female directorial candidates for corporations to consider.[10] It is unclear whether companies

---

[6] Amendment to the Public Limited Companies Act, Ot. prp. Nr. 97 (2002–03) (Nor.).

[7] CHRISTA TOBLER, '*Going Global in Sex Equality Law: The Case of Gender Representation Rules for Company Boards*', in ECONOMIC LAW AND JUSTICE IN TIMES OF GLOBALISATION 894 (Mario Monti et al. eds., Nomos, Vienna, 2007).

[8] Section 16-15 of Norwegian Public Limited Liability Companies Act of 13 June 1997 No 45.

[9] See Morten Huse, *The 'Golden Skirts': Lessons from Norway about Women on Corporate Boards of Directors*, in DIVERSITY QUOTAS, DIVERSE PERSPECTIVES: THE CASE OF GENDER 16–17 (Stefan Gröschl & Junko Takagi eds., Routledge, 2012). See also Marianne Bertrand, Sandra E. Black, Sissel Jensen, & Adriana Lleras-Muney, *Breaking the Glass Ceiling? The Effect of Board Quotas on Female Labour Market Outcomes in Norway* 86(1) REV. ECON. STUD. 191 (2019).

[10] Kenneth R. Ahern & Amy K. Dittmar, *The Changing of the Boards* 127 Q. J. ECON 137, 145 (2011).

did not consider those on the database to be ready for the board. Still, knowingly appointing a person who is already sitting on multiple boards and thus time-poor means that the director is not being appointed for their potential contributions. This tells us that the companies subject to the quota had engaged in what is called as 'check-the-box' compliance, meaning that they were uninterested in embracing the spirit of the law. In fact, when we look at how the law was initially received, we see that some public companies chose to convert into private companies rather than comply with the new measure.[11] Judging by the nature of compliance by those firms that did remain subject to the law, we can conclude that the idea behind it had not been accepted.

Apart from simply raising the percentage of women directors, another expectation from any measures to improve the number of women (or other types of diversity) on the board is that it should translate into a higher number of women (or diverse members) in the firm's C-suite and workforce more generally. This did not happen in Norway.[12] Dhir explains, based on interviews of Norwegian directors he conducted prior to 2015, that some women had to leave management positions for directorships as a result of the quota law.[13] However, since the trend has continued since then, it would appear that new women executives were not appointed. It is not clear whether the female board members failed to champion female candidates for C-suite jobs, and women-friendly policies in the firm, or if their efforts failed for other reasons. In any case, championing diversity comes with costs for diverse people, in terms of how they are perceived by their employees,[14] peers, and bosses.[15] Not only this, people within a

---

[11] Beate Sjåfjell, *Gender Diversity in the Boardroom and Its Impacts: Is the Example of Norway a Way Forward?* 20 DEAKIN L. REV. 25, 28 (2015).

[12] See, e.g., Marianne Bertrand, Sandra E. Black, Sissel Jensen, & Adriana Lleras-Muney, *Breaking the Glass Ceiling? The Effect of Board Quotas on Female Labour Market Outcomes in Norway* 86(1) REV. ECON. STUD. 191 (2019).

[13] AARON A. DHIR, CHALLENGING BOARDROOM HOMOGENEITY 162 (Cambridge University Press, 2015).

[14] For instance, when Indra Nooyi was the CEO of PepsiCo, it was apparently assumed that any Indian American person hired at the company was a contact of Nooyi.

[15] JOAN C. WILLIAMS, BIAS INTERRUPTED: CREATING INCLUSION FOR REAL AND FOR GOOD, 12 (Harvard Business Review Press, 2021) 138. [A study found that 'diversity champions were seen as less competent when they hired someone like themselves ... except when the champions were white men'.]

minority group often (although not always) report experiencing conflicts from within the group, possibly because they are pitted against each other.[16] Irrespective of whether or not these dynamics were at play in Norway, they are useful to note as possible factors in other countries that consider quota laws at the board level. In Norway, this lack of impact on firm diversity more generally again suggests that merely the letter of the law had been complied with. There was no push to conceptualise and give effect to innovative strategies to enhance diversity beyond the board.

This inertia regarding gender issues might suggest that there was no social pressure like in the United States after #MeToo hit. Indeed, although #MeToo spread to Norway with stories of sexual harassment in politics and media companies breaking, the movement did not gain as much traction, with members of the older generation terming it a 'witch hunt'.[17] Further, while #BLM did have an echo in Norway in the form of anti-racism protests, this has not led to responses from companies in the way that we saw in the United States.[18] So far, it remains that the focus on firm diversity in Norway has been limited to increasing the representation of women on corporate boards.

After Norway, other European countries like France, Belgium, Italy, Germany, and Spain introduced quotas for women on corporate boards.[19] Interestingly, Spain, which imposed a 40% gender quota but did not impose a penalty for non-compliance, did not see

---

[16] *Id.*, at 140. Williams says both women and people of colour face these issues and provides a telling extract from one of her interviewees. 'There is a definite white boys club here. And even some of the women that were able to make it, they have the attitude of "suck it up buttercup. I went through it too, so you have to go through it"'.

[17] Mette Wiggen, *Scandinavia's #MeToo Problem*, FAIR OBSERVER (Dec. 10, 2019), www.fairobserver.com/360_analysis/scandinavia-gender-equality-me-too-movement-norway-sweden-finland-news-73651/.

[18] David Nikel, *Norway Fears Coronavirus Return as Anti-Racism Protest Fills Oslo Streets*, FORBES (June 6, 2020), www.forbes.com/sites/davidnikel/2020/06/06/norway-fears-coronavirus-return-as-anti-racism-protest-fills-oslo-streets/?sh=5fee47e0504c. See Nerijus Adomaitis, *'Climate before Cash': How Young Norwegians Are Driving Change in the Country's Oil Industry*, NBC NEWS (Apr. 12, 2021), www.nbcnews.com/business/energy/climate-cash-how-young-norwegians-are-driving-change-country-s-n993761.

[19] For a discussion of the varying levels of enforcement measures in each of these countries, see Heike Mensi-Klarbach & Cathrine Seierstad, *Gender Quotas on Corporate Boards: Similarities and Differences in Quota Scenarios* 17(3) EUR. MANAG. REV. 615 (2020).

a substantial increase in female board directors.[20] In fact, as little as 9% of the firms subject to the requirement complied with it.[21] This is reminiscent of Norwegian firms being reluctant to comply with the quota in the period before it became mandatory. At the end of the two-year period before Norway's quota became mandatory, only about 15.5% of the directors on all public companies were women and this was much lower than what the government had intended.[22] Clearly, only a hard quota induced compliance, albeit with the letter rather than the spirit of the law.

In most of the other countries, the number of women directors increased just like it did in Norway.[23] But again, there is no evidence to show that there were more women appointed to the C-suite or in the rest of the workforce because of such quotas. As discussed in Chapter 2, C-suite diversity is perhaps even more useful than board diversity for the company and its workforce to be able to benefit from diversity.

With a view to addressing the lack of women in the C-suite, Germany, which has a two-tier board system (consisting of the management board and the supervisory board), has imposed a gender quota on the management board. The law requires companies with a management board having more than four seats to fill at least one of these seats with a woman.[24] This is the equivalent of trying to impose a quota on executive directors in a unitary board system (which is what United States and other common law countries have). Under Section 76(4) of the German Stock Corporation Act, these companies were previously only required to set their own targets for the proportion of women on the management board, although a target of zero was also permissible.[25] This quota for management boards is in addition

---

[20] Articles 75, 78, Spanish Gender Equality Act, 2007.

[21] See Ruth Mateos de Cabo, Siri Terjesen, Lorenzo Escot, & Ricardo Gimenoe, *Do 'Soft Law' Board Gender Quotas Work? Evidence from a Natural Experiment* 37(5) *EUR. MANAG. J.* 611 (2019).

[22] Sjåfjell, *supra* note 11.

[23] Helena Vieira, *Quotas Have Led to More Women on Corporate Boards in Europe*, LSE Business Review (Sept. 30, 2016), https://blogs.lse.ac.uk/businessreview/2016/09/30/quotas-have-led-to-more-women-on-corporate-boards-in-europe/.

[24] Second Leadership Positions Act, 2021 (Germany), which would make amendments to the Stock Corporation Act, 1965 (Germany).

[25] Stock Corporation Act, 1965 (Germany) s 76(4).

to Germany's 30% quota for women on the supervisory board that has been a requirement since 2015.[26] While focusing on executive directors might have more of an impact than rules only applicable to non-executive board positions, it is too early to tell if this will bring changes to company culture and eventually to workforce diversity. Only if these changes are brought about will the quota have been a success, if one were to assess the requirement from the perspective of addressing the root of the problem.

Like Germany, France first imposed a quota in 2011 for women on the board of directors or the supervisory board in case of companies that have opted for the dual board model via what is known as the Copé-Zimmerman law.[27] Then, finding that the increased percentage of women on directors did not have any trickle-down impact on management positions, France proposed a bill to impose similar quotas for women in senior management positions in 2021.[28] Known as the Rixain-Castaner bill, this will require companies with more than 1,000 employees to have 30% representation of each sex in positions of 'senior managers and members of management bodies' by 2027, and 40% by 2030.[29] In addition to this, companies subject to the Rixain-Castaner bill are also required to annually publish the proportion of women and men in senior management positions.[30] Thus, the bill seems to be employing a mix of quota and disclosure requirements to ensure that companies are compliant. Here too, the success of the bill, once it becomes law, will depend on whether it can address the causes of the problem. Further, one is left to wonder what the solution will be if diversity in management positions is unable to have trickle-down effects to the rest of the workforce. Will there be quotas at every level?

[26] Act on Equal Participation of Women and Men regarding Leadership Positions within the Sectors of Private Economy and Public Service, 2015 (Germany). This is now reflected in s 96 of the Stock Corporation Act, 1965 (Germany).

[27] LAW No. 2011-103 of January 27, 2011 on the balanced representation of women and men on boards of directors and supervisory boards and on professional equality, www.legifrance.gouv.fr/dossierlegislatif/JORFDOLE000021716835/. See Veronique Magnier & Darren Rosenblum, *Quotas and the Transatlantic Divergence of Corporate Governance* 34 NW. J. Int'l L. & Bus. 249, 255 (2014) for a discussion of the law.

[28] Article 7, Bill 4000 aiming to accelerate economic and professional equality, www.assemblee-nationale.fr/dyn/15/textes/l15b4000_proposition-loi.

[29] *Id.*

[30] *Id.*

The industry reactions to the new quota for management boards in Germany and France have been mixed. In Germany, Hiltrud Werner, a Volkswagen AG board member was of the view that the quota was long overdue. However, another company, MTU Aero Engines AG, said that the law 'encroaches considerably on companies' freedom of decision' but then also added that the requirement was 'a building block towards promoting women to management positions and encourages us to strengthen the measures we have already implemented'.[31] This double-speak is interesting and something that resonates in the United States too, as will be discussed later in this chapter. In France, Geoffroy Roux de Bézieux, head of the bosses' union (Medef), seems to echo MTU Aero Engines AG, minus the double-speak, when he said that there was no need for an extension to the Copé-Zimmermann law and that the Rixain-Castaner bill was interfering with company decisions.[32]

4.1.2 California: Looking beyond Gender

Although the United States has taken the route of requiring companies to voluntarily disclose diversity information, one state, California, has recently introduced board quotas. It would seem that the impact of #MeToo, particularly in Hollywood, might have provided the necessary push to overcome the quota hesitancy, although there is no real evidence to prove that that was the cause.[33] The state initially introduced a gender quota and then followed it up with a quota for racial minorities.

A bill passed in 2018 set out a requirement for companies with principal executive offices in California to appoint at least one woman director by the end of 2019. The requirement would then increase by

---

[31] Kim Richters & Dieter Holger, *Germany Readies Quota for Women Board Members*, WALL ST. J. (Mar. 16, 2021), www.wsj.com/articles/germany-readies-quota-for-women-board-members-11615887001?mod=searchresults_pos14&page=1.

[32] Alison Hird, *French MPs Approve Quotas for More Women in Corporate Management*, RADIO FRANCE INTERNATIONALE (May 13, 2021), www.rfi.fr/en/france/20210513-french-mps-approve-quotas-for-more-women-in-corporate-management.

[33] But see Joan MacLeod Heminway, *Me, Too and #MeToo: Women in Congress and the Boardroom*, 87(5) GEO. WASH. L. REV. 1079, 1088 (2019). Heminway says that such a causal relationship between the social movements and the quota law might be in the eye of the beholder.

the end of 2021 for companies with five or more directors. Companies with six or more board members would need to appoint at least three women directors, those with five board positions would need to appoint two women directors.[34] Non-compliance would result in monetary penalties ($100,000 for the first violation and $300,000 for each subsequent violation) and the fact of non-compliance being made public. Out of 625 affected companies, only 282 reported that they had complied by the end of 2019.[35] However, no fines were levied because regulations regarding this are yet to be adopted. Even when fines are levied, as Fried notes, these amounts would be less than the cost of appointing new board members.[36] It is not clear that the shame sanctions are effective either. On the contrary, one study found that there was a negative share price reaction to the gender quota law.[37] However, the study also found that female board nominees got more votes than male nominees both before and after the gender quota law. The authors of the study explained that this apparent paradox meant that the negative share price reaction was in fact a reflection of 'the concern that the board will sub-optimally replace high quality male directors with new female directors'.[38] In other words, the reaction was to the forced intervention rather than a lack of confidence in the ability of female directors.

California, however, did not stop at a gender quota. In 2020, the state passed a bill to impose a quota for 'underrepresented communities' to the same companies targeted by the previous bill.[39] The term was defined to mean anyone who self-identified as 'Black, African American, Hispanic, Latino, Asian, Pacific Islander, Native American, Native Hawaiian or Alaska Native or as gay, lesbian, bisexual or

---

[34] Bill SB 826 Corporations: boards of directors (2017–18). This Bill would amend the California Corporations Code.

[35] Cydney S. Posner, *New Report on California Board Gender Diversity Mandate*, HARVARD LAW SCHOOL FORUM ON CORPORATE GOVERNANCE (Mar. 18, 2020), https://corpgov.law.harvard.edu/2020/03/18/new-report-on-california-board-gender-diversity-mandate/.

[36] Jesse M. Fried, *Will Nasdaq's Diversity Rules Harm Investors?*, European Corporate Governance Institute – Law Working Paper No. 579/2021 6 (Mar. 31, 2021), https://papers.ssrn.com/sol3/papers.cfm?abstract_id=3812642.

[37] Marina Gertsberg, Johanna Mollerstrom, & Michaela Pagel, *Gender Quotas and Support for Women in Board Elections*, 19 (2021), www.nber.org/papers/w28463.

[38] *Id.*, at 19–20.

[39] Bill AB-979 Corporations: boards of directors: underrepresented communities (2019–20).

transgender'. This bill would require companies to hire at least one director from the underrepresented communities by the end of 2021 and three (if they have more than nine directors on the board) or two directors (if they have between four and nine directors on the board) by the end of 2022. Monetary penalties would apply for non-compliance of this quota, as was the case for non-compliance with the gender quota.

The term 'underrepresented communities' has been questioned in terms of how the categories of communities were chosen. For example, one commentator asks why people of middle eastern origin cannot be included when Asians have been included.[40] Such questions are bound to arise whenever an attempt is made to define something as broad as underrepresentation. However, when some types of diversity get left out, the purpose of the law is defeated. Ultimately, it is good to see policymakers' view facets of diversity beyond gender, but a blunt tool like the quota will require us to commit to a definition of diversity which might prove troublesome. There have been a few constitutional challenges of the quotas from some organizations, but companies have refrained. This reticence to challenge the law may be partly because of pressure from institutional investors and partly because it would appear to go against #MeToo and BLM which companies publicly supported.[41] Even beyond the architecture of the quota itself and constitutional issues, the official reasoning provided for the law is problematic because it makes claims about women directors and racial minority directors being able to increase firm profits. As discussed in Chapter 2, not only are such claims resting on flimsy evidence,[42] they

---

[40] David A. Bell, Dawn Belt, & Jennifer J. Hitchcock, *New Law Requires Diversity on Boards of California-Based Companies*, HARVARD LAW SCHOOL FORUM ON CORPORATE GOVERNANCE (Oct. 10, 2020), https://corpgov.law.harvard.edu/2020/10/10/new-law-requires-diversity-on-boards-of-california-based-companies/.

[41] Courtney Murray & Eric Talley, *Racial Diversity and Corporate Governance: Assessing California's New Board Diversity Mandate*, CLS BLUE SKY BLOG (Oct. 28, 2020), https://clsbluesky.law.columbia.edu/2020/10/28/racial-diversity-and-corporate-governance-assessing-californias-new-board-diversity-mandate/.

[42] The studies only show correlation between women/racial minorities and higher profits but no evidence that women/racial minorities were the cause of such rise in profits. Krawiec makes these arguments regarding Bill SB 826. See Kimberly Krawiec, *Board Diversity in The News Again* (Sept. 1, 2018), http://kimberlydkrawiec.org/board-diversity-in-the-news-again/. See also Akshaya Kamalnath, *California's Proposed Quota for Women on Corporate Boards*, OXFORD BUSINESS LAW BLOG (Sept. 24, 2018), www.law.ox.ac.uk/business-law-blog/blog/2018/09/californias-proposed-quota-women-corporate-boards.

are also harmful to the very women and minority individuals that the law seems to be aiming to help.

The initial Bill to introduce the quota for women specifically mentioned that many technology companies in California went public without having any women on their boards.[43] However, since technology companies in the United States have fewer women entering the workforce to begin with, it might then be worth asking whether the board should have gender parity or simply reflect the demographics of the rest of the company.[44]

The bigger problem that probably needs to be addressed in the technology sector is that many companies reportedly have a work culture hostile to women, and this makes it difficult to retain women in the workforce.[45] An example of this problem is the work culture at Uber that eventually gave rise to the Holder Report.[46] A more recent example of this problem is the culture at Activision Blizzard, a video game company whose employees staged a walk out in July 2021 in protest against widespread harassment and discrimination and an alleged rape that came to light when a lawsuit was filed.[47] These problems cannot be addressed by mandating a quota at the top. Further, details coming to light later about Activision Blizzard seem to point to a governance issue, that is the CEO not reporting serious issues of harassment to the board of directors.[48] Simply increasing the number of diverse members on the board of such a company via quota law would not have helped address the issue of CEO monitoring. Even if one makes the

---

[43] Bill SB 826 § 1(f)(3).

[44] Susan Pinker, *Why Aren't There More Women in Science and Technology?*, WALL ST. J. (Mar. 1, 2018), www.wsj.com/articles/why-arent-there-more-women-in-science-and-technology-1519918657.

[45] Elephant in the Valley, www.elephantinthevalley.com/.

[46] See discussion in previous chapters on this.

[47] Zoe Schiffer, *Activision Blizzard Employees Walk out of Work to Protest Rampant Sexism and Discrimination*, THE VERGE (July 28, 2021), www.theverge.com/2021/7/28/22598410/activision-blizzard-employee-walk-out-protest-sexism-discrimination-lawsuit. The California Department of Fair Employment and Housing brought a lawsuit against the company alleging that 'the company had a pervasive "frat boy" culture where female employees were constantly harassed, discriminated against, and underpaid'.

[48] Kirsten Grind, Ben Fritz, & Sarah E. Needleman, *Activision CEO Bobby Kotick Knew for Years about Sexual-Misconduct Allegations at Videogame Giant*, WALL ST. J. (Nov. 16, 2021), www.wsj.com/articles/activision-videogames-bobby-kotick-sexual-misconduct-allegations-11637075680.

claim that a diverse board would have monitored the CEO better and ensured that relevant information was transmitted to the board, that is a deeper issue that needs to be examined. As discussed in Chapter 2, not all diverse board members bring diverse perspectives; and even when they do, not all of them are psychologically independent of the CEO. This would mean that the discussion should go beyond simple board quotas. Further, diversity in the management team might also act as a check against rogue CEOs.

Finally, while the board and management may create and put in place risk management systems, the impact of such frameworks on corporate culture should also be scrutinized when assessing a firm's commitment to diversity. Ensuring a firm culture that does not allow wrongdoing, including harassment and discrimination, is probably more important than asking companies to hire a minimum number of women directors. An emphasis on culture will help diversify the sector more organically than simply having diversity at the top. More discussion on this is present in Chapter 5.

4.1.3 The Report Card on Quotas

While it is too early to tell how California's board quotas will play out, it would seem from the European experiences that the number of diverse board members will increase, provided that the penalties are enforced. Otherwise, we might have a situation of poor compliance like in Spain. However, the European experience would also suggest that improved board diversity will not result in improved diversity in the C-suite and the wider workforce. On the other hand, the quota imposed by California might fare better because there is more ostensible support for the underlying issues from both firms and other market participants in the aftermath of #MeToo and BLM. However, if firms merely support social causes outwardly, without sincere intent, the quota law might incentivise them to simply do the minimum required to comply, especially once the social movements lose momentum.

There are also other issues with using quotas as a regulatory tool. They can lead to token appointments, that is a phenomenon where women are appointed merely to fulfil the legal requirement, rather than for the value they bring. This is reflected in the golden skirts in Norway: such over-extended female directors might not have enough time to contribute substantially on every board they are part of. Another manifestation of tokenism is when women who are related to existing directors or members of the top management are hired as directors, just to fulfil the quota requirements. This has been observed in France[49] and India (which has a form of gender quota for corporate boards and has a sizeable number of family owned firms).[50] A more subtle manifestation of tokenism has also been observed – one where women directors are not appointed to key board committees such as in the audit, nomination, and compensation committees.[51] As Ford has said, 'bright line rules are the easiest to game and hardest to tailor properly' to each situation, and the quota is definitely a bright line rule that corporations have gamed by making token appointments.[52] Each type of company might have to address different issues and a blunt tool like the quota is indeed incapable of addressing every scenario and so might lead to unintended consequences. Also, any type of regulation, not just a quota, will have unintended consequences.[53]

[49] See Rosenblum (California Dreaming), *supra* note 5, at 1454. Rosenblum interviewed current and former corporate board members from the largest and most actively traded companies listed on France's stock exchange-in 2011 when the Copé-Zimmerman law was introduced. Some of his interviewees said that smaller firms might comply with the quota by appointing 'marionettes', that is 'a female relative or paramour' so as to pay a smaller salary than other women would demand as a result of the quota.

[50] Because companies mostly appointed family members to comply with the quota requirement, a new listing rule was introduced which required at least one woman director who is also an independent director to be appointed to the board. See Akshaya Kamalnath & Annick Masselot, *Corporate Board Gender Diversity in the Shadow of the Controlling Shareholder – An Indian Perspective*, 19 OXFORD U. COMMW. L.J. 179 (2019).

[51] Yaron Nili, *Beyond the Numbers: Substantive Gender Diversity in Boardrooms*, 94 IND. L.J. 145, 178 (2019). ['Females are more likely than their male colleagues to serve on the Corporate Governance and Compensation committees and less likely than males to serve on the Audit Committee after controlling for Age and Industry'.] See also Ruth V. Aguilera, Venkat Kuppuswamy, & Rahul Anand, *What Happened When India Mandated Gender Diversity on Boards*, HARV. BUS. REV. (Feb. 5, 2021), https://hbr.org/2021/02/what-happened-when-india-mandated-gender-diversity-on-boards. In India, after the listing rules made it clear that listed companies should have at least one independent director who is a woman, companies appointed qualified members who were not related to the family of the controlling shareholders. However, these women directors were not appointed to important board committees.

[52] CHRISTIE FORD, INNOVATION AND THE STATE: FINANCE, REGULATION, AND JUSTICE 26 (Cambridge University Press, 2017).

[53] ALEX EDMANS, GROW THE PIE: HOW GREAT COMPANIES DELIVER BOTH PURPOSE AND PROFIT 255 (Cambridge University Press, 2020).

A significant unintended consequence of quota rules is the stigmatisation of women or other individuals who are their beneficiaries.[54] The fact that these directors, even well-qualified ones, were appointed as a result of quota laws might result in negative perception by their peers.[55] Further, colleagues who are not the targets of the quota might view the measure as unfair, which will have negative follow-on effects of lower workplace engagement, particularly with individuals appointed as a result of the quota.[56] This is unfortunate because research suggests that supportive colleagues, particularly of the dominant groups (men, whites, etc. depending on the context) can generate feelings of inclusion for members of minority groups.[57] Further, as discussed in Chapter 3, researchers have identified mentoring and networking as two ways in which women have been able to overcome barriers and gain leadership positions.[58] However, resentment generated by a quota law might discourage men or those from the dominant group from championing women or racial minority colleagues via mentoring or networking.

Another unintended consequence that would be comic if it were not so unfortunate is apparent in an incident in France, albeit outside the corporate sector. It was reported in December 2020 that the mayor of Paris, Anne Hidalgo, was fined 90,000 euros for appointing eleven women out of sixteen upper management positions in the

---

[54] This is true for quotas of any sort. In India, where there are quotas for various castes and religions in educational institutions and public sector jobs, the term quota has taken on a negative connotation. A great illustration of this is a dialogue from an Indian movie (titled 83), which shows the journey of the Indian cricket team which was very much an underdog in the 1983 Cricket World Cup. When the team surprises everyone by qualifying for the finals, a news article calls it a fluke. Some of the team members are irritated by this and discuss the article internally. One team member angrily says in that discussion that they have won the required number of games to qualify, rather than qualifying through a quota. The dialogue is indicative of the negative connotation that quotas bring with them.

[55] Lisa M. Leslie, David M. Mayer, & David A. Kravitz, *The Stigma of Affirmative Action: A Stereotyping-Based Theory and Meta-Analytic Test of the Consequences for Performance,* 57(4) *ACAD. MANAG. ANN.* 964 (2014).

[56] *Id.*

[57] Charlotte E. Moser & Nyla R. Branscombe, *Male Allies at Work: Gender-Equality Supportive Men Reduce Negative Underrepresentation Effects among Women,* SOC. PSYCHOL. PERSONAL SCI. (2021, online first).

[58] Cindy A. Schipani, Terry M. Dworkin, Angel Kwolek-Folland, & Virginia G. Maurer, *Pathways for Women to Obtain Positions of Organizational Leadership: The Significance of Mentoring and Networking,* 16 *DUKE J. GENDER L. & POL'y* 89 (2009).

city government because it violated the 40% quota for the 'under-represented sex'.[59] In this situation, the underrepresented category became men rather than women, thus giving rise to what Hidalgo called an 'absurd and unfair' fine.[60] Of course the fine was justified in terms of what the law required, but it also seems curious to penalise the mayor for appointments that improved women's representation in leadership positions at a point in time when women are still held down by the glass ceiling. Further, one could argue that the eleven women might have been the most meritorious candidates. My argument here is not that men should be underrepresented, but rather that the quota is an instrument that is too blunt to avoid consequences that are adverse to equality within corporations. Although this story from France is not from the corporate world, it may well have been, considering that hard quotas are being imposed there, as well as in many other jurisdictions.

In the private enterprise world, there would also be an argument that if an entrepreneur decides to create a company with only women on the board or in C-suite, they should be able to do it. This is similar to the argument the German company MTU Aero Engines AG was making when it said that the quota law 'encroaches considerably on companies' freedom of decision'. Of course, the same company went on to add that the quota was 'a building block towards promoting women to management positions and encourages us to strengthen the measures we have already implemented'. But even this second comment indicates that the firm is keen to have its own agency in promoting equality rather than to simply comply with an external rule.

Ultimately, the broader goal of improving equality within the firm is not achievable via the quota route. This is best illustrated by the metaphor of a track race used by Choobineh. She asks us to imagine a track race where men and women start at the same point, but only

---

[59] Darren Rosenblum, *When the State Levies Fines on Feminism*, FORBES (Dec. 17, 2020), www.forbes.com/sites/darrenrosenblum/2020/12/17/when-the-state-should-levy-fines-on-feminism/?sh=1356f2ce25b8.

[60] *Anne Hidalgo Denounces an 'Absurd and Unfair' Fine*, HUFFPOST (Dec. 15, 2020), www.huffingtonpost.fr/entry/anne-hidalgo-invite-les-femmes-a-venir-avec-elle-regler-lamende-pour-non-respect-de-la-parite_fr_5fd8ba45c5b663c37599d8b4.

women encounter obstacles along the path thus causing some to get tired and leave the race, while men run straight ahead.[61] Then she brings the quota solution into this track race[62]:

> Every so often, a referee drives next to the running competitors in a golf cart, picks up a few women who are still in the process of completing the race, places them in the passenger's seat, and drives them to the finish line.

Even though the referees might think that this ensures equality, Choobineh points out that the male athletes who do not win an award might feel cheated because they have run the whole race while the women have been dropped off in the golf cart.[63] Not only this, those men who do win an award might look down on the women who win because they did not run the full race.[64] Further, Choobineh rightly concludes that the golf cart policy (or quota) 'simply places women at the finish line, thereby entrenching the focus on gender rather than ensuring that the track & field abilities of both men and women are equally measured in the race'.[65] This metaphor really helps draw attention to the fact that quota laws do not address the problems that give rise to inequality in the workplace but instead makes a cosmetic fix at the top of the corporation which in fact gives rise to further problems like tokenism and resentment against women or whichever group is eligible to benefit from the quota.

To be able to address the actual obstacles on the track hampering women, the more general barriers like care obligations society imposed on women, toxic work cultures that may drive women to leave the company, and discrimination because of conscious or unconscious bias should be addressed. While some of these inequalities may be addressed by corporations, the external issues like the social expectations of care-giving placed on women are to be solved by forces external to the corporation. As Lim argues on the issue of gender diversity in corporate boards, quotas will not solve the root of the problem,

---

[61] Neeka Choobineh, *Gender Quotas for Corporate Boards: A Holistic Analysis*, 33, https://repository .upenn.edu/cgi/viewcontent.cgi?article=1004&context=joseph_wharton_scholars.

[62] *Id.*

[63] *Id.*, at 34.

[64] *Id.*

[65] *Id.*

that is systemic and structural disadvantages that women face. He further adds that these should be addressed by the state.[66] Choudhury too notes that there has to be some state responsibility to solve the structural problems faced by women. Simply requiring companies to appoint more women on their boards is not enough to solve them.[67]

As far as bias and discrimination within the firm is concerned, corporations can attempt to address these issues within the workforce. However, this cannot be achieved through quotas. As Fuith rightly says, 'the difficulty lies in attempting to legislate the hearts and minds of individuals in a society that has long viewed women as secondary'.[68] The difficulty also exists for discrimination and bias for reasons other than gender – race, national origin, disability, etc. For instance, recall the story of Shefaly Yogendra who said that, as an immigrant and a person of Indian origin in UK, she often found that recruitment firms did not believe her resume.[69] There is also research to show that people who speak English with certain accents find it difficult to obtain senior executive positions.[70] Fuith hits the nail on the head when she says that 'corporations are less likely to authentically and fully embrace the issue of gender and other types of diversity on their corporate boards when

---

[66] ERNEST LIM, SUSTAINABILITY AND CORPORATE MECHANISMS IN ASIA 113–114 (Cambridge University Press).

[67] Bernali Choudhury, *New Rationales for Women on Boards*, 34(3) *OJLS* 511, 541 (2014).

[68] Leanne Fuith, *Achieving Diversity on Corporate Boards: Engagement and Education; Not Legislation,* 45 *MITCHELL HAMLINE L. REV.* 112, 132 (2019). [Quoting Martin Luther King, Jr. who described the need for civil rights legislation while acknowledging its limitations:

> Now the other myth that gets around is the idea that legislation cannot really solve the problem and that it has no great role to play in this period of social change because you've got to change the heart and you can't change the heart through legislation. You can'tlegislate morals. The job must be done through education and religion. Well, there's half-truth involved here. Certainly, if the problem is to be solved then in the final sense, hearts must be changed. Religion and education must play a great role in changing the heart. But we must go on to say that while it may be true that morality cannot be legislated, behavior can be regulated. It may be true that the law cannot change the heart but it can restrain the heartless.]

[69] LaToya Harding, *'People Didn't Believe My CV', Says Board Director*, BBC NEWS (June 16, 2021), www.bbc.com/news/business-57486592. See also the discussion in Chapter 2 where Yogendra's story was mentioned earlier.

[70] See Laura Huang, Marcia Frideger, & Jone L. Pearce, *Political Skill: Explaining the Effects of Nonnative Accent on Managerial Hiring and Entrepreneurial Investment Decisions,* 98(6) *AM. J. APPL. PSYCHOL.* 1005, 1014 (2013). ['Non-native accent, not race, best explained executive hiring recommendations and new venture funding.']

they are forced to do so'.[71] This is consistent with the post-quota law developments in Germany and France where firms did the bare minimum of appointing the required number of directors without internalising the idea of enhancing opportunities for women. As a result, there were no trickle-down effects of the law to management positions and new quotas needed to be imposed for management positions.

Another important point Choobineh makes and one that is often overlooked is that the golf cart solution may crowd out potentially qualified men for the awards.[72] This sounds like an unfair argument considering that qualified women are left out of top positions because of the obstacles they face; until we recall the example from France discussed above where it seems like the appointment of women leaders was questioned. These sorts of outcomes are bound to create resentments across identity groups. As discussed in Chapter 3, this is detrimental to the very individuals that the quota is supposed to help. Further, when the quota does not cover certain groups within the broad category meant to be addressed (as we see in the California quota which only includes some groups within 'underrepresented groups') or when it is only targeted at one group (as in the case of gender quotas), other disadvantaged people will be left out. Of course, there is no way to cover all types of disadvantages in a quota law.

Beyond equality issues, the benefits of diversity in terms of improved team outcomes and decisions throughout the company are not gained if board quotas do not translate into diversity across the entire firm. Even at the board, if the quota simply brings more insiders – whether those holding multiple directorships or family members of members of the management team – to the table, it is unlikely to result in much cognitive diversity. Further, any diverse thinking that these candidates bring, by virtue of their identity as women or other minority status, can only provide results if the board and CEO are genuinely interested in hearing and considering their views, that is they do not consider them as tokens.

For all the above reasons, quotas are not useful and might result in unintended negative consequences. The snowball needs to be stopped.

---

[71] Fuith, *supra* note 68, at 133.
[72] Choobineh, *supra* note 61, at 34.

4.2 DISCLOSURE LAWS

Can sunlight do better than the snowball? Disclosure requirements are often justified by the famous quote 'sunlight is the best disinfectant',[73] referring to the fact that making the information public will allow investors to demand change. In time, corporate disclosures, particularly those regarding social and sustainability issues, have also become a source of information for other stakeholders.[74] While prescriptive laws like the ones imposing quotas incentivise compliance in name only, the idea with disclosure requirements is that they force companies to pay attention to the issue; and the reputational impact of the diversity information that will be disclosed is supposed to incentivise better behaviour. Further, they allow companies more flexibility to tailor programs to suit their needs. The 'softness' of such laws might also ensure buy-in from firms in that they would understand and try to give effect to the spirit of the law – improving opportunities and work conditions for diverse employees.

However, as I discuss in this section, disclosure rules about diversity coupled with various external pressures take on the form of aspirational quotas and thus also come with some of the costs of actual quotas. Also, not all disclosure rules are equal. Some may genuinely be aimed at encouraging corporate involvement and creativity in solving the problem of lack of diversity. Others may act as a warning for corporations to voluntarily comply with the minimum expectation (for instance, appoint 30% women on their boards) or expect mandatory legislation in this regard. As Rosenblum notes, 'the fear of legislation may prove nearly as powerful as legislation itself'.[75] I would add that if companies respond to the threat of quotas as if there was a quota law, then such threats will also give rise to the costs of quotas.

This section will discuss the diversity disclosure requirements in the United States.

---

[73] LOUIS D. BRANDEIS, OTHER PEOPLE'S MONEY AND HOW THE BANKERS USE IT (1914).

[74] Umakanth Varottil, *A Dose of Sunlight Therapy: Using Corporate and Securities Laws to Treat Climate Change* 7 (2009), https://papers.ssrn.com/sol3/papers.cfm?abstract_id=1570346 (accessed Nov. 26, 2009); Ann M. Lipton, *Not Everything Is about Investors: The Case for Mandatory Stakeholder Disclosure*, 37 YALE J. ON REG. 499 (2020).

[75] Rosenblum (California Dreaming), *supra* note 5, at 1435.

4.2.1 United States: The 'Comply and Explain' Rule

The Securities Exchange Act of 1934 requires that shareholders of a company whose securities are listed on a national stock exchange receive a proxy statement prior to a shareholder meeting, whether an annual or special meeting.[76] The information contained in the statement must be filed with the SEC before soliciting a shareholder vote on the election of directors and the approval of other corporate action.[77] Companies are required to provide certain information in the proxy statement.

After the financial crisis of 2008, certain additions were made to these disclosure requirements and the law was amended accordingly.[78] Following this amendment, listed companies, from February 2010, are required to disclose their diversity policy for nomination of directors if they have one in place, and describe its implementation, in their annual proxy and information statements.[79] The relevant portion of the law states that companies are to disclose a range of details regarding their director nomination process. The item corresponding to diversity states as follows:

> describe the nominating committee's process for identifying and evaluating nominees for director ... and whether, and if so how, the nominating committee (or the board) considers diversity in identifying nominees for director. If the nominating committee (or the board) has a policy with regard to the consideration of diversity in identifying director nominees, describe how this policy is implemented, as well as how the nominating committee (or the board) assesses the effectiveness of its policy.[80]

Thus, the disclosure about diversity is with reference to whether diversity is a consideration for the company in the nomination process. Where such a diversity policy exists, the rule also requires companies to disclose its implementation and its effectiveness as assessed by the nomination committee of the board. Thus, while there is no need

---

[76] 15 USC § 78a (1934).
[77] 15 USC § 78a (1934).
[78] Securities Exchange Commission, *Proxy Disclosure Enhancements*, www.sec.gov/rules/final/2009/33-9089.pdf.
[79] Regulation S-K, 17 CFR 229.407(c) (vi).
[80] Regulation S-K, 17 CFR 229.407(c) (2).

to explain why there is no diversity policy in place if the company does not have one, more detailed disclosures are required where the company does have a diversity policy. In other words, it is a 'comply and explain' rule. Fairfax has rightly noted that the need to explain the implementation and effectiveness of the diversity policy where one exists would incentivise companies to adopt policies that would yield results.[81] Conversely, firms that are uninterested in focusing on diversity will not adopt a diversity policy. The voluntary nature of this would prevent greenwashing, provided that there was no external pressures to show a commitment to diversity.

Significantly, the rule does not define the term 'diversity', and it is up to companies to explain how they understand the term. In its proposal, the SEC anticipated that companies might define diversity in different ways. While some might define diversity in terms of demographic aspects like race, gender, and nationality, other companies might define it in terms of diversity of viewpoint, educational qualifications and professional experience.[82] The proposal document explains that 'companies should be allowed to define diversity in ways that they consider appropriate', and thus, the SEC specifically chose not to define the term.[83] This is a useful approach because it avoids the pitfalls of providing a definition which excludes some categories (as seen in the California provision). Further, it allows each company to identify the aspects of diversity that are most relevant to its operations and workforce.

Dhir, in a content analysis of proxy disclosures on diversity published in 2015, found that firms mainly defined diversity to mean non-identity-based factors like prior experience rather than identity-based factors like race or gender.[84] However, the number of firms that used gender as one of the definitions of diversity has gradually climbed.[85] Nili's study considered data up to 2016 and so pre-dates the #MeToo and BLM movements. We can infer from this that companies did not

---

[81] Lisa M. Fairfax, *Board Diversity Revisited: New Rationale, Same Old Story*, 89 *N.C. L. REV.* 855, 874 (2011).
[82] SEC (Proxy Disclosure Enhancements), *supra* note 271.
[83] *Id.*
[84] Dhir, *supra* note 13, at 213.
[85] Nili, *supra* note 51, at 185.

consider gender diversity to be very important but gradually began to do so as awareness and investor pressure grew. In any case, the SEC seems to have intended a broader idea of diversity. It alluded to the link between board diversity and independence when it stated that while looking for diverse candidates, boards might be forced to look outside of their existing networks and that the resulting board might be more independent.[86] Further, it stated that where the company was in need of more independence, the result of a more diverse and thus independent board would be improved governance.[87] It is explained that such improved governance might be the result of the availability of different viewpoints.[88]

In his 2019 article, Nili criticised the fact that very few firms even defined diversity.[89] However, he noted that some firms did meaningfully engage with diversity through a well-framed policy and subsequently with changes to board composition. Since Nili's focus in the article was gender, those are the examples he provides. In any case, the nature of soft law (which is what the disclosure rule is) is that it brings about gradual change as companies learn from the disclosures of their peers and through investor engagement and also engagement by other kinds of audiences.[90] Indeed, large institutional investors began to pressure companies specifically on gender diversity by 2017. More on that in the section on market initiatives below.

4.2.2 Nasdaq's 'Comply or Explain' Rule

In August 2021, the US SEC approved a listing rule applicable to companies that are listed on the Nasdaq stock exchange.[91] Although this rule is in the form of a disclosure rule, it is quite a different animal from the SEC diversity disclosure rule both because of its content and because of the way in which it is structured.

---

[86] SEC (Proxy Disclosure Enhancements), *supra* note 78, at 80.
[87] *Id.*
[88] *Id.*, 81.
[89] *Id.*, 185–86.
[90] Lisa M. Fairfax, *Board Diversity Revisited: New Rationale, Same Old Story*, 89 N.C. L. REV. 855, 873 (2011).
[91] Securities Exchange Act Release No. 34-92590 (Aug. 6, 2021) (order approving SR-NASDAQ-2020-081 and SR-NASDAQ-2020-082).

The rule requires Nasdaq-listed companies (with some exceptions) to have at least two directors who are 'diverse', including at least one director who self-identifies as female and at least one director who self-identifies as an 'underrepresented Minority or LGBTQ+'.[92] The term 'diverse' is defined quite differently from the way this book defines it. Per the Nasdaq rule, it means 'an individual who self-identifies in one or more of the following categories: (i) Female, (ii) Underrepresented Minority, or (iii) LGBTQ+'. Then 'underrepresented minority' is in turn defined as 'an individual who self-identifies as one or more of the following: Black or African American, Hispanic or Latinx, Asian, Native American or Alaska Native, Native Hawaiian or Pacific Islander, or Two or More Races or Ethnicities'.[93] Clearly, there is no place for viewpoint diversity, or age diversity, or experiential diversity in this definition. Also, the definition of 'underrepresented minority' can be attacked with the same argument as in the California law by asking why Arabs or some other category of people are not included.[94] Non-compliant companies must explain the reasons for their non-compliance. Not only this, such companies are then provided with a network of diverse (as defined in the Nasdaq rule) and board-ready candidates to recruit from.[95]

Structurally, it is different from the SEC's 'comply *and* explain' rule because the Nasdaq rule requires companies to either comply *or* explain reasons for non-compliance. The content of the rule is also different inasmuch as there is a clear stipulation of what diversity means and specification of the target number of diverse (as defined by the rule) directors to be appointed. This makes the rule an aspirational quota. I use this phrase because the specified target then becomes the number that investors and activists will ask for and will take away the focus from other innovative diversity-related measures that a company

---

[92] *Id.*, at 4.
[93] *Id.*, at 5–6.
[94] See generally David E. Bernstein, *The Modern American Law of Race*, 94 S. CAL. L. REV. 171 (2021) for a discussion of how racial and ethnic minorities in the United States were categories for various purposes. ['The few records that exist suggest that (1) even the bureaucrats who made the decisions were unable to articulate why certain groups were included and others were not, or why they included or excluded groups with particular cultural backgrounds or countries of origin;…'.]
[95] Securities Exchange Act Release No. 34-92590 (Aug. 6, 2021) (order approving SR-NASDAQ-2020-081 and SR-NASDAQ-2020-082) 8.

might want to pursue. Additionally, the option to explain rather than comply is illusory because firms will hesitate to signal a disinterest in diversity, especially in the wake of #MeToo and BLM.[96]

Concerns have been raised about the Nasdaq rule pushing more companies to avoid going public, or about the rule harming investors if one expects the negative stock price reaction to the California gender quota to be replicated here as well.[97] The constitutional validity of the Nasdaq rule has also been challenged (as was the case with the California quota) by some think-tanks and the issue is yet to be ruled upon.[98] Again, here too it is not corporations that are challenging the rule, because they would most likely be hesitant to publicly show their displeasure with any rule about diversity. Finally, Fried has criticised Nasdaq for selectively relying on studies or parts of studies where the outcome appears to support its proposed regulation and ignoring other studies where it is not.[99] This has unfortunately been a common problem with law and policy discussions on the issue of gender and race diversity even beyond Nasdaq, I had discussed some of these issues in Chapter 1 while arguing that the empirical foundations of the business case are shaky. In light of the California quota and the Nasdaq rule, the importance of the policy rationale informing law and regulation become clear. Had the discussions delved more into the specific problems faced by diverse candidates, the rules might have been less rigid and possibly attempted to address issues of bias, lack of access to networks, bullying, harassment, etc.

4.2.3 UK–Principles Based Disclosure against the Backdrop of Targets

In the UK, diversity disclosures are required (in a comply or explain format) by the Corporate Governance Code, 2018 (referred to in

---

[96] Fried, *supra* note 36, at 7.

[97] *Id.* See also Andrew Ackerman, *Nasdaq's Plan for Diversity on Corporate Boards Is Decried by Senate Republicans*, WALL ST. J. (Feb. 12, 2021), www.wsj.com/articles/nasdaqs-plan-for-diversity-on-corporate-boards-is-decried-by-senate-republicans-11613160390.

[98] Tracy Thomas, *NASDAQ Board Diversity Regulations Challenged in Court*, GENDER AND THE LAW PROF BLOG (Oct. 27, 2021), https://lawprofessors.typepad.com/gender_law/2021/10/nasdaq-board-diversity-regulations-challenged-in-court.html.

[99] See generally Fried, *supra* note 36.

this book as the UK Code). The UK Code sets out the recognised corporate governance standards, for companies listed in the UK.[100] Companies in the UK which have premium listing[101] on the London Stock Exchange (LSE) have to report on how they applied the principles set out in the UK Code. Hence, it is known as principles-based disclosure. At the outset, the UK Code emphasises[102]:

> The ability of investors to evaluate the approach to governance is important. Reporting should cover the application of the Principles in the context of the particular circumstances of the company and how the board has set the company's purpose and strategy, met objectives and achieved outcomes through the decisions it has taken.

Further, explaining the rationale for such a principles-based approach rather than rigid requirements, the Code says that its approach is meant to offer flexibility and that companies should use it wisely.[103]

The principles in the UK Code are categorised into five main heads – (i) board leadership and company purpose; (ii) division of responsibilities; (iii) composition, succession, and evaluation; (iv) audit, risk, and internal control; and (v) remuneration. While the principles most relevant to diversity are contained in the third category, there are other principles in the UK Code that are of relevance. I will pick up on some of these in Chapters 5 and 6.

Before getting into the details of the requirements set by the UK Code, it is worth recalling (from Chapter 1) that the UK Code's definition of diversity is perhaps the most in line with how this book conceives of diversity because it seeks to promote 'diversity of gender, social and ethnic backgrounds, cognitive and personal strengths'.[104] So it goes beyond gender when considering demographic diversity and at the same time avoids the California and Nasdaq rules' common pitfall of trying to exhaustively define the term 'underrepresented minority'. Even more significantly, it expressly mentions cognitive diversity.

---

[100] UK Code, 2018.
[101] As per 2010 changes to the Financial Services Authority (FSA), only voting equity shares can have premium listing.
[102] UK Code, 2018, 2.
[103] UK Code, 2018, 1.
[104] UK Code, 2018, Principle J.

Interestingly, diversity is not meant to be an overriding consideration, but rather to be considered within the context of merit. Thus, it seems to be a matter of favouring diverse candidates who are equally meritorious,[105] balanced against merit. Principle J in its entirety is as follows:

> Appointments to the board should be subject to a formal, rigorous and transparent procedure, and an effective succession plan should be maintained for board and senior management. Both appointments and succession plans should be based on merit and objective criteria and, within this context, should promote diversity of gender, social and ethnic backgrounds, cognitive and personal strengths.

The provisions of the UK Code that explain how this principle can be given effect to focus on the appointment process and say that the 'board should establish a nomination committee to lead the process for appointments, ensure plans are in place for orderly succession to both the board and senior management positions, and oversee the development of a diverse pipeline for succession'.[106] Further, to ensure that the members of the nomination committee do not just appoint their friends or the friends of other board members, the provisions note that the board should use 'open advertising and/or an external search consultancy' for the appointment of non-executive directors and the board chair. Further, where an external search consultancy is used, the board should identify the agency in its annual report 'alongside a statement about any other connection it has with the company or individual directors' to ensure that the search process is not indirectly captured.[107]

Principle K goes on to add that the 'board and its committees should have a combination of skills, experience and knowledge'. Thus,

---

[105] Readers will recall the discussion in Chapter 1 where I counter the argument that the push to hire diverse candidates is anti-merit – this argument is made surprisingly often!. The framing of Principle J clarifies that diversity will not be at the cost of merit. Of course, it depends on how companies implement this principle. Token hires (to satisfy targets or virtue-signal) may not consider merit. As we saw earlier in this chapter, some companies in France and India appointed family members of existing directors and C-suite members to comply with diversity quotas. Obviously, merit is not the primary consideration in such cases.

[106] UK Code, 2018, Provision 17.

[107] UK Code, 2018, Provision 20.

there is a further emphasis on other facets of diversity here. Further, it says that board membership should regularly be refreshed. This is significant because regular refreshment can drive both diversity and independence on the board.[108] The provisions giving effect to this principle set out that all directors should be up for re-election annually. During this, the board should set out 'the reasons why each director's contribution is important to the company' long-term sustainable success' in the papers accompanying the resolutions to elect each director.[109] The focus then moves on from appointment and board refreshment to evaluation of directors, which I will discuss in Chapter 5. The evaluation process, whether internal or external, is meant for the board to be able to engage with its strengths and weaknesses. Although this is not explicitly stated, diversity should be one aspect against which the review should be conducted.

The diversity-related disclosure that is required from the company, based on the principles discussed so far, in essence consists of four things. First, companies should disclose their appointments process and approach to succession planning and how both of these support developing a diverse pipeline. Thus, even though the emphasis is on board appointments, the requirement to discuss how the approach will develop a pipeline would mean that companies also address issues relevant to levels below that of the board.

Second, the companies should disclose their 'policy on diversity and inclusion, its objectives and linkage to company strategy, how it has been implemented and progress on achieving the objectives'. This implies that companies should not only focus on numbers but also ensure that the diverse employees feel included. It is relevant to note here that the introduction of the UK Code states that 'a company's culture should promote integrity and openness, value diversity and be responsive to the views of shareholders and wider stakeholders'.[110] Altogether, there seems to be a push towards thinking about the impact of company culture on employees, particularly those who can

---

[108] Darren Rosenblum & Yaron Nili, *Board Diversity by Term Limits*, 71 ALA. L. REV. 211 (2019). [Term limits maintain the pool of institutional knowledge on boards but rotate members to ensure new perspectives and independent thinking.]

[109] UK Code, 2018, Provision 18.

[110] UK Code, 2018, 1.

be categorised as diverse either due to demographic characterises or due to views and perspectives.

Third, companies are required to disclose the gender balance of those in the senior management (i.e., executives just below the board level) and their direct reports. The fourth and final diversity-related requirement is that companies should disclose details of board evaluations including 'the outcomes and actions taken, and how it has or will influence board composition'.[111] While this final requirement does not directly mention diversity, it seems to be inviting investors to engage with issues relating to board performance and refreshment.

Overall, the principles-based framework and the issues that the principles and disclosure requirements require companies to focus on seem to be well considered and broad. However, these disclosure requirements are complicated by diversity (gender and ethnicity only) targets set by various government committees in the UK. For gender diversity, the Davies Report, published in 2011, set a target of 25% women on boards of FTSE 100 companies by 2015, and this was successfully achieved.[112] This target was increased to 33% women on boards of FTSE 350 companies in 2015 by the Davies Review, Five Year Summary Report.[113] This report also encouraged companies to focus on the percentage of women in the executive level.[114] Since then, the issue of gender diversity in senior leadership positions has been addressed by the Hampton-Alexander Reports, the latest of which calls for 33% women on boards and in senior leadership positions of all companies.[115]

Ethnic diversity has been addressed by the Parker Review Committee, which in 2017 recommended that 'each FTSE 100 company should have at least one director of colour by 2021; and each

[111] UK Code, 2018, Provision 23.

[112] LORD DAVIES, WOMEN ON BOARDS (2011).

[113] DAVIES REVIEW, FIVE YEAR SUMMARY, IMPROVING THE GENDER BALANCE ON BRITISH BOARDS 7 (2015), https://assets.publishing.service.gov.uk/government/uploads/system/uploads/attachment_data/file/482059/BIS-15-585-women-on-boards-davies-review-5-year-summary-october-2015.pdf.

[114] *Id.*

[115] HAMPTON-ALEXANDER REVIEW FTSE WOMEN LEADERS, IMPROVING GENDER BALANCE – 5 YEAR SUMMARY REPORT, 11 (2021), https://ftsewomenleaders.com/wp-content/uploads/2021/02/HA-REPORT-2021_FINAL.pdf.

FTSE 250 Board should have at least one director of colour by 2024'. In line with the UK Code's focus on the appointment process, the Parker Review Committee also recommended that FTSE 100 and FTSE 250 companies should (either themselves or via search firms) 'identify and present qualified people of colour to be considered for Board appointment when vacancies occur'.[116] This is somewhat similar to the Rooney Rule (from American football) that many scholars on both sides of the Atlantic have recommended. The rule required teams seeking to interview at least one minority applicant for the position of coach. Choudhury has argued that, although this sort of rule looks like a quota, it is quite different because it simply ensures that the minority candidate gets an interview rather than assuring their appointment.[117] However, even the Rooney rule is easy to game. Employers can go through the motions of interviewing diverse candidates without intending to hire them. In any case, what the Parker Review committee sets forth is a target rather than a rule with sanctions attached to it. There are also some recommendations regarding the code of conduct applicable to executive search firms which we will look at in Chapter 5. There are also recommendations about developing the pipeline for people of colour internally via mentorship and other programs.[118] In 2020, the same committee conducted a survey, based on which they updated their 2017 recommendations. A key message from the update was an exhortation to companies that did not respond to the survey to take the reporting recommendations seriously.[119]

This sort of pressure from a government committee on certain targets is bound to focus companies on meeting those and away from other firm-specific efforts. Indeed, Hickman notes that a majority of the companies 'referred to at least one of the three key diversity reports (i.e. the Davies Review, the Hampton-Alexander Review

---

[116] PARKER REVIEW COMMITTEE, A REPORT INTO THE ETHNIC DIVERSITY OF UK BOARDS, 49 (2017), https://assets.ey.com/content/dam/ey-sites/ey-com/en_uk/news/2020/02/ey-parker-review-2017-report-final.pdf.

[117] Bernali Choudhury, *Gender Diversity on Boards: Beyond Quotas*, EBLR 229, 241 (2015).

[118] Parker Review Committee (2017), *supra* note 116, at 49.

[119] PARKER REVIEW COMMITTEE, ETHNIC DIVERSITY ENRICHING BUSINESS LEADERSHIP AN UPDATE REPORT FROM THE PARKER REVIEW, 61 (2020), https://assets.ey.com/content/dam/ey-sites/ey-com/en_uk/news/2020/02/ey-parker-review-2020-report-final.pdf.

and the Parker Report)' in their diversity disclosures.[120] Although Hickman's inference from this is that most companies are engaging with the diversity issue, my own inference is that the race and gender targets are weighing heavily on their diversity agenda. Despite this, a review by Professor Ruth Sealey on behalf of the Financial Reporting Council (FRC) found that about 20–30% of the FTSE 100 and 10% of the FTSE 250 seemed to have embraced the spirit of the principles by providing rich narratives about their approach to diversity in the board and the wider workforce.[121] The report also noted that many of the companies understood 'diversity as a much broader concept that encompasses a range of sources of difference, including social and educational background, disability and other "protected characteristics"'.[122] Although such broad surveys are not available for more recent disclosures, it has been noted that not many companies have disclosed information regarding appointment of ethnically diverse board members, as recommended by the Parker Review Committee.[123]

Unfortunately, UK's market regulator, the Financial Conduct Authority (FCA) is seeking to introduce changes to the listing rules that would in effect require specific disclosures about compliance with gender and diversity targets, similar to Nasdaq's diversity rule. The rule would apply to the UK and overseas listed companies that have securities admitted to listing or trading on a regulated market in the UK.[124] The targets sought to be introduced are threefold. First, at least 40% of the board should consist of women (including those self-identifying as women) directors. Second, one of the senior board

[120] Eleanor Hickman, *Diversity, Merit and Power in the C-Suite of the FTSE100*, 213–306 (2019), www.ucl.ac.uk/judicialinstitute/sites/judicial_institute/files/eleanore_hickman_post_viva_thesis_0.pdf305.

[121] FINANCIAL REPORTING COUNCIL, BOARD DIVERSITY REPORTING, 2–3 (2018), www.frc.org.uk/getattachment/62202e7d-064c-4026-bd19-f9ac9591fe19/Board-Diversity-Reporting-September-2018.pdf.

[122] *Id.*

[123] Maitane Sardon, *U.K. Investment Managers Push for More Diversity on Boards*, WALL ST. J. (Feb. 24, 2021), www.wsj.com/articles/u-k-investment-managers-push-for-more-diversity-on-boards-11614200970. ['Three-quarters of companies in the FTSE 100 index failed to report the ethnic makeup of their boards in last year's annual meeting season [2020], according to the association.']

[124] FCA CONSULTATION PAPER, DIVERSITY AND INCLUSION ON COMPANY BOARDS AND EXECUTIVE COMMITTEE, 5 (2021).

positions like Chair, CEO, CFO, or the senior independent directors (similar to lead independent director in the United States) should be a woman (including those self-identifying as a woman). Third, at least one member of the board should be a non-white ethnic minority person.[125] In addition to these targets, the FCA also proposes to require companies to publish data about 'the composition of their board and the most senior level of executive management by gender and ethnicity' in their annual reports.[126]

These proposals can be criticised for the same reasons that the California quota and the Nasdaq quota were, in the discussion above. Specifically, in the UK context, these rules take away from the expansive definition of diversity that the UK Code allowed. Further, a big criticism of such aspirational quotas is that they would undo the work of the principles-based disclosure regime which has allowed companies to engage with the spirit of the diversity disclosure requirements.

4.2.4 Market Initiatives

The UK Code specifically states in its introduction that it is the responsibility 'of investors and their advisors to assess differing company approaches thoughtfully'.[127] There has indeed been considerable engagement on diversity from investors, and the market more generally. In February 2021, the Investment Association (whose members manage $12 trillion in assets) announced that it would issue warnings to FTSE 350 companies that did not publish information on the ethnic and racial composition of their boards and also to those that did not have a plan to appoint at least one director from an ethnic minority background by the end of 2022.[128]

Even in the United States, investors play an active role in mounting campaigns on corporate governance issues including on diversity. As early as in 2012, the California State Teachers' Retirement System (CalSTRS) publicly expressed dissatisfaction when Facebook, Inc

---

[125] *Id.*, at 6.
[126] *Id.*
[127] UK Code, 2018, 1.
[128] Maitane Sardon, *supra* note 123.

(now Meta, Inc) for its all-male board.[129] Since then, the pressure has grown exponentially, with the number of board diversity proposals in the United States reaching an 'all time high' in 2017.[130] Proxy advisors have also become supportive of the movement. This was even before the #MeToo and BLM movements impacted the corporate sector and also before the California quota law was introduced. In February 2020, the investment bank Goldman Sachs announced that it would 'only underwrite IPOs in the US and Europe of private companies that have at least one diverse board member' from July 2020 and at least two diverse board members from 2021.[131]

Grundfest has argued, while discussing problems with the California quota, that investor activism can achieve superior results to legislation.[132] The problem with this approach is that the focus on institutional investors is often limited to whatever has captured public sentiment the most – gender diversity initially, and now diversity in terms of race and ethnic minorities. Companies will usually signal support for these campaigns precisely because of the public support for the campaigns, and the reputational costs of not getting behind whatever the issue of the day is. However, there is no guarantee of sustained change. Further, since institutional investor campaigns are often in terms of numerical targets for women and racial minorities on the board, they crowd out other firm-specific efforts to attract and retain diverse candidates at various levels in the pipeline and to prioritise different facets of diversity. In the bargain, corporations loose flexibility to tailor measures to their circumstances, which is one of the goals of using disclosure as a regulatory tool. The flip side is that

---

[129] Matt Stevens, *Facebook's All-Male Board Criticized by California Pension Fund*, L.A. TIMES (Feb. 7, 2012), www.latimes.com/business/la-xpm-2012-feb-07-la-fi-calsters-facebook-20120207-story.html.

[130] Ronald O. Mueller & Elizabeth Ising, *Shareholder Proposal Developments during the 2017 Proxy Season*, HARVARD LAW SCHOOL FORUM ON CORPORATE GOVERNANCE (July 12, 2017), https://corpgov.law.harvard.edu/2017/07/12/shareholder-proposal-developments-during-the-2017-proxy-season/.

[131] David Solomon, *Diverse Leadership Is Needed More Than Ever – Here's What We're Doing* (Feb. 4, 2020), www.goldmansachs.com/our-commitments/diversity-and-inclusion/launch-with-gs/pages/commitment-to-diversity.html.

[132] Joseph A. Grundfest, *Mandating Gender Diversity in the Corporate Boardroom: The Inevitable Failure of California's SB 826*, 10 (2018), https://papers.ssrn.com/sol3/papers.cfm?abstract_id=3248791.

disclosure requirements can become meaningless in the absence of investor engagement if companies simply engage in check-the-box compliance or alternatively use the reporting as a public relations tool by making selective disclosures.[133]

Since institutional investor activism on social issues is not only guided by law and regulation but also by the discussion in society, the answer perhaps lies in educating the general public, especially millennials and Gen Zers who are actively participating in these debates, about the various pieces of the diversity jigsaw.[134] An understanding beyond simplistic numerical representation is required for the public to be able to appreciate the unintended consequences of both quotas and aspirational quotas. When the public is better educated and the diversity discourse becomes more informed, institutional investors will also tailor their activism accordingly. Regulators, stock exchanges, professional bodies, and consultancies would also do well to look at all the research on the issue (whether or not it matches their proposals) and engage with experts and commenters with different views.

---

[133] Bernali Choudhury & Martin Petrin, *Corporate Governance That 'Works for Everyone': Promoting Public Policies through Corporate Governance Mechanisms*, 18(2) JCLS 381, 409–10 (2018).

[134] It is not at all clear that institutional investors are motivated by genuine concern for diverse members of the workforce. If they were, they would have practiced what they preached and implemented effective diversity programs and measures for their own employees. Instead, they simply seem to be signalling virtue by promoting issues that seem to have caught the public imagination. See Aziza Kasumov, *BlackRock under Pressure to Live up to Its Promises on Diversity*, FINANCIAL TIMES (Mar. 22, 2021), www.ft.com/content/6476e681-4154-43a6-93e4-f5c86ae30dd9. The article details the experiences of a female Muslim employee who faced harassment and discrimination at Blackrock, along with similar experiences faced by others including a black gay employee, a former employee who was Kenyan, and a Black woman employee. Most tellingly, the article quotes a black employee saying 'as far as the senior leadership of this team is concerned the only reason you're here is to boost the diversity numbers'. Along with making the point about the proponents of market initiatives themselves not cleaning house, this final statement also underscores how counter-productive it is to focus on numbers. See also Attracta Mooney & Madison Darbyshire, *Race and Finance: Asset Managers Fail to Walk the Walk*, FINANCIAL TIMES (Dec. 28, 2021), www.ft.com/content/59d8f7c4-cc9e-41a4-b739-c43c4195d592. ['…asset managers are struggling to live up to their professed ideals. Black employees and members of other minority groups remain dramatically under-represented in the sector – particularly in senior roles – and industry executives say it could take years to mount the recruitment efforts needed to make their workforces truly diverse.']

4.2.5 The Report Card on Disclosure Measures

As the above discussion has shown, disclosure measures, coupled with targets and institutional investor pressure, have started to operate like aspirational quotas, and particularly focus on demographic characteristics, while ignoring cognitive diversity altogether. One reason why institutional investors and regulators seem to focus on gender and race (and other underrepresented categories in some cases) but not on cognitive diversity, experiential diversity, etc., is that the former is easy to measure. Another reason is that gender and race are issues that have captured the public interest in a way that diversity in educational and professional backgrounds have not.

However, even as far as gender and race is concerned, the focus is only on numerical representation even under disclosure rules. As Edmans rightly notes, selectively focusing on some data not only provides an incomplete picture but also 'creates incentives to focus on only the aspects that are reported'.[135] Whether it is driven by hard quotas, or by soft law mechanisms (disclosure requirements) complemented by investor activism, or by social media activism, the focus on percentages and numbers means that other types of diversity issues will be neglected and that there will be no efforts directed towards removing systemic barriers faced by diverse candidates.

When viewed in isolation, the US SEC disclosure rule and the UK's principles-based disclosure rules have both done well to either not prescribe how firms should define diversity or to provide an expansive definition of diversity. One could argue that these measures alone have not shown measurable change and are therefore not working. But since only gender and racial diversity at the board and senior management levels are being measured, there is no way to see if the rules helped bring improvements in diversity at all levels of the workforce, and for all types of diverse candidates. One way that disclosures could provide information about these sorts of measures is if firms provide details about the

---

[135] Alex Edmans, *Response to FCA Discussion Paper DP21/2 on Diversity and Inclusion in the Financial Sector*, 6 (2021), https://alexedmans.com/wp-content/uploads/2021/09/FCA-Diversity.pdf. He provides examples of bias in favour of good looking people, and bias against people with tattoos as examples of issues that fall by the wayside when we exclusively focus on quantitative data.

policies and measures introduced within the company. This will work only if institutional investors that truly care about diversity engage with the qualitative information where firms provide this. In any case, firms would do well to focus on long term issues to avoid future costs.

Ultimately, if the goal of disclosure is to nudge companies to consider relevant issues and to allow flexibility in addressing them, encouraging qualitative disclosures is the best path forward. To complement this, research, discussion, and policy papers, whether they are put out by the government, market players, or academics should address the many facets of diversity and how they can be addressed at all levels of the corporation. Best in class reports should focus on innovative programs that corporations operationalise rather than on whether numerical targets for gender and race diversity are met at the upper levels of the firm. Another way to assess the effectiveness and suitability of firms' diversity measures is to conduct employee surveys that can provide first-hand experience of whether diverse members feel included and have opportunities to work and rise up the ladder. This focus will, in turn, incentivise companies to expend resources on impactful measures rather than on cosmetic changes. Shifting the conversation about diversity will eventually shift the focus away from short-term metrics and towards real change that might bear fruit in the long run both for corporations and for society.

4.3 INCENTIVISING FIRM-SPECIFIC SOLUTIONS

If after discussing quotas and disclosures – the two main types of measures used to address diversity in corporations – the assessment has been that both types of measures are not useful, we are left to wonder what the alternative is. Indeed, I have been asked this at conferences where I have discussed the costs of quotas and disclosure mechanisms. Before casting for an alternative type of regulation, it is apposite to ask if regulation should be the answer, at all. Irrespective of the type of regulation used, if the effect is that corporations seek to hire diverse candidates merely to comply with the law, then the outcome is not desirable. A scene from the Netflix show Superstore where a retail store manager who is called by 'corporate' and asked to apply for an executive role finds that all the candidates to be interviewed happen to be Latinas, is instructive. One candidate tells her that management probably realised they were missing a colour in the crayon box while another says that she was not above rolling her Rs to get the job. The aforementioned store manager is then shown answering the interviewer intelligently only to be nudged towards her ideas regarding 'customers of colour'. We then see the candidate struggle to improvise and throw in phrases like 'as a Latina' and 'cultura' with a pronounced accent and the interviewers immediately sound impressed. Obviously, the show is tongue in cheek but the scene also has some truth about the reality of today's diversity hiring.

Edmans is of the view that regulators might not be best placed solve the diversity problem, not least because it is difficult to measure the different facets of diversity.[136] The present analysis of various regulatory measures in different jurisdictions falling short goes to support Edmans' argument. However, firms may also engage in token hiring of diverse candidates because of social media pressure or investor activism. Fuith, drawing from Martin Luther King Jnr's work, writes (in the context of board diversity) that the problem of board diversity can be solved by 'changing the hearts and minds of corporate leaders, shareholders and employees through education and engagement' because prescriptive laws will not incentivise corporations to 'authentically and fully embrace' diversity.[137]

I agree with both Edmans and Fuith on the point that regulators may not be best placed to solve diversity issues within the corporation. However, they can join the effort to educate both corporations and society about the many pieces of the diversity jigsaw. As Jena and Hari note in their book that 'popular literature on diversity and inclusion is full of unsubstantiated claims...' and this should be rectified.[138] As the discussion in this chapter and earlier in this book has shown, regulators have also been promoting spurious claims about diversity. Not only are these claims unsubstantiated by rigorous empirical studies; it has become anathema to criticise these claims or in fact the regulations

---

[136] *Id.,* at 5.
[137] Fuith, *supra* note 68, at 132–33.
[138] Swati Jena & T. N. Hari, Diversity Beyond Tokenism: Why Being Politically Correct Doesn't Help Anyone 19 (Sage, 2021).

that are introduced based on these claims. This is evident from the corporate double-speak, that is corporations making statements in support of diversity without following through with relevant measures (as discussed in Chapter 3). It is also evident from knee-jerk reactions of firms in response to social media activism. Recall the example of the Apple employee who was fired because of online activism against something he had written in the past and which Apple already knew about before hiring him.[139] The inability to discuss the merits and demerits of diversity-related measures is also obvious when firms hesitate to be openly critical of diversity quotas and disclosure requirements (recall statements by firms in Germany and France).[140]

While this uneasiness with discussing diversity frankly has been reinforced in the current climate of social media activism, it is certainly not new. In a 2011 publication that conducted qualitative interviews of women and minority directors, Broome, Conley, and Krawiec find that most of their respondents spoke of functional benefits of diversity rather than the fairness rationale. Even more concerning was the fact that respondents were not able to provide evidence to substantiate the claims about the functional benefits of diversity by means of examples and, in many cases, backed away from the initial claims. Based on this, the authors make an astute observation that diversity seems to evoke 'universal acclaim in the abstract' but at the same time, it also seems too dangerous to talk about concretely.[141] They explain this paradox by pointing out that a focus on the functional benefits of diversity would imply that diversity is a proxy for difference. However, such a claim is open to stereotyping and other invidious claims.[142] The authors further explain this as follows[143]:

> Everyone in the debate has a vested interest in not walking through that door. Those who are not members of the excluded groups do not want to be heard to say that 'they' are all alike, whereas those who are members do not want to point to fundamental differences

---

[139] See discussion of this incident in Chapter 3.
[140] Richters & Holger, *supra* note 31; Hird, *supra* note 32.
[141] Lissa L. Broome, John M. Conley & Kimberly D. Krawiec, *Dangerous Categories: Narratives of Corporate Board Diversity*, 89 N.C. L. REV. 759, 760–61 (2011).
[142] Recall Damore's memo discussed in Chapter 1.
[143] Broome, Conley, & Krawiec, *supra* note 141, at 762.

that might be translated as 'less qualified' or 'needing assistance'. So we are left with narratives that simultaneously extol difference and express embarrassment with it.

A decade since the publication of that article, it has not become any less dangerous to discuss concrete issues about diversity. Various pieces of the diversity jigsaw are still left out of the conversation because of this awkwardness. Ironically, the conversation about diversity must become open enough to tolerate different viewpoints. What is required, then, is responsible and honest discussions on all relevant aspects and perspectives about diversity from the media, academics, and regulators. In such an environment, states could incentivise firm-specific solutions across the corporate hierarchy by promoting a thoughtful consideration of diversity issues relevant to each company and its stakeholders.

As discussed in Chapter 3, each firm is best placed to identify and assess the problems faced by its workforce and find ways to fix them. This is because the workforce in each company is different, and so are the circumstances of each company. For instance, a company that sells face cream will have to deal with a set of challenges that are very different from a company that creates virtual reality products. Similarly, a company with a young workforce has to deal with very different issues from one with a much older demographic as its workforce. A regulator cannot anticipate the issues faced by every type of diverse candidate in every type of company. This is what Hayek called, 'the knowledge of the particular circumstances of time and place'. Hayek says about such knowledge:

> It is with respect to this [knowledge] that practically every individual [or corporation] has some advantage over all others because he possesses unique information of which beneficial use might be made, but of which use can be made only if the decisions depending on it are left to him or are made with his active coöperation [sic].

For the present purpose, such knowledge can be called 'firm-specific knowledge'. Hayek says that decentralised solutions are more apt where firm-specific knowledge is important.[144] This is extremely relevant for diversity issues. Company management not only have firm-specific

---

[144] Frederick Hayek, *The Use of Knowledge in Society*, 35 AM. ECON. REV. 519–30 (1945).

Table 4.1 Diversity measures

Quotas	No flexibility
	Does not solve the root of the problem
Disclosures	Flexible but sometimes works as an aspirational quota or target.
	Does not solve the root of the problem.
Market initiatives	No flexibility when the focus is on numbers. Also work as aspirational quotas.
	Does not solve the root of the problem.
Firm-specific solutions	Flexible – companies could decide and take steps that are most appropriate to solve its diversity problems.
	There is scope for innovation.
	There is also scope for greenwashing.

knowledge about the demographic that works for them, they also have the means to gather more information about the specific challenges faced by their employees through surveys and other internal mechanisms (see Chapter 5 for more on this).[145] Additionally, the company's management is able to fashion solutions that best address the twin goals of employee well-being and value-maximization because they have (or can gather) firm-specific knowledge about employee information and firm performance. This approach can lead to social justice innovation within forms and also allow different firms to compete with each other to provide favourable work conditions for all employees. To an extent, the after-effects of the pandemic are helping firms realise the value of using employee-centric innovation as a means to attract talent.[146]

Only the lightest of involvement from regulators, if at all, is useful. Regulators could encourage companies to provide qualitative

---

[145] This intentional information-gathering is required because 'employees … will quite simply know and discover things about which their boss have no idea'. See Nicolai J. Foss, *The Use of Knowledge in Firms* 155(3) J. INSTITUTIONAL THEOR. ECON. 458, 472 (1999).

[146] Emma Jacobs, *Family-Friendly Leave Policies Are Key to Staff Retention*, FINANCIAL TIMES (Dec. 5, 2021), www.ft.com/content/b14b4e7a-e87d-4aee-a267-8100661e4b57.

disclosures about how they are addressing diversity (as defined by the company) issues in the entire workforce. This can help investors and other stakeholders[147] to scrutinise the nuts and bolts of how different firms address and promote diversity. In turn, this will incentivise companies to assess the needs of their workforce and expend resources to solve them. Prioritising detailed disclosures over numbers will hopefully redirect social media activism towards long-term change. Companies could also learn from peer experiences in terms of how different measures fare and then adapt them to suit their own workforce needs. However, sole reliance on the information disclosed by firms on the policies and programs undertaken might mean that a number of firms will use it as a public relations exercise. Thus, there have to be other channels of information gathering to prevent greenwashing. Employee surveys are an example and companies like Glassdoor already provide this. Employees themselves are active on social media and so corporate hypocrisy is unlikely to go unnoticed, as we have seen in Chapter 3.

Chapter 5 will discuss issues of corporate culture and board culture, both of which are also unique to each firm and reinforce the idea that form-specific solutions to diversity are the most appropriate (Table 4.1).

---

[147] While the aim of the disclosure regime is to inform investors about important issues, various stakeholders have also relied on corporate disclosures especially on issues of public interest like sustainability and diversity. Consulting firms often digest diversity information about the top firms in different jurisdictions and provide reports for public consumption. These reports are then used by regulators, media, and academics like myself. Thus, it is communicated to the public through various channels.

5 CORPORATE CULTURE, BOARD CULTURE, AND BOARD CONSULTANTS

This chapter looks at three pieces of the diversity jigsaw – corporate culture, board and management culture, and the potential role of consultants providing board advisory services in improving board and management culture for diverse directors and executives. It argues that culture at all levels of the company is crucial for attracting and retaining diverse talent and discusses a range of ways by which companies can cultivate good culture.

Before we begin, a note about terminology in this chapter is useful. The phrase 'corporate culture' will be used interchangeably with 'firm culture', 'organizational culture', and 'workplace culture'. The terms board advisory services, and board consultants will be used interchangeably. Since executive search firms essentially offer a type of board advisory service, and since many of these services are offered together by consulting firms, the term executive search firm may also be used interchangeably with board consultants or board advisory services.

5.1 CORPORATE CULTURE

As Chapters 3 and 4 have pointed out, knee-jerk reactions to social media pressure and tick-the-box compliance with law and regulation that imposes board quotas or requires disclosures will not bring about long-term change. Sustained change is only possible when there is a cultural shift in the company.

But what is culture? The term is becoming increasingly commonplace in corporate governance discussions, even if it does not feature in the content of corporate regulation in most jurisdictions. It is a fuzzy term with multiple definitions. One definition of the term is that it is the way people act when no one is looking, suggesting that it is something ingrained in the people of an organization.[1] Another definition is that culture is the bridge between a company's purpose and its people.[2] A third definition is that it is a 'pattern of behavior that is reinforced by systems and people, and is manifest in the norms or expectations that people have for how they need to behave to fit in and succeed in the corporation'.[3] While the first two definitions provide the basic idea, the third definition speaks to the mechanism through which it is created and reinforced. I will return to the third definition later while talking about the board of directors and management. But for now, let us work with the first two definitions. In essence, these two definitions suggest that corporate culture is a concept that focuses on a firm's people. Thus, diversity should be an important consideration within it. Chapter 3 discussed some links between firm culture and diversity in the context of corporate responses to social movements, and how these responses are often unsustainable in the long term. The discussion here looks at corporate responses to culture issues in the aftermath of the pandemic and then at how the board can address culture and diversity together.

At present, none of the regulations specifically attempting to address diversity either directly mention the term culture or indirectly reference the issue by a consideration of how the company can support and retain diverse candidates at various levels of the workforce including the board and management levels.

The UK Code uses the term, culture, in its introduction.[4] When assessed by the context in which it is used, culture seems to focus

---

[1] Blacksun, Reporting on Corporate Culture: What We See and What We Suggest 2, www.blacksunplc.com/content/dam/black-sun/corporatecomms/Documents/Research/research_reportingoncorporateculureresearch_pdf.

[2] Deloitte, Annual Report Insights 2020: Surveying FTSE Reporting 14, www2.deloitte .com/content/dam/Deloitte/uk/Documents/about-deloitte/deloitte-uk-annual-report-insights-2020.pdf.

[3] Gary B. Gorton, Jillian Grennan, & Alexander Zentefis, *Corporate Culture* (2021), https:// papers.ssrn.com/sol3/papers.cfm?abstract_id=3928972.

[4] UK Code, 1. The term is used in the following context:

> Companies do not exist in isolation. Successful and sustainable businesses underpin our economy and society by providing employment and creating prosperity. To succeed in the long-term, directors and the companies they lead need

on relationships with stakeholders including employees and especially diverse employees. The 2018 survey of corporate disclosures on diversity shows that a few companies have used the term culture while discussing diversity.[5] The survey extracted one company's (Tate and Lyle) diversity-related disclosure as an example of how some companies went above and beyond because it also provided details of how the board viewed diversity. Part of the extract is below[6]:

> The Board believes that a diverse and inclusive culture is a driver of superior business performance, growth and innovation.

This part of the statement claims that the company was aiming for a 'diverse and inclusive culture' meaning that its culture will prioritise employee diversity and inclusion. This is an important link between diversity and culture that this company has articulated. It is only when the culture of the company supports diversity that the idea of diversity becomes ingrained in the systems and people. That is when a company moves from short-termism to a longer-term engagement with diversity. Chapter 3 discussed corporate short-termism on diversity issues and outlined a range of possible mechanisms to create a culture that accepts and welcomes diversity – specifically gender and racial diversity. Here the discussion will focus more broadly on work culture and how diversity should be an important consideration within that concept.

Despite the current emphasis on it, 'corporate culture' is not a new term in the governance literature. Nadler, in a 1993 publication, noted that the culture of an organization included, amongst others, the following six components: (i) respect for each individual and their contribution to the firm, (ii) accepting and valuing diversity, (iii) every individual having an equal opportunity to achieve their potential, (iv)

---

to build and maintain successful relationships with a wide range of stakeholders. These relationships will be successful and enduring if they are based on respect, trust and mutual benefit. Accordingly, a company's culture should promote integrity and openness, value diversity and be responsive to the views of shareholders and wider stakeholders.

[5] Financial Reporting Council, Board Diversity Reporting, 2–3 (2018), www.frc.org.uk/getattachment/62202e7d-064c-4026-bd19-f9ac9591fe19/Board-Diversity-Reporting-September-2018.pdf.

[6] *Id.*, Referencing the disclosure by Tate & Lyle in its annual report for 2017.

concern and fair treatment of all individuals by the firm management; (v) employees are kept informed, and (vi) employees are enthusiastic and proud to work for the firm.[7] All these components speak to employee well-being generally.

Now to look at what the term signifies in recent times, especially to younger employees, I refer to Comparably's list to top twenty-five companies for culture in 2021 and employee quotes from these companies as provided by Comparably to Business Insider.[8] I have compiled these quotes in Table 5.1 (but excluded those that did not provide concrete information) and matched them to Nadler's list of components for company culture. As can be seen in Table 5.1, these quotes not only match some of the components in Nadler's list but also bring up some additional components. The components on Nadler's list that find purchase in the employee quotes from 2021 are: (ii) accepting and valuing diversity; (vi) employees are enthusiastic and proud to work for the firm; and (i) respect for each individual and their contribution to the firm. The additional components of culture that employees seem to value are a strong mission that drives culture, ability to work remotely, teamwork and helpfulness of colleagues, and an ethic of care that permeates from the company leadership. Of course, some of these components are indicative of the issues raised by the pandemic, but they cannot be dismissed because issues like the ability to work remotely when needed have been raised even before and can be especially important to parents (especially mothers) who have young children. The focus on a company's mission can be quite important to attract and retain talent and, in a sense, sits well with employees being proud to work at the firm.

I also think it is interesting to note those components of Nadler's list that are missing from the employee quotes: (iii) every individual having an equal opportunity to achieve their potential, (iv) concern and fair treatment of all individuals by the firm management; and (v) employees are kept informed. While you could argue that (iv) is the

---

[7] Paul S. Nadler, *Cultivating Corporate Culture*, 9 COM. LENDING REV. 75, 76 (1993).
[8] The full list of top 100 companies for work culture is here. The quotes were provided by Comparably to Business Insider and can be found here: www.businessinsider.in/careers/news/the-25-global-companies-with-the-best-workplace-cultures-according-to-employees/slidelist/81934993.cms#slideid=81935005.

Table 5.1 Component of company culture-based employee quotes in 2021

Rank	Company	Quote	Corresponding component on Nadler's list
2	Adobe	'The team genuinely cares about their employees and seek to have a positive impact on the world.'	[Mission Driven]; [General ethic of caring for employees].
4	Microsoft	'We have great diversity (including geographical diversity), strong work ethic, and crazy smart co-workers.'	Accepting and valuing diversity; Employees are enthusiastic and proud to work for the firm.
9	Boston Consulting Group	'I feel so proud to work for a globally recognized leader in the business consulting field. BCG is a fantastic place to work.'	Employees are enthusiastic and proud to work for the firm.
12	Zoom	'I love that we can work remote, yet make connections with our own awesome tools with any coworker anywhere in the world.'	Employees are enthusiastic and proud to work for the firm [and to work with each other]; [Mission Driven]; [Remote work]
14	Apple	'Apple gives massive amounts of time and effort to spotlight all the different experiences and perspectives we have access to, and go out of their way to encourage us all in our creativity.'	Accepting and valuing diversity; Respect for each individual and their contribution to the firm.
16	TaskUs	'Recognition is freely given on a regular basis up to the founder level. Tremendous teamwork in the face of the pandemic.'	Respect for each individual and their contribution to the firm; Employees are enthusiastic and proud to work for the firm [and to work with each other].

(*continued*)

Table 5.1 (continued)

Rank	Company	Quote	Corresponding component on Nadler's list
17	IBM	'I appreciate the inclusion of all types of people and the respect shown between others both laterally and vertically.'	Accepting and valuing diversity; Respect for each individual and their contribution to the firm.
18	Medallia	'We are a global team, in multiple time zones, and we always help each other out to work as a team to accomplish our tasks and projects.'	Employees are enthusiastic and proud to work for the firm [and to work with each other].
19	LexisNexis Legal & Professional	'Our company's purpose is to globally promote and support the Rule of Law in all that we do. This makes for an inspiring and uplifting workplace.'	[Mission driven culture]
20	Dynatrace	'We have collaboration, the will to help each other, a wide mosaic of skills that fit fantastically together, and great international teammates.'	Respect for each individual and their contribution to the firm.
24	Adidas	'I love the work and being part of a successful global brand.'	Employees are enthusiastic and proud to work for the firm.
25	PepsiCo	'Allows you to grow and gain a very diverse experience, working with amazing people'.	Respect for each individual and their contribution to the firm.

same as the ethic of care that I have listed as one of the newer component of culture, in reality, it is not. I interpret (iv) to mean that there is no discrimination in the firm. Similarly, (iii) also speaks to the absence of discrimination in the company. Finally, (v) speaks to employees being given the relevant information to be able to understand the reasons behind firm decisions. However, since this is based on a single employee quote that has been provided for each company, we cannot make inferences based on this alone. So, I looked at the previous year's survey on work culture by Comparably and found more analyses on that data. Peart notes, in a Forbes article that even amongst the top ranked companies for 2020, there were issues of culture that needed to be worked on. Although '84%–98% of the employees from small and large company culture winners felt company leaders do what they should do to retain them as an employee' apparently only '57%–59% of the women and people of color who took the survey across all companies could say the same'. Similarly, while '80%–88% of the overall employees from small and large company culture winners felt their company provide meaningful advancement opportunities', 'only 49%–53% of the women and people of color who took the survey across all companies could say the same'.[9] This data clearly shows why (iii) and (iv) on Nadler's list seem to be missing from the employee quotes and tells us that there is work to be done even in the top companies.

Now let's unpack these components. Respect for each individual and their contribution to the firm would imply that each individual should be able to make suggestions and voice their disagreements and concerns on pertinent issues. Similarly, pay disparities, harassment and bullying, and other such practices go against the need to accept and value diversity and treat all employees fairly. Not only this, when a different view is expressed, or a problem is reported, the employee should not face negative consequences for doing so. On the contrary, employees with diverse perspectives, and those who face issues and report them, should be treasured. Such employees help prevent missteps – whether in operational matters, compliance matters, or equity issues.

An example of a company that retaliated against an employee who raised issues that needed to be addressed and eventually had to face reputational and financial consequences for its action is Pinterest. The employee in question was the former chief operating officer of Pinterest, Francoise Brougher. Ms. Brougher, in a lawsuit, had alleged

---

[9] Natalia Peart, Meet The Best Company Workplace Culture Awards 2020 – According to Comparably, FORBES (Dec. 14, 2020), www.forbes.com/sites/nataliapeart/2020/12/14/best-company-workplace-culture-awards-2020/?sh=5501fe2b34d3.

that Pinterest excluded her from meetings after she pushed for equal pay and that she was ultimately fired after she raised concerns about sexist comments by a colleague to the company. Overall, her complaint said that Pinterest created an 'unwelcoming environment for women and minorities'. Eventually, Pinterest publicly announced an agreement to pay $22.5 million to settle these claims and also issued a statement saying that it 'recognizes the importance of fostering a workplace environment that is diverse, equitable and inclusive and will continue its actions to improve its culture'.[10] Apart from the fact that the company that does not pay attention to culture, and retaliates against employees that report issues, will face consequences *ex post*, such companies are also unable to retain talented employees. In fact, the same company has an example to offer on that count as well. Prior to Ms. Brougher's lawsuit, two black employees of Pinterest, Ifeoma Ozoma and Aerica Shimizu Banks, resigned from their jobs at Pinterest and publicly alleged pay discrimination and retaliation for advocating for social change.[11] Incidentally, Ozoma had been instrumental in leading policy change on misinformation related to vaccines at Pinterest that had brought Pinterest public acclaim.[12] The culture issues at Pinterest ultimately resulted in it losing talented employees. Bad work culture also means that it is difficult for the company to attract newer talent since the information tends to eventually leak out of the organization.

---

[10] *'Pinterest in $22.5m Gender Discrimination Payout'*, BBC NEWS (Dec. 15, 2020), www.bbc.com/news/business-55311470.

[11] Banks' problems at Pinterest began when she 'discovered the company wasn't paying holiday pay to its lowest-paid contract workers doing hospitality, security, janitorial jobs', many of whom were people of colour and some were disabled. She drafted a proposal to change this, in conjunction with some members of the legal team. However, the proposal apparently 'embarrassed' a senior executive. The retaliation she faced after this even included being interrogated by a private investigator hired by Pinterest. See Julie Bort & Taylor Nicole Rogers, *The Two Black Employees Who Took on Pinterest Explain Why They Quit, Their Fight for Pay, the Death Threats, the Private Investigator: 'It Was a Torturous Experience'*, BUSINESS INSIDER (June 24, 2020), www.businessinsider.in/tech/news/the-two-black-employees-who-took-on-pinterest-explain-why-they-quit-their-fight-for-pay-the-death-threats-the-private-investigator-it-was-a-torturous-experience/articleshow/76563329.cms.

[12] Julia Carrie Wong, *Pinterest's New Vaccine Search Will Offer Something Rare on Social Media: Facts*, THE GUARDIAN (Aug. 28, 2019), www.theguardian.com/society/2019/aug/28/pinterest-anti-vaccine-combat-health-misinformation?CMP=Share_iOSApp_Other.

SpaceX offers us a contrary example where good firm culture helps retain employees, even when the company is unable to offer salaries on par with its competitors. This was the case in SpaceX' early days. A 2010 study found that half of the best students from the University of Michigan's graduate program in space engineering had ended up working for SpaceX rather than the 'industry's leading companies'. Apparently, they took pay-cuts to work at SpaceX because they 'believed in the mission'.[13] This reflects a corporate mission or purpose that employees could be invested in, and feel proud of.[14] If the mission statement was mere window dressing, it would not impress employees enough to take pay cuts. However, company culture is also part of the story. One of the reasons Elon Musk enjoyed a stellar approval rating as CEO of SpaceX on Glassdoor in 2017 is that he encourages his employees to speak up and especially so, to tell him when he is wrong.[15] This also goes to the point about every employee's contribution being valued. Recall the story of an employee at Amazon coming up with the idea of Amazon Prime and sending it to management through a digital suggestion box. It goes to the point about each employee being valued and encouraged to contribute ideas for the business.[16] It is not only about seeking out employee ideas. Yamini Ranjan, CEO of software company HubSpot said that she prioritised meeting with all levels

---

[13] ERIC BERGER, LIFTOFF (William Collins, 2021). See also Charlotte Villiers, *Boardroom Culture: An Argument for Compassionate Leadership*, 30(2) EUR. BUS. L. REV. 253, 272. Villiers notes that according to Aventr (a software company specialising in providing software and analytics designed to help companies to increase employee engagement and improve communications between managers and employees), SpaceX' organizational structure is 'fairly flat when it comes to hierarchy and generation of ideas'. This is not something specific to SpaceX but rather a more general observation about employee choices. See 'Culture over Cash? Glassdoor Survey Finds More Than Half of Employees Prioritize Workplace Culture Over Salary' (April 14, 2020, INSIDE Public Accounting), https://insidepublicaccounting.com/2020/04/culture-over-cash-glassdoor-survey-finds-more-than-half-of-employees-prioritize-workplace-culture-over-salary/.

[14] Villiers, *Id.* ['According to Aventr, the environment at SpaceX isn't about comfort and ease; the company culture is mission driven. Everyone at the company believes they are responsible for "getting humans to Mars." Their ultimate goal is to help humanity become a multi-planetary species. They set aggressive, arguably unrealistic goals, yet the people of SpaceX keep getting the work done because their mindset is on the mission. The general working assumption at SpaceX is that everything is possible.']

[15] *Id.*

[16] VIVEK WADHWA, ISMAIL AMLA, & ALEX SALKEVER, FROM INCREMENTAL TO EXPONENTIAL 132–33 (Harper Business, 2020).

of her workforce regularly when the company was forced to shift to hybrid working due to COVID-19.[17] (Incidentally, HubSpot was voted as the firm with the fifth best culture on Comparably and fourth best place to work at, by Glassdoor in 2021.[18]) Thus, management taking time to engage with employees whether through on online suggestion box (which is more practical in a large company) or personally meeting with employees (more likely in a smaller company) go towards respecting employees and their contributions.

In addition to employees wanting to feel valued in the company, they also want to work in a company where acting ethically is the norm.[19] This is particularly important to younger employees. A Gallup survey conducted in 2018 reveals that the second most important thing that young millennial and Gen Z employees want in their job is ethical leadership.[20] To look at an example, Algolia, an API Platform for Search & Discovery, got 'Great Place to Work' to survey its employees in December 2021.[21] The results of the survey are instructive[22]:

97% of employees believe that management is honest and ethical
97% of employees are proud to work at Algolia
95% of employees report on having a flexible schedule and work-life balance
94% of employees believe management is competent at running the business
94% of employees responded that they are given a lot of responsibility

---

[17] Richard Waters, *HubSpot's Yamini Rangan on the Challenges of Sudden Power*, FINANCIAL TIMES (Dec. 19, 2021), www.ft.com/content/ad61f2cd-2f8b-42c4-a40b-7e951898ad2c.

[18] Glassdoor, '2021 Best Places to Work', www.glassdoor.com/Award/Best-Places-to-Work-LST_KQ0,19.htm. One of the reviews say: 'The support leadership has shown through thoughtful programs, WFH reimbursement, and flexibility has been next level.'

[19] See, e.g., Hian Chye Koh & El'fred H Y Boo 42 (5/6) MANAG. DECIS. 677 (2004). The study finds significant and positive links between ethical culture (comprising of control mechanisms that specifically aim at influencing organisational outcomes) and job satisfaction.

[20] Ed O'Boyle, '*4 Things Gen Z and Millennials Expect from Their Workplace*, (Mar. 21, 2021, Gallup), www.gallup.com/workplace/336275/things-gen-millennials-expect-workplace.aspx.

[21] Great Place to Work provides certification to companies by conducting employee surveys. Great Place to Work, www.greatplacetowork.com/.

[22] *Algolia Named a Great Place to Work for the First Time*, BUSINESS WIRE (Dec. 16, 2021), www.businesswire.com/news/home/20211216005737/en/Algolia-Named-A-Great-Place-To-Work-For-The-First-Time.

Clearly, honest and ethical management is as important as being valued at work and being able to have work–life balance. All of this goes towards employees feeling proud of where they work.

All of the components listed by Nadler and the components I have identified based on the 2021 Comparably survey are important for diversity, broadly construed. While some of these points directly speak to diversity, other more general points like having a core inspiring mission, respecting each individual and ensuring that employees feel proud to work in the organization speak more generally to employee well-being. Ultimately, when employee well-being is focused on every employee, irrespective of whether they belong to the in-group or not, the firm's culture can be said to support diversity. However, measures that are tailored to a specific group of people or to diverse individuals more generally might be required based on the specific circumstances of each company.

5.1.1 Corporate Culture Insights from the Pandemic

The current focus on culture has coincided with the debate about the purpose of the corporation and stakeholder-centric governance[23] and then with the #MeToo and BLM movements,[24] and again with the pandemic.[25] While the core components that Nadler identified remain relevant, solutions suited to each firm's need at a specific moment in time (as this book has advocated in Chapters 3 and 4 with regard to addressing diversity) have begun to emerge. Consider the examples of two different US companies responding to the impact of the pandemic on its employees.

The first is that of a life-sciences company Illumina 'provided a "COVID Care" cash payment to help address our employees'

---

[23] More details on this topic are found in Chapter 6. For a detailed discussion on the interaction between the corporate purpose movement and an emphasis on corporate culture, see Akshaya Kamalnath, *The Corporate Purpose Debate, 2018–20 Edition*, GNLU L. REV. (2020), https://ssrn.com/abstract=3688027.

[24] See, e.g., Mengqi Sun, Papa John's Looks to Improve Corporate Culture after Founder Flap, WALL ST. J. (Mar. 1, 2019), www.wsj.com/articles/papa-johns-looks-to-improve-corporate-culture-after-founder-flap-11551477189.

[25] See, e.g., Jonathan Pearce, Amid Pandemic, Illumina Invests in 'Culture of Care' WALL ST. J. (Dec. 6, 2021), https://deloitte.wsj.com/articles/amid-pandemic-illumina-invests-in-culture-of-care-01638730575?mod=Deloitte_riskcompliance_wsjarticle_h2&tesla=y.

unanticipated financial needs' and that they 'increased emergency backup childcare allowances and offered up to 30 days of paid leave to employees for emotionally significant events'.[26] Not only this, the company moved from its previous practice of conducting a semi-annual employee survey to a quarterly survey to be able to understand and respond to employee problems. Illumina terms it as a 'culture of care' and says that the company's commitment to culture 'fosters innovative and breakthrough technology'.[27] Thus, the company seems to view an investment in culture as something that benefits employees, and eventually the company.

Another example is that of Goldman Sachs introducing paid family leave for any employees 'facing issues related to Covid-19', paid bereavement leave for the loss of family members, paid leave if they, their spouse, or surrogate have a miscarriage or still birth, and unpaid sabbaticals for long-serving employees.[28] The latter was unheard of in big corporate firms, which was the reason women dropped out of the race when they took on family responsibilities. Goldman Sachs seems to have been prompted in this direction after a group of first-year analysts complained about the increased workload and the toll it had taken on their mental and physical health and the ensuing media attention on the firm.[29] Specifically in response to the junior analysts concerns, Goldman Sachs said it would hire more employees and enforce boundaries around working hours.[30] One might say that the reputational fallout spurred the company into action, and they would probably be right. Even so, these responses by Goldman Sachs, a leading wall street firm could herald a wider industry wide change.

These two examples of companies addressing culture issues may seem like they have nothing to do with diversity. It is true that they were

[26] *Id.*

[27] *Id.*

[28] Charley Grant, Goldman Sachs Rolls out New Worker Benefits to Combat Employee Burnout, Wall St. J. (Nov. 29, 2021), www.wsj.com/articles/goldman-sachs-rolls-out-new-worker-benefits-to-combat-employee-burnout-11638210617.

[29] Hugh Son, *Goldman's Junior Bankers Complain of Crushing Workload amid SPAC-Fueled Boom in Wall Street Deals* CNBC (Mar. 18, 2021), www.cnbc.com/2021/03/18/goldman-sachs-junior-bankers-complain-of-crushing-work-load-amid-spac-fueled-boom-in-wall-street-deals.html.

[30] *Id.*

not particularly aimed at hiring or retaining diverse employees. Yet, they have the potential to change the definition of 'the ideal employee', which will make it easier for firms to retain diverse members – particularly women. If flexible work, leave for emotionally significant events, etc. can be offered to the entire workforce, then one set of diverse members – women, will greatly benefit from it. One major reason for women to drop out of the work force is the lack of flexible work hours and the inability to take time off for childcare or other responsibilities. If diversity had been a consideration within the corporate culture discussion, perhaps these sorts of arrangements would have become available sooner. Incidentally, since these measures have been introduced in the context of the pandemic and have been made available to all employees, women may be more likely to use them. Otherwise, women might have worried that they will be taken less seriously if they opt for these benefits. Recognizing that many employees will hesitate to take these options, a Goldman Sachs representative has said that the company planned to highlight senior managers who take the sabbatical.[31] In addition to the measures discussed above, in the post-COVID-19 lockdown period, when employees returned to work, many firms including those on wall street were encouraging employees to dress more informally. However, even here some employees reportedly said they would wait to take cues from senior management.[32] Thus, it is important to set the tone at the top, like Goldman Sachs proposes to do.

The fact that both these companies conducted internal surveys to understand employee problems meant that they could provide solutions to the specific issues.[33] A firm with other problems, for instance persistent sexual and racial discrimination, would require other

---

[31] *Id.*

[32] Suzanne Kapner, You're Finally Going Back to the Office. What Are You Going to Wear?, WALL ST. J. (June 4, 2021), www.wsj.com/articles/youre-finally-going-back-to-the-office-what-are-you-going-to-wear-11622799041?st=u5fum91tey9gzcw& reflink=article_copyURL_share&mod=article_inline. [Quoting one employee who said that 'engineering is historically a men's field' and that she would 'take cues from more senior women in the company as to what they are wearing, because they've earned the respect of their peers'.]

[33] Martin, the chief research officer at the Institute for Corporate Productivity, identifies listening to employees as one of the key aspects to focus on when overhauling company culture. See Kevin Martin, *How to Future-Proof Company Culture*, FINANCIAL TIMES (Feb. 13, 2020), www.ft.com/content/39db7e82-3947-11ea-ac3c-f68c10993b04.

solutions. Recall the Holder Report's recommendations (discussed in Chapter 3), which made suggestions to combat sexual harassment and bullying because those were the problems that emerged from Uber, the company in question. In that case, the recommendations sought to ensure that management reinforces to employees that bad conduct will not be tolerated and to provide multiple channels through which employees could report problems to HR, management, and the board. The broad principles behind the Holder Recommendations could also be used to design measures for problems like retaliation against employees who seek to highlight problems and wrongful conduct. If firms commit to a no tolerance approach to wrong doing of any sort, then they should constantly listen to employees – both through targeted surveys and by allowing platforms for employees to report matters, anonymously if needed. Setting up internal whistleblowing systems that incentivise reporting of issues without fear of retaliation is also an effective tool to glean information about misconduct.[34] However, to bring cultural change, employees should see that these policies are being implemented and that there will actually be no retaliation for bringing an issue to light internally. Recall the retaliation seen in the Pinterest example discussed earlier.

5.1.2 Culture (and Diversity) as a Board Responsibility

From an employee perspective, a corporation that listens to their concerns and addresses them, irrespective of whether or not they belong to the majority group in the workforce, would ensure well-being and work satisfaction. From the board's perspective, paying attention to stakeholder needs and building and maintaining

---

[34] Janet Austin & Sulette Lombard, *The Impact of Whistleblowing Awards Programs on Corporate Governance*, 36 WINDSOR Y.B. ACCESS JUST. 63, 74 (2019). ['...it is advantageous for the corporation itself to have well-developed systems of internal reporting, in that this serves to encourage insiders with information about wrongdoing to report internally first, rather than reporting to a regulator or the media, thus potentially preventing or limiting financial and reputational harm to the organization. In addition, the behaviour of directors and managers are likely to be influenced by an awareness of a greater likelihood of wrongdoing being disclosed by whistle-blowers, thus resulting in enhanced corporate accountability.']

an effective corporate culture helps identify problems *ex ante* and mitigate risks before they escalate.[35] So, one could even argue that setting an appropriate corporate culture is part of the board's monitoring role. Also, information about a company's culture is available to potential employees via forums like Glassdoor and Comparably, which means that companies with bad culture will not be able to hire the best candidates. Unsurprisingly, studies suggest that firm culture leads to increased firm value in the long term.[36]

It seems like a no-brainer then that culture should be a board imperative. The question is how this can be done. It is now useful to recall the third definition of culture listed at the beginning of this chapter: 'a pattern of behavior that is reinforced by systems and people, and is manifest in the norms or expectations that people have for how they need to behave to fit in and succeed in the corporation'. This would mean that the board should ensure that there are systems that incentivise certain desired behaviour and disincentivise other conduct and that the top management leads by example.

The UK Code rightly describes culture as a board responsibility and states that the board should 'establish the company's purpose,

---

[35] Jennifer G. Hill, *Legal Personhood and Liability for Flawed Corporate Cultures*, 8 ['…flawed corporate cultures can result in serious harm to corporate stakeholders, including employees, creditors, customers and shareholders. In some cases, the damage was to society at large.']

[36] John R. Graham, Jillian Grennan, Campbell R. Harvey, & Shivaram Rajgopal, *Corporate Culture: Evidence from the Field*, 18–22 (2021), https://papers.ssrn.com/sol3/papers.cfm?abstract_id=2805602. The authors surveyed executives from large firms in North America about firm culture and found that 92% of the respondents said they believed 'that improving corporate culture would increase their firm's value'. The authors also supplemented the surveys with qualitative interviews to help explain the responses. One interviewee's answer about the importance of culture is that it is 'the most important thing because in some ways it can influence your ability to come to solutions to all the unknown problems and challenges that you will face from inception to growth'. Other interviewees explained the link between culture and firm performance saying that 'culture enhances firm performance because it enables superior execution' and that culture reduces agency costs 'because you have an invisible hand at work inside of each of the employees that helps to guide their decisions and judgments in a way that the overall corporation would desire it to be'. Additionally, 77% of executives suggested in the survey, 'that culture has a moderate or big effect in compliance decisions' One of the interview responses explains that 'if the culture promotes or tolerates "rogue" behavior then [it is] less likely to have compliance'. See also Alex Edmans, *The Link between Job Satisfaction and Firm Value, with Implications for Corporate Social Responsibility*, ACAD. MANAG. PERSPECT. 1 (2012).

values and strategy, and satisfy itself that these and its culture are aligned'.[37] The board itself should lead by example and promote the desired culture.[38] Recall that the board not only sets company strategy but has the job of monitoring management. Thus, the UK Code states that the board should assess and monitor culture in the company and, where 'is not satisfied that policy, practices or behaviour throughout the business are aligned with the company's purpose, values and strategy, it should seek assurance that management has taken corrective action'.[39] Since executive compensation is one of the key tools with which the board can monitor management, the UK Code also provides that compensation package for executives should be designed in a manner that ensures that setting and maintaining desirable firm culture is incentivised.[40] This requirement clearly reflects an understanding of the important role played not only by the board but also by the CEO and other executives who are in charge of day-to-day operations of the company. In fact, the UK FRC, in its 2016 report on culture (which was based on a roundtable with the chairs of the FTSE 100 and other discussions with various stakeholders) observed that a common theme coming from most participants was that the CEO has the greatest influence on firm culture.[41] In other words, the company should set the tone at the top – with the board, CEO, and executives playing important roles.

Another mechanism adopted to monitor management is to ensure that the workforce is able to raise concerns to the board and that this can be done anonymously where required. The UK Code requires the board to have such a mechanism in place and also to ensure that such concerns are followed up and investigated where required.[42] As seen in the discussion above about insights on firm culture from the post-pandemic examples, it is important to listen to employees. However, it is not enough to simply create avenues for employees to report problems. Employees being able to communicate directly with

---

[37] UK Code, Principle B.
[38] *Id.*
[39] UK Code, Provision 2.
[40] UK Code, Provision 33.
[41] Financial Reporting Council, Corporate Culture and the Role of Boards: Report of Observations, 14 (2016).
[42] UK Code, Principle E, Provisions 6 and 7.

the CEO and other executives on everyday work-related issues makes employees feel valued. Such interaction will also help senior management gauge staff morale informally and to respond accordingly.[43]

Since the UK Code follows a comply or explain regime, the only direct obligations flowing from these principles is for companies to report in the annual report on activities in this regard and any action taken. It also specifically states that 'an explanation of the company's approach to investing in and rewarding its workforce' should be included in the annual report.[44] A 2020 study of company reporting on culture found that 90% of the companies had described the mechanisms used to monitor company culture, and the most prominent measure used was employee surveys. Other measures include review of whistleblowing reports, internal audits, town halls where directors directly meet with staff, and directors being designated for workforce engagement. A few companies also included exit interviews for employees, customer surveys, and supplier feedback as additional sources of information to draw from while assessing and developing strategy for firm culture.[45] In addition to reporting engagement mechanisms, over half the companies reported how employee feedback influenced board decision-making.[46]

Almost all of these mechanisms can help diverse employees (across all facets of diversity) voice their specific concerns and make sure that their views are heard by the board. Acting upon employee concerns, even if it is the concern of a very small percentage of employees, will assure diverse employees that they are equally valued in the firm. Creation of gender-neutral toilets and help accessing information or networks required for promotion might be some examples. Channelling whistleblower complaints pertaining to diversity issues (for instance, an employee that makes racist comments or bullies diverse employees) to the chief diversity officer who is empowered to act on the matter is another way in which diverse employees see that they are valued by

---

[43] Villiers, *supra* note 13, at 277.
[44] UK Code, Provision 2.
[45] Deloitte, 'Annual Report Insights 2020: Surveying FTSE Reporting' 14, www2.deloitte .com/content/dam/Deloitte/uk/Documents/about-deloitte/deloitte-uk-annual-report-insights-2020.pdf.
[46] *Id.*, 15.

the organization. Similarly, attrition statistics that are attuned to diversity issues might help companies understand whether there is a problem with retaining certain types of employees in the company. For instance, a company might see that female employees tend to leave the company at a certain point in the corporate hierarchy. Or that minority employees are leaving the company after short stints. Obviously, such quantitative metrics can only indicate that there is a problem but cannot explain the cause of the problem. Further information gathered via exit interviews of those leaving or through surveys of existing employees can help the company learn the reasons for patterns that emerge from metrics.[47] Williams provides the example of Clorox where very few minority employees received high ratings as a result of which promotion rates were low for such employees. This in turn resulted in high turnover of minority employees. Williams notes that Erby Foster, the diversity and inclusion director of Clorox, identified this by paying attention, not just to outcome metrics but also to the reasons behind these outcomes.[48]

Diversity is an important consideration even when information is gleaned from other stakeholders like customers or suppliers. Paying attention to diverse groups within these stakeholder categories will help the company support diversity outside the organization. Thus, formally integrating diversity issues within a corporation's assessment of culture is necessary. This will help diversity considerations become part of a firm's DNA, thereby allowing for long-term change.

In the United States, the SEC introduced new disclosure requirements about HCM in 2020.[49] It has not defined HCM but instead allowed companies to decide what metrics are relevant to report under this head. So, companies are now simply required to include a discussion of HCM in their annual reports. The SEC has, however, provided some guidance. The rule states that companies should include a description of their 'human capital resources, including the number of persons employed by the registrant [company], and any human capital

---

[47] Joan C. Williams, Bias Interrupted: Creating Inclusion for Real and for Good, 12 (Harvard Business Review Press, 2021) 159.

[48] Id.

[49] Modernization of Regulation S-K Items 101, 103, and 105, Securities Act Release No. 33-10825, Exchange Act Release No. 34-89670, 85 Fed. Reg. 63,726, 63,739 (Oct. 8, 2020).

measures or objectives that' the company 'focuses on in managing the business (such as, ... measures or objectives that address the development, attraction and retention of personnel)'.[50] Thus, although culture is not explicitly mentioned, the guidance provided focus on many aspects relevant to firm culture. The rule does not come out of the blue, but rather follows efforts institutional investors and other industry bodies like the Conference Board to push companies to think about human resource issues.[51] Just before the rule was introduced in 2020, many companies were already making voluntary HCM disclosures that included information about workforce diversity, workforce compensation, workforce health and safety, workforce skills and capabilities, and culture initiatives.[52] However, the disclosures in this regard were not detailed and many disclosures were lacking in clarity.[53] Further, commentators seem critical of the disclosures that have been made in the 2020–21 reports.[54] However, as emphasized in Chapter 4, disclosure rules aim to get companies to recognise and pay attention to a particular issue and so the impact of the rule will be gradual. Besides, disclosure for the sake of disclosure is not useful. The question to ask is whether companies will use the rule, coupled with investor activism and social activism, to implement a change in culture that benefits all employees including those that are diverse.

Recent institutional investor activism has focused specifically on prevention of sexual harassment under the categories of both HCM and company culture.[55] This focus, alongside #MeToo, has already pushed many US company boards to pay attention to culture through the compensation committee. The name of the committee itself seems to be transforming with some companies calling it 'the culture and compensation committee'.[56] These committees seem to be concerned with disincentivising sexual harassment in the company by means of

---

[50] *Id.*
[51] For a detailed discussion on this, see George S. Georgiev, The Human Capital Management Movement in U.S. Corporate Law, 95 TUL. L. REV. 639 (2021).
[52] *Id.*, at 676–77.
[53] *Id.*, at 677.
[54] Id., at 682–83.
[55] Blackrock, Investment Stewardship Annual Report, BLACKROCK (2019) 20, www.blackrock.com/corporate/literature/publication/blk-annual-stewardshipreport-2019.pdf; Amelia Miazad, *Sex, Power, and Corporate Governance*, 54 UC DAVIS L. REV. 1913 (2021).
[56] Miazad, *Id.*, 1974.

specific clauses in CEO compensation agreements.[57] Additionally, compensation is also being tied to the numerical increase in diversity at the firm. For instance, executives at Starbucks Corp. will reportedly be awarded more shares if diversity of the company's managerial positions is increased by 2024.[58]

While use of compensation arrangements to effect culture changes might be a positive development[59] (and consistent with one of the principles in the UK Code in this regard), the focus needs to be more systemic and should go beyond issues of sexual harassment, and numerical representation. Instead, the focus must shift to a firm-wide review and improvement of company culture if all forms of diversity are to be addressed. Recall (from Chapter 3) that companies made statements on race and commitments to hire more black people, in the context of the killing of George Floyd and subsequent focus on BLM. These announcements were typically silent about examining the company's culture to ensure that the newly hired diverse people would have the same opportunities to achieve their full potential, as other employees.[60] Similarly, firms that focus on achieving representation

---

[57] *Id.*, 1975. ['According to employment lawyers and executive compensation consultants, the #MeToo movement has caused companies to contemplate changes to their executive compensation agreements. A handful of companies have already made these changes, which fall into four categories: (1) the addition of "sexual harassment" within the definition of cause for termination; (2) the addition of sexual harassment as a "trigger" to allow the clawback of compensation paid; (3) the addition of a representation & warranty to address prior misconduct; and (4) the inclusion of diversity and inclusion as a metric for assessing executive bonuses.']

[58] Other companies like McDonald's Corp and Nike Inc. made similar announcements. See Emily Glazer & Theo Francis, *CEO Pay Increasingly Tied to Diversity Goals*, WALL ST. J. (June 2, 2021), www.wsj.com/articles/ceos-pledged-to-increase-diversity-now-boards-are-holding-them-to-it-11622626380.

[59] Since the compensation structure and incentives is an indication of what the firm indicates, tying compensation to diversity issues sends a clear message to executives. Further, since the compensation structures are currently geared towards short-term profits, baking in a focus on employee well-being is seen as a way to reorient what executives focus on. See, e.g., Leo E. Strine Jr. & Kirby M. Smith, *Toward Fair Gainsharing and a Quality Workplace for Employees: How a Reconceived Compensation Committee Might Help Make Corporations More Responsible Employers and Restore Faith in American Capitalism*, 76 BUS. LAWYER 43 (2021).

[60] Bowdeya Tweh, Patrick Thomas, & Sebastian Herrera, Apple, Google Join Roster of Companies Pledging to Donate, Change Practices on Race, WALL ST. J. (June 12, 2020), www.wsj.com/articles/in-corporate-reckoning-executives-pressed-to-improve-racial-equity-in-workplaces-11591917711.

of women and other categories of people in board and senior management positions, to comply with quota laws or disclosure-based targets, will not really be bringing long-term change unless diversity issues are part of their assessment of firm culture.

A significant issue that has not been the focus of regulation or investor attention in both the UK and the United States, but something that is responsible for much unhappiness, especially amongst younger employees, seems to be that of hierarchical structures in the workplace and how they unequally impact employees who are diverse. This is perhaps why younger employees prefer flatter structures with less hierarchy.[61] They not only want to see career progression but also an acknowledgement of their work and ideas.[62] In many cases, hierarchy might mean that a junior employee painstakingly prepares a document or presentation and the senior takes credit for it. Or it could be an idea that a senior colleague unfairly takes credit for. Hierarchy could also result in ideas of junior employees not being taken seriously, irrespective of the merit of the idea. It could also result in female employees noticing that they do not have access to the same pay or perks as their male colleagues of similar ranks, but not being able to raise these issues with their managers and not being taken seriously even if they do. All these examples not only run counter to employee well-being but also result in meritorious candidates being overlooked for promotions because someone else has taken credit for their work or because they were not able to access the same perks and facilities that helped their colleagues do better.

While these are issues that affect all employees, diverse candidates[63] find it much harder to navigate hierarchy because it is less likely that they will become part of cliques (or network of friends,

---

[61] Viv Groskop, *Hierarchy Matters at Work, So Why Aren't We Talking about It?*, FINANCIAL TIMES (Aug. 15, 2021), www.ft.com/content/7116b638-3e96-47c3-b26a-1e6f78ea0bdc.

[62] Layli Foroudi, *Workplace Culture Is a 'Rude Awakening' for New Graduates* FINANCIAL TIMES (Mar. 9, 2020), www.ft.com/content/439bcfec-4362-11ea-9a2a-98980971c1ff.

[63] A reminder that diversity is not restricted to race and gender. As Joan C. Williams rightly notes, although the in-group in most contexts will be composed of white men, not all white men will be part of it. Whether they are part of it or left on the fringes will depend on other characteristics like their educational background, whether they were the first generation in their family to be college educated, etc. See Williams, *supra* note 47, at 12.

to use a less negative term) that include more influential people in the firm.[64] These cliques are usually formed based on commonalities like graduating from the same university, having the same hobbies outside work, or taking smoke breaks, with one's manager or some other senior colleagues. Such commonalities result in social access to one's boss and other senior members in the workplace which can, in turn, result in the usual hierarchical culture becoming relaxed for the junior employees that are part of these cliques.[65]

The increasing focus on identity groups by quota requirements, targets, and social movements, might even make it harder for diverse candidates to find mentors and champions across these divisions.[66] Even if there is no intention to discriminate against women or racial minorities or some other type of diverse group, if employees belonging to these groups are unable to find ways to navigate the hierarchical structure, they are likely to be overlooked for promotions. While mentorship and sponsorship programs are often suggested to help diverse members gain visibility, and consequently promotions,[67] these

---

[64] 'Across industries, women and people of colour are fourteen percentage points less likely than white men to think performance evaluations are fair. While men are roughly fifteen to thirty percentage points more likely to feel that pay and opportunities to advancement are fair, with women of all races and black men vying for the most dissatisfied group.' See Williams, *supra* note 47, at 148.

[65] See, e.g., Zoë Cullen & Ricardo Perez-Truglia, *The Old Boys' Club: Schmoozing and the Gender Gap*, NBER (2021). Based on data from one large firm in Asia (where the gender gaps in pay and promotion rates are similar to those documented for other corporations in both developed and developing countries), the authors found, amongst other things, that 'increased social interactions due to co-smoking leads to significantly faster career progression'. They also found that 'employees may use interactions with their managers to gain their managers' favor and use these moments for self-promotion'. Both employees and managers learn useful information during these interactions. While 'employees may learn useful information, such as which tasks or training are more conducive to promotions', managers may learn more about their employees which helps them identify the employees' 'effort, accomplishments and potential'.

[66] Cindy A. Schipani, Terry Morehead Dworkin, & Devin Abney, *Overcoming Gender Discrimination in Business: Reconsidering Mentoring in the Post #Me-Too and COVID-19 Eras*, 23 U. Pa. J. Bus. L. 1072 (2021).

[67] See, e.g., Monika Hamori & Rocío Bonet, *How Companies Can Ensure Women Get the Top Jobs, Too*, Financial Times (Mar. 22, 2021), www.ft.com/content/bb1b4b61-fa27-491a-a121-f41786654bfb. ['Among the most effective practices to help women move ahead are sponsorship initiatives, such as the Breakthrough Leadership Programme at accountancy firm PwC and the Women in Leadership Sponsorship and Development Programme at broadcaster Sky. These foster the development of networks in the workplace, make the performance of women visible, and ensure that they gain access to challenging jobs.']

programs are not always successful.[68] Addressing the overall structure will be a more significant change and unlock benefits both to diverse and to other employees.[69] Thus, the board and CEO should consciously strategise and implement policies that create flat or less hierarchical structures that makes the contributions of junior employees visible.

A related issue is that some types of contributions are not given due credit, and this has become even more apparent in the wake of the COVID-19 pandemic. During this time, women have not only had to deal with more care responsibilities at home (due to childcare services becoming unavailable) but also have taken up more responsibility at work to help colleagues deal with work–life challenges.[70] However, this extra work often goes unrecognized.[71] Companies would do well to recognise and reward employees that take initiatives to care for their colleagues and fill-in for gaps in the firm's benefits programs. This would also incentivise other employees to step forward and support their colleagues.[72] Table 5.1 shows employees value working in a place with helpful colleagues. Also, as firms start to build work flexibility into their culture, based on lessons from the pandemic, it will be important to ensure the visibility of contributions from colleagues who choose

---

[68] *Id.* Hamori and Bonet note that mentoring programs have been challenged by the impact of COVID-19, which made working from home the norm for almost a year in many countries. However, I think it is possible to make this work online, like we have done with so many other things during 2020 and 2021. The real problem of mentoring and sponsorship programs is that the mentor–mentee relationship cannot be built based on whom one is assigned to. Often, these are more organic relationships that develop. This is not to say that mentoring and sponsorship programs will not work. Rather, it is merely to say that they are not always effective.

[69] As Joan C. Williams says, '…we need to stop focusing nigh exclusively on helping people navigate systems that remain fundamentally unfair'. We need to instead focus on changing the systems. See Joan C. Williams, *supra* note 47, at 3.

[70] MCKINSEY & COMPANY, WOMEN IN THE WORKPLACE 2021 (Sept. 27, 2021), www.mckinsey.com/featured-insights/diversity-and-inclusion/women-in-the-workplace.

[71] *Id.* The study notes that 'less than a quarter of companies are recognizing this work to a substantial extent in formal evaluations like performance reviews'.

[72] Edmans rightly notes that employees have the ability to 'go the extra mile' even if this is not required or rewarded in employment contracts. As the McKinsey evidence shows, some employees already are. However, explicitly recognizing such behaviour in performance evaluations will indicate that the management views this positively. Eventually, this will seep into the culture of the company. See ALEX EDMANS, GROW THE PIE: HOW GREAT COMPANIES DELIVER BOTH PURPOSE AND PROFIT 34 (Cambridge University Press, 2020).

to avail of sabbaticals, leave to care for a sick relative, etc., and of those who step up and fill in during their colleagues' absences. This type of culture will help the company identify and promote responsible and talented employees, irrespective of their background, race, gender, hobbies, work location and timings or other characteristics unrelated to their work output. Having said this, we should acknowledge that problems can and do arise even in flatter structures and when that happens, the reporting and other mechanisms are useful.

To sum up the argument on corporate culture, the board and management should together address corporate culture by making systemic changes, and leading by example. Any consideration of corporate culture is incomplete if issues of diversity are not part of that consideration. While the SEC's broad disclosure rule on HCM may not provide specific guidance on culture and employee concerns, market forces have directed companies along these lines. The UK's disclosure rules are more explicit on both culture and employee engagement. However, as the discussion here has shown, there is scope for firms to look beyond the legal and investor mandates and aim for best-suited solutions to their employees. It is ultimately less important that companies provide detailed disclosures on these issues and more important that they genuinely pay attention to issues of culture and diversity. Companies that do this will be able to attract and retain the best talent and avoid corporate governance failures.

From a theoretical perspective, all the ideas and mechanisms to improve corporate culture discussed here can fit within a paradigm that integrates compassion and empathy into corporate governance.[73] While compassion can help the board management to be sensitive to the issues of workers, empathy will help focus on the specific needs of diverse employees. The COVID-19 pandemic and the consequent hardships have forced corporate leaders to countenance many employee concerns, along with the realization that addressing these is in the interests of the company. Carrying this realization forward into corporate governance thinking, and then integrating it into systems and culture will be important. More on this in the next chapter.

---

[73] See generally Villiers, *supra* note 13. Villiers argues for compassion in corporate leadership. I take that idea and add empathy to it, to ensure that diverse candidates are specifically considered in the corporate culture discussion.

5.2 BOARD AND MANAGEMENT TEAM CULTURE

The discussion thus far has focused on corporate culture generally. Board culture matters for board directors to function effectively and for the well-being of directors in the same way that corporate culture matters for the workforce. So also does management team culture for executives. Further, the same way that a bad work culture is more likely to affect diverse employees adversely, the culture on the board and management teams are most likely to negatively impact diverse directors and executives.

The culture of the board not only includes the environment in which board members interact with each other but also board members' interactions with senior management since these interactions are, in large part, the means through which information flows to the board. Important questions to ask about board culture are whether it allows the best candidates to be hired as directors, whether it allows all directors to contribute meaningfully, whether it encourages diverse views and if yes, whether these views are taken seriously, and finally whether all members are actively contributing to the board's functioning. For the diversity discourse, the important questions are whether the board's culture allows diverse candidates to be hired and if so, are such candidates able to contribute effectively? These are important questions to ask because the right culture is required for the board to be effective and because difficult board cultures will impact the well-being of diverse candidates on such boards. The focus here is specifically on gender and racial diversity which are touted as a means to enhancing board effectiveness as if they were fairy dust. However, the discussion will also be applicable to many other forms of diversity on the board.

The UK Code rightly notes that the board chair has a duty to promote a culture of openness and debate on the board.[74] The chair is also responsible for facilitating 'constructive board relations and the effective contribution of all non-executive directors, and ensures that directors receive accurate, timely and clear information'.[75] In other words, all directors should be able to access relevant information and then contribute effectively to the work of the board.

---

[74] UK Code, Principle F.
[75] UK Code, Principle F.

In practice however, as the interviews of board members of Netflix (discussed in Chapter 2) demonstrates, it is not common for the board to have a culture where dissentient views are encouraged.[76] If this is the reality, board diversity, with all its supposed promise of bringing diverse perspectives to discussions, will not be able to improve the board decision-making process. In this scenario, expecting diverse board members to overcome a culture where alternate views are discouraged, to enhance the monitoring function of the board, is unreasonable. It is as if the diverse candidates are being set up to fail.

Why would corporations hire diverse directors and then not allow dissentient views? There could be two possible reasons for this. The first is that, as mentioned in Chapter 4, many firms seem to be pushed to comply with diversity quotas or targets without genuine education about the benefits of diversity. The second reason is that much of this – the culture that prevents diverse candidates from contributing effectively – is unconscious. As Fulp noted, male directors are often not aware that they are creating unfriendly and sometimes hostile culture for women on the board.[77] Consistent with this, women directors in a study said that they were not treated as full members of the group and that 'many male directors seem unaware that they may create hostile board cultures, fail to listen to female directors or accept them as equals, and require them to continually re-establish their credentials'.[78] The same could be said for the in-group directors (even if some of them happen to be women or ethnically diverse) creating an undesirable culture for any member that does not belong to this group. In one extreme case, it was publicly reported that a woman director, Liz Dolan quit the board of Quicksilver in protest because she was excluded from conversations that led to the replacement of the CEO.[79]

---

[76] David F. Larcker & Brian Tayan, *Diversity in the C-Suite – The Dismal State of Diversity among Fortune 100 Senior Executives*, STANFORD CLOSER LOOK SERIES 4 (Apr. 1, 2021), www.gsb.stanford.edu/sites/default/files/publication-pdf/cgri-closer-look-82-diversity-among-f100.pdf.

[77] CAROL FULP, SUCCESS THROUGH DIVERSITY: WHY THE MOST INCLUSIVE COMPANIES WILL WIN 70 (Beacon Press, Boston 2018).

[78] Boris Groysberg & Deborah Bell, *Dysfunction in the Boardroom*, HARV. BUS. REV. (June 2013), https://hbr.org/2013/06/dysfunction-in-the-boardroom.

[79] Joann S. Lublin, *Quiksilver Director Exits Amid Spat*, WALL ST. J. (June 4, 2015), www.wsj.com/articles/quiksilver-director-exits-amid-spat-1433460219.

Despite the UK Code's emphasis on the Chair, the CEO is often influential and plays a role in setting the culture of board meetings and other interactions between the board and management. Afterall, the CEO controls the flow of information to the board in most cases. Again, the interviews of the Netflix directors rightly illustrate how the CEO must prioritise a culture both within the board and management teams that allows open discussion and transparency. Dominant CEOs who discourage diverse views are largely responsible for negative culture in top management teams. Recall the examples of AIG and Massey (discussed in Chapter 2) where the CEOs were not questioned by other executives, which ultimately made it easy for them to conceal information from the board.[80] Thus, it is important for the culture in both the management team and the board to be one that encourages diverse views.

Board and management culture is not only important for the corporation to be able to maximise the effectiveness of its senior leadership, including its diverse members, but also for the diverse candidates who take on these positions. While a lot of literature has been devoted to how diversity benefits companies, not as much literature focuses on why diverse candidates might want to serve as board directors or even remain in the workforce in executive roles. Often businesses and law firms lament that the pool of diverse candidates is too shallow[81]; however, recent diversity databases show that this is not the case.[82] Instead, there might be a problem of women and minority candidates opting out of workplaces where racism, sexism, bullying, and discrimination are prevalent.[83] Similarly, as potential board members, they would want to opt out of boards where they are merely hired as tokens to signal that the company cares about diversity, rather than as members whose contributions are valued.

There is also the issue of 'glass cliffs' where women and members of minority groups are often appointed as directors or CEOs or to

---

[80] See discussion in Chapter 2.
[81] Eli Wald, *In-House Myths*, WIS. L. REV. 407 (2012).
[82] See, e.g., Derek T. Dingle, *Power in the Boardroom: Registry of Black Corporate Board Members* (Sept. 12, 2018), www.blackenterprise.com/registry-black-corporate-board-members-2018/.
[83] Cheryl L. Wade, *Gender Diversity on Corporate Boards: How Racial Politics Impedes Progress in the United States*, 26 PACE INT'L L. REV. 23 (2014).

other executive positions only when the company is in crisis.[84] In any kind of crisis and especially when the crisis involves an issue of sexual harassment or racism going unaddressed, the newly appointed woman director or director belonging to a racial minority faces more scrutiny. For instance, when Ariana Huffington was appointed to the board of Uber after the allegations of sexual harassment created a reputational crisis for the company, some news articles discussed her appointment with negative undertones.[85] Especially with appointments that respond to high publicity events about company specific or systemic problems, it becomes increasingly important for these diverse candidates to be able to make informed assessments about the culture of the board, and the wider company. Being part of a board that does not in fact facilitate discussion of different perspectives on issues will mean that diverse candidates will not make a difference to the board's decisions.[86] Further, to have an impact on issues like harassment and discrimination, directors need to perform both monitoring and advisory roles. It is then important to know whether the CEO and board culture facilitates such involvement. Such information will allow board candidates to assess whether they will be able to make a real contribution to the company. This is particularly important for diverse candidates who are hired in the context of social pressure resulting from #MeToo and BLM movements because the expectation from such candidates seems to be that they will help address problems of racism and sexism within the firm.

If candidates are in fact able to make such assessments, then companies will also be incentivised to pay attention to these issues in order to

[84] Douglas M. Branson, *Pathways for Women to Senior Management Positions and Board Seats: An A to Z List*, Mich. St. L. Rev. 1555, 1568 (2012); Terry Morehead Dworkin, Aarti Ramaswami, & Cindy A. Schipani, *A Half-Century Post-Title VII: Still Seeking Pathways for Women to Organizational Leadership*, 23 UCLA Women's L.J. 29, 46 (2016).

[85] See, e.g., 'Can Arianna Huffington Help Uber Recover from Sexual Harassment Claims?' (Market Watch, Mar. 24, 2017), www.marketwatch.com/story/can-arianna-huffington-help-uber-recover-from-sexual-harassment-claims-2017-03-24-9884450.

[86] Ravi S. Kudesia, *Diversity Is Not Enough: Why Collective Intelligence Requires Both Diversity and Disagreement*, HETERODOX BLOG (July 21, 2021), https://heterodox-academy.org/blog/diversity-is-not-enough-why-collective-intelligence-requires-both-diversity-and-disagreement/?fbclid=IwAR0UDywCGHKk5SpFz0hqFYQbVlZJqwu KAv_WCytogK0IHkSktdiHrG9WVzQ. Kudesia reports on a co-authored study that finds that diversity alone will not improve decision-making in a team if the team cannot 'leverage the wisdom of disagreement'.

be able to attract the diverse candidates. This presents the issue of how potential directors may be able to make these assessments accurately. The answer could lie with consulting firms that typically provide supplemental board services like executive and director search functions, board evaluations, and other board advisory services. These consulting firms already play a role in improving board culture for many large companies, and when they begin to service the supply side of the market (diverse candidates), the demand side (client companies) could also become more attuned to issues of board and management team culture.

5.2.1 Role of Consulting Firms in Building Effective Board Culture

Consulting firms act as intermediaries in the labour market for executive talent since they facilitate transactions between companies and potential executives.[87] In the executive and director search space, these consulting firms fill information gaps between companies and potential executives/directors, although as any third-party involvement naturally does, it comes with costs.[88] The fact that companies are using them shows that the benefits[89] exceeds any costs and as we will see below, for diverse candidates too, the benefits will be even more valuable, thus making the costs worthwhile.

Board consulting firms not only research, identify, screen, interview, verify candidate qualifications, and negotiate offers, they also provide leadership consulting, succession planning, and board assessment services.[90] Interestingly, the larger executive search firms also offer 'culture shaping' as a service.[91] One of the big executive search firms recently bought a leadership consulting firm to consolidate its 'culture shaping' offering.[92] Thus, there is already a focus on culture.

---

[87] Omari Scott Simmons, *Forgotten Gatekeepers: Executive Search Firms and Corporate Governance*, 54 WAKE FOREST L. REV. 807, 815 (2019).

[88] *Id.*, at 816.

[89] Amongst other things, the benefits to the company include signalling good governance practices and shifting accountability. *Id.*, at 817–19.

[90] *Id.*, at 820.

[91] *Id.*, at 825–26.

[92] Staffing Industry Analysts, *Heidrick Buys 'Culture Shaping' Firm for $53 Million* (Jan. 3, 2013), www2.staffingindustry.com/site/Editorial/Daily-News/US-Heidrick-Buys-Culture-Shaping-Firm-for-53-Million-24168.

5.2.2 Recruitment

Within the director-hiring process, executive search firms are responsible for 22% of all independent director nominations in the United
States.[93] The emphasis on diversity in recent times coupled with pressure from social movements like #MeToo and BLM indicates that
executive search firms are likely to be used more in the coming days.[94]
Companies are also getting behind other intermediaries who are offering bootcamps to make diverse candidates board ready.[95] According
to the board search guiding principles of the Association of Executive
Search and Leadership Consultants (AESC), a self-regulatory body,
diversity is one of the factors that executive search firms engage with,
in the board consultation process.[96] They work to manage unconscious
bias on the company side and on the other side, prepare candidates by
briefing them about the company's culture and strategy.[97] Relatedly,
they also focus on board refreshment practices and succession planning.[98] In the aftermath of #MeToo, BLM, and various new diversity

---

[93] Ali C. Akyol & Lauren Cohen, *Who Chooses Board Members?* 16 ADVANCES FIN. ECON.
43 (2013).

[94] Patrick Temple-West & Andrew Edgecliffe-Johnson, Push for Diversity Brings Rush of
Business for Executive Headhunters, FINANCIAL TIMES (Dec. 23, 2020), www.ft.com/
content/dbbc0f46-163e-4cce-abfa-31d2f9e44230. [Quoting Margot McShane, a board
and CEO hiring specialist at Russell Reynolds saying that her firm had 'seen "a dramatic
uptick" in demand for more diverse lists of board candidates since this summer's Black
Lives Matter protests'. The same trend of increase in demand for diversity in the executive
and board search process was reported by Lyndon Taylor, head of Heidrick & Struggles'
diversity and inclusion practice.] See also Nina Trentmann, *Racially Diverse CFOs Are
in High Demand, but Challenges Persist,* WALL ST. J. (May 25, 2021), www.wsj.com/
articles/racially-diverse-cfos-are-in-high-demand-but-challenges-persist-11621942201.
['Many companies and boards now insist on being presented with a diverse slate of candidates when filling C-suite positions and are tweaking how they assess candidates. They
also are taking steps to better retain and promote diverse internal talent.']

[95] Emily Glazer & Theo Francis, As Corporate Boards Pursue Diversity, Director
Training Programs Spring Up, WALL ST. J. (Dec. 31, 2021), www.wsj.com/articles/
as-corporate-boards-pursue-diversity-director-training-programs-spring-up-
11640946604?mod=Searchresults_pos13&page=1. For example, companies like
Amazon and Microsoft have provided financial support to the Black Boardroom Initiative,
started by law firm Perkins Coie LLP.

[96] Association of Executive Search and Leadership Consultants, www.aesc.org/sites/default/
files/uploads/documents-2015/AESC_Board_Search_&_Advisory_Guiding_Principles
.pdf, 2, 3.

[97] *Id.,* at 4.

[98] *Id.,* at 3.

requirements, American companies are reportedly also seeking advice about how to talk to people about sexual orientation, and other facets of diversity from executive search firms.[99]

Executive search firms have also become significant in the UK. Recall (from Chapter 4) that the UK Code mentions the use of executive search firms in the context of board appointments. The UK's standard voluntary code of conduct for executive search firms ('Code of Conduct') also emphasises diversity.[100] It requires executive search firms to consider the company's aspirations about diversity and 'explore with the client if recruiting women and/or ethnically diverse individuals is a priority both generally and on this occasion'.[101] The executive search firms themselves are asked to have an informal target of 40% female candidates on any longlist or shortlist of candidates being provided to the client company and if this target cannot be met, to explain why this is the case to the client company.[102] Even though it is not part of the Code, the Parker Review has recommended that each FTSE 100 company should have at least one director of colour by 2021; and each FTSE 250 Board should have at least one director of colour by 2024.[103]

Apart from reiterating the focus on numbers, executive search firms are also advised to help the client company with the interview and selection process so as to ensure that the process is objective and unconscious bias is eliminated as much as possible.[104] This, coupled with the inclusion of diverse candidates in the longlist and short list, might indeed help boards appoint candidates that are less like themselves, and outside their existing networks. The Code of Conduct does provide guidance about supporting candidates (especially first-time candidates) through the process by helping them prepare for interviews.[105] While these practices will be useful, the diverse candidates will struggle to be effective if the board culture is not ready for them.

[99] Temple-West and Edgecliffe-Johnson, *supra* note 94.
[100] Standard Voluntary Code of Conduct for Executive Search Firms, 2021 (UK).
[101] *Id.*
[102] *Id.*
[103] Parker Review Committee, *Ethnic Diversity Enriching Business Leadership: An Update Report from The Parker Review*, 61 (2020), https://assets.ey.com/content/dam/ey-sites/ey-com/en_uk/news/2020/02/ey-parker-review-2020-report-final.pdf.
[104] Standard Voluntary Code of Conduct for Executive Search Firms, 2021 (UK).
[105] *Id.*

There is also some suggestion that the executive search firms should work with client companies to help on-board the new hires.[106] However, there is no mention of any support being provided on the other side of the market – that is to the candidates being hired, and particularly to diverse candidates. Diverse candidates – for both board and executive positions – would benefit by executive search firms providing services like matching them with other diverse directors or executives holding positions in other companies so that they can receive guidance on navigating difficult board cultures and glass cliffs. Recall the example of Margaret Keane, the first CEO of Synchrony, discussed in Chapter 3, who mentions that she valued the help she received in dealing with uncooperative colleagues and advice about getting the most out of board members.[107]

The executive search firms could also conduct workshops on how individual directors can contribute to a board that resists diverse perspectives. New directors, whether they are younger than the other directors, or belong to a different race, ethnicity, gender, or simply do not belong to the same social networks as the other directors and CEO, are often hesitant to challenge things that the rest of the group takes for granted. This can especially be true in boards that are unwilling to take the new member seriously or resist any disagreement. The solution offered up for this problem is that a critical mass of women directors is required on the board, and it has become accepted that this critical mass is 30%.[108] But it would not be practical to attempt a critical mass of every kind of diverse director a board decides to agree. Besides, not every woman director will have the same view. What if one director has an outlier view and other directors, including other diverse directors, espouse the majority view? Psychology professor, Bohns, writes in her book that even a single individual expressing disagreement or even expressing doubt has an impact. More impact than they might think anyway. Bohns says that the speaker, irrespective of how powerful they are, will care about how they are perceived. If one person is doubtful, they will attempt to persuade them. The

---

[106] *Id.*
[107] Lublin, *supra* note 79.
[108] Alison M. Konrad, Vicki W. Kramer, & Sumru Erkut, *Critical Mass: The Impact of Three or More Women Directors* 37(2) ORGAN. DYN. 145, 150 (2008).

fact that one extra person has to be convinced means that the person proposing the decision will have to work harder, that is present more arguments to convince the doubter. The extra work needed to win that person might lead the group to move towards a less extreme view than they started out with, Bohns says.[109] It could also be the case that a second director, even if they belong to the in-group, might also espouse the diverse perspective once they see the new director taking that view.[110] These and other insights by experts in various fields and diverse candidates with board experience will be useful for the first time and sometimes even experienced board members to be able to counter difficult work cultures.

These services should be available even after the candidates have been appointed. This will help them during the on-boarding process and perhaps even afterwards. With the pressure to appoint diverse directors mounting (because of laws, targets, and pressure from investors and the general public), diverse candidates will be in demand and will need to be careful about what positions they take on. While diverse candidates bring reputational value to the firm, they should be aware that they might be likely to take the fall when an issue relating to problematic culture in the company comes to light. Diverse candidates would therefore find that the costs of preparing themselves to swim in choppy waters (as boards that are not used to diverse candidates can be) are worth incurring.

---

[109] VANESSA BOHNS, YOU HAVE MORE INFLUENCE THAN YOU THINK (2021). As I was reading Bohns work on this, I found myself nodding in agreement because I had been on a panel that was charged with assessing a certain academic work. Another, more senior panel member had, in his written report, assessed the work in a way that I thought was unfair. It took a great deal of my mental energy to argue against that view. I had prepared for a lot of resistance because I was the outside member (from a different university) on that panel and because I am a woman from a different country. However, to my surprise, the other member moderated his own comments after listening to my view. Although I did not find the panel particularly welcoming to a different view, I was able to make a difference when I pushed ahead.

[110] Dale A. Oesterle, *Should Courts Do Behavioral Analysis of Boardroom Conduct*, 9 J. BUS. & TECH. L. 51 (2014). Discussing the problem of board members feeling misplaced loyalty to an authority figure, Oesterle notes that an assigned 'devil's advocate' on the board may be able to present different views without actually being seen as disloyal to the CEO. Then the other members could join in the discussion. A diverse director who is aware of these dynamics might be able to present their alternative view, knowing that others will be more willing to discuss it so long as the view is not seen to come from them.

Further, candidates, particularly diverse candidates who are unable to glean this information through informal networks, might want to ascertain whether the culture of the board and management team that they are invited to join is one that is welcoming. While employees are able to access market information about a company's culture before deciding to work there via platforms like Glassdoor, board culture is less easily gauged by those without inside sources. Since firms are under pressure to hire them, diverse candidates will be in demand and will likely want to assess board culture before accepting the position. A recent *Wall Street Journal* article reports that diverse candidates are already in a position to choose between a number of offers for board positions. The article quotes Jan Fields, chair of the nominating and governance committee of women's clothing retailer Chico's FAS Inc., saying that diverse candidates are 'mulling offers from two or three others, or they're deciding if they even want to go and be a part of a company'.[111]

Executive search firms might be able to solve this information gap by offering services like matching diverse candidates with other more experienced diverse candidates (as suggested above), and where the client company agrees to this, providing confidential reports about the culture of the board and steps taken and likely to be taken by the board chair and CEO to allow the diverse candidates being hired to contribute. Even where a candidate is willing to take on a board position despite red flags in the firm's board culture, the candidate may be able to negotiate better terms to join the firm. Client companies that are truly interested in diversity (rather than token appointments) are likely to be interested in these conversations. Not only this, the existence of such a service will alert client companies to issues of board culture and will encourage them to review their board culture. The time is therefore ripe for executive search firms to offer their services to the other side of the market.[112]

---

[111] Emily Glazer & Theo Francis, As Corporate Boards Pursue Diversity, Director Training Programs Spring Up, WALL ST. J. (Dec. 31, 2021), www.wsj.com/articles/as-corporate-boards-pursue-diversity-director-training-programs-spring-up-11640946604?mod=Searchresults_pos13&page=1.

[112] Although diversity consultancies, either as part of the executive search form or as a different firm, have mushroomed, the only address the companies' side of the market and do not offer specialised services of the sort proposed in this chapter for diverse candidates.

5.2.3 Board Evaluation

Executive search firms also consult with boards to provide advisory services that includes assessing board culture, creating an inclusive board culture, inducting new board members, improving the relationship between the CEO and the board, and clarifying the role of the board and its committees and members.[113] Crucially, it also includes board evaluation services.[114] While external board evaluation is not a new idea in the UK and some other countries,[115] most company boards in the United States only conduct a self-assessment.[116] Outsourcing it to a third-party firm can bring objectivity to the process. The UK Code recommends that the Chair of the board should have an externally facilitated board evaluation regularly (every three years if it is a FTSE 350 company).[117] The results of the external evaluation should then be used to address the weaknesses that are identified by the process.[118]

Since these same consultancy firms also act as intermediaries for director appointments, the metrics about board culture that emerge from the evaluation process, and the subsequent improvement made can also be used as a metric for candidates to assess the company, where the company agrees to make this available to the candidates. Thus, executive search firms, through the range of supplemental board services they provide, are well placed to act as intermediaries between boards and candidates for board directorships.

To ensure that these intermediaries are efficiently serving both sides of the market – companies and diverse candidates for board positions – it is necessary for them to focus in their evaluations of company culture, on issues that diverse board members might find particularly challenging. Issues such as whether dissentient views are frowned upon or whether board members have timely access to information to be able to contribute effectively in both monitoring and advisory

---

[113] Association of Executive Search and Leadership Consultants, *supra* note 96, at 5.

[114] *Id.*

[115] Australia, Singapore, and South Africa also recommend external evaluation at regular intervals.

[116] The NYSE now requires companies to conduct self-evaluations at least annually. See NYSE, Inc., Listed Company Manual § 303A.09 (2004), www.nyse.com/pdfs/governance guidelines.pdf.

[117] UK Code, Provision 21.

[118] UK Code, Provision 22.

capacities should be included in the evaluation metrics. These issues speak to board culture and diverse directors will particularly value these metrics while making decisions. Even information about the companies' board refreshment policies and succession planning can be useful to potential candidates to assess the culture of the board. The more refreshment there is, the more open the board is to hear from newer members. These factors might also help candidates fulfilling other facets of diversity, for instance those from a different experiential background, deciding whether to take on the board position.

Even though the monitoring role of the board is most emphasised, since diverse board members usually bear the burden of being appointed after a crisis (harassment, bullying, etc.) within the company or a social movement drawing attention to systemic problems, such directors cannot be as under-committed to the company as other independent directors currently are. Eventually, such involvement of diverse directors coupled with pressure from intermediaries providing board advisory services has the potential to change expectations from all independent directors.

There is, however, danger in relying on these evaluations to assure investors and others of board effectiveness on various measures including culture. This is because the company whose board is being evaluated is the one who pay's the evaluator. As one CEO put it, 'paid external advisers will not jeopardise future fees with harsh truths'.[119] It is precisely because of this that it is important to understand that the purpose of board evaluation is self-assessment that can help reflection and improvement rather than for the process to act as a check against negligence and misconduct.[120] No external consultant can help a company that does not want to help itself. The CEO and board chair of a client company should help the executive search firm help them (as Tom Cruise famously said in the movie Jerry Maguire[121]). Even a

---

[119] Andrew Hill, *Could Do Better: The Need for Tougher Board Reviews*, FINANCIAL TIMES (Jan. 25, 2021), www.ft.com/content/ec65340c-3b71-4e52-8861-3c4b60fc9953.

[120] There is a counter view that 'the purpose of evaluation is to provide an assessment of whether the board is or is not effective, in either absolute or relative terms, and that the purpose of disclosure is to provide assurance as to the future performance of the board and company'. See Chartered Governance Institute UK & Ireland 'Review of the effectiveness of independent board evaluation in the UK listed sector' (2021) 10. The Institute does not agree with this view. It merely presents the counter view.

[121] Playing a sports agent in the movie, Cruise is seen to be saying to his client, 'help me help you help yourself'.

consultancy that provides the 'harsh truths' cannot control what the board chooses to disclose in the annual report, and also whether the board uses the results of the evaluation to make improvements. As an analysis of reporting on board evaluations in 2020 shows, 'only 46% of FTSE 350 companies outlined their outputs and actions' resulting from the evaluations.[122]

What this means is that the usual playbook of relying on investors to engage with companies on disclosures regarding board evaluations will not be effective. While investors can ask companies to provide more detail, the solution, particularly for board culture and diversity issues, is to educate various players about the various pieces of the diversity jigsaw. The players here are companies, consultancies, and diverse candidates. When board consultancies start to provide meaningful diversity-related solutions, some client companies that are keen on effecting real change will see the value in them. Diverse candidates will also choose to work with consultancies that provide services tailored to their needs. This will in turn lead more companies to work with the consultancies that are able to attract diverse candidates. The executive search firm/consultancy market is ripe for a disruption on these lines. When a few firms start to service the other side of the market (diverse candidates) and also focus their board services to effect cultural change, such firms will start to become market leaders and others will follow.

Despite the many advantages of the model outlined above, it is not advisable for mandatory regulations requiring companies to engage board consultancies for director nomination, board evaluation, and other board advisory services; or for board consultancies to be required to service diverse candidates. Mandatory requirements, as we saw in Chapter 4, are likely to result in tick-the-box compliance rather than genuine engagement in the process.[123] Since evaluations are merely used as a tool for the board to assess and make changes to its culture where necessary, it is a means to an end and a tick the box exercise will serve no one. Similarly, mandating how board consultancies/executive search firms do their job would neither secure buy-in from the

---

[122] Chartered Governance Institute UK & Ireland (Review of board evaluation), *supra* note 120, at 15.

[123] Luca Enriques & Dirk Zerzsche, Quack Corporate Governance, Round III: Bank Board Regulation under the New European Capital Requirement Directive, 16 THEORETICAL INQ. L. 211 (2015).

consultancies nor from the client companies. Instead, a market-driven process where the demand for board diversity results in intermediary firms refining their board evaluation processes based on the needs of diverse candidates, who make up the other side of the market is more efficient. However, the informational needs of diverse candidates are under-researched and need to be highlighted. Once the importance of board culture and their potential to allow board diversity to 'work' is understood, institutional investors (many of whom are already active on the diversity agenda) will begin to engage with companies along those lines, and consulting firms who are able to address board culture with a specific focus on diverse candidates' needs will be in demand.

5.3 BOARD CULTURE AND COMPANY CULTURE AS PART OF THE DIVERSITY JIGSAW

This chapter has shown that the right culture – at the board, management team, and the entire workforce – is important both for company level benefits and for the well-being of diverse directors, executives, and employees. Culture, then, is an important consideration for the diversity discourse and one that should be assessed separately for the workforce and for directors and executives. While the impact of COVID-19 and subsequent lockdowns has helped corporations focus on issues of employee well-being, many of those issues are especially relevant to diverse candidates. However, as this chapter has shown, a deliberation examination of culture that goes beyond responding to the pain points that COVID-19 highlighted is required for culture to be an effective tool to hire, retain, and promote the right employees. Further, when the board and management team are able to ensure a culture that attracts and allows diverse candidates to contribute effectively, the firm's senior leadership will be able to set the tone from the top for an effective corporate culture. Although this chapter has highlighted the role of board consulting services, it has also underscored that the buck ultimately stops with company leadership.

PART III

6   A PROPOSAL TO RECONCILE
CORPORATE LAW AND
CORPORATE GOVERNANCE
WITH DIVERSITY

The final piece of the diversity jigsaw that I discuss in this book is one that is fundamental not only to an understanding of diversity but also to all other issues at the intersection of corporate law and society, like climate change and other ESG issues. Thus far, the book has discussed the meaning of diversity, why it is important at all levels of the corporation, its specific importance for corporate governance, the impact of social movements and legal and market initiatives on how corporations deal with diversity, and how corporate culture and board culture are important determinants of how a corporation deals with diversity. This chapter attempts to reconcile corporate law with diversity and other societal issues.

After surveying the basic theories underpinning the purpose of the corporation, this chapter argues firstly that corporate law is in fact not averse to corporations addressing diversity and other societal issues; it is rather the operation of the entire corporate governance ecosystem that needs to be reconciled with these issues. This can be done by finding a middle ground between the two competing theories informing ideas of corporate purpose, and then ensuring that all actors within the corporate governance ecosystem are willing to allow this. Second, the chapter looks ahead through the peephole of corporate responses to the pandemic and argues that this could be the catalyst for firms to constructively address diversity issues on the lines of what I've discussed in Chapters 1–4. However, a crisis is only an impetus for action – whether or not effective and sustained actions will be indeed taken will again depend on a range of factors. Third, this chapter argues that corporations should be seen as part of the solution, rather than pushing them into a corner by constantly painting them as villains. The latter narrative will simply encourage woke-washing.

6.1 CORPORATE PURPOSE AND DIVERSITY

The debate about what the purpose of a corporation should be is an old and crowded one. It is also one that is important for how the diversity discourse has been shaped.

To first describe the debate, there are broadly two narratives that seem to sit in opposition with one another. On one side is shareholder primacy, according to which the purpose of the corporation is to maximise shareholder value; and on the other is stakeholder theory, which advocates for the maximization of value for all stakeholders. The debate between these two models is far from resolved. On the contrary, it becomes louder every time a new issue in corporate law, or a wider systemic issue like a financial crisis, or an external shock like a pandemic, forces us to think about various ESG issues that corporations have to deal with.

In the context of diversity-related laws and regulations, the issue of whether diverse boards will be able to maximise shareholder wealth, that is whether there is a business case for diversity, becomes important when one views the purpose of the corporation from a narrow understanding of the shareholder value maximization. On the other hand, it seems that fairness- and equality-based arguments are only useful when one uses a stakeholder theory lens. However, as I will argue here, there can in fact be a meeting point for these two seemingly extreme models. But there is some rubble to be cleared before that path can be clearly seen and used. We will return to this after a quick tour of how shareholder primacy and stakeholder theories have developed over time.

6.1.1 Shareholder Value Maximization as the Corporate Purpose

The debate between the shareholder primacy model (or shareholder value maximization model[1]) and the stakeholder model is crystalized in

---

[1] The shareholder primacy theory is conceptually not the same as the shareholder value maximization model. However, because shareholder primacy theory suggests that the interests of the shareholders should be given primacy, and because it is commonly

the famous exchange between Adolph A. Berle and E. Merrick Dodd in 1968. Berle said that the powers of the corporation or the management of the corporation are 'at all times exercisable only for the ratable benefit of all the shareholders as their interest appears'.[2] Dodd responded that corporations not only have a profit-making function but also a social service function and, therefore, the corporate purpose was more than just to make money for shareholders and included securing the welfare of employees, consumers, and the community as a whole.[3] Although Dodd did not use the term, he advocated for a stakeholder-oriented model. However, as he himself clarified, Dodd's view of designating a 'social responsibility' for businesses was 'merely a more enlightened view as to the ultimate advantage of the stockholder-owners [or shareholders]' and thus did not require a departure from the traditional goal of shareholder wealth maximization.[4]

By the early 2000s, it seemed like shareholder primacy was the model accepted in corporate law.[5] In a 2001 paper, Hansmann and Kraakman said that 'as a consequence of both logic and experience, there is convergence on a consensus that the best means to this end (that is, the pursuit of aggregate social welfare) is to make corporate managers strongly accountable to shareholder interests and, at least in direct terms, only to those interests'.[6] They went on to explain that opting for this shareholder primacy model did not mean that other constituencies would go unprotected. A concern raised was that the corporate board, if charged to only maximise shareholder returns,

---

assumed that shareholders are interested in wealth maximization, these two models are often conflated. We can live with this conflation for now, just to avoid getting into the theoretical woods too much.

[2] Adolf Berle, *Corporate Powers as Powers in Trust* 44 (7) HARV. L. REV. 1049 (1931).

[3] E. Merrick Dodd, *For Whom Are Corporate Managers Trustees?*, 45 HARV. L. REV. 1145, 1148 (1932).

[4] *Id.*, at 1156.

[5] Henry Hansmann & Reinier Kraakman, *The End of History for Corporate Law*, 89 GEO. L.J. 439 (2001); JONATHAN R. MACEY, CORPORATE GOVERNANCE: PROMISES KEPT, PROMISES BROKEN 51 (Princeton University Press, 2008); FRANK H. EASTERBROOK & DANIEL R. FISCHEL, THE ECONOMIC STRUCTURE OF CORPORATE LAW 36 (Harvard University Press 1991).

[6] Hansmann & Kraakman, *supra* note 5. The idea that managers are accountable to shareholders can also be seen in the influential paper by Jensen and Meckling where they explain that managers are the agents of shareholders. Michael C. Jensen & William H. Meckling, *Agency Costs and Ownership Structure*, 3 J. FIN. ECON. 305, 308 (1976).

would do so by externalizing costs to non-shareholders like employees, consumers, or the environment. Proponents of the shareholder primacy model respond to this concern by arguing that such negative externalities are addressed by appropriate legislation (e.g. labour law, consumer protection law) outside of corporate law.[7] The only exception to this are creditors since corporate law provides for their protection in certain situations.[8]

Milton Friedman also (in)famously[9] endorsed the view that protection of other constituencies is best achieved by laws outside corporate law. Although his 1970 statement that 'the social responsibility of business was to increase its profits' in a New York Times Magazine article became very (un)popular, it has often been quoted out of context.[10] His statement was as follows:

> In a free-enterprise, private-property system, a corporate executive is an employee of the owners of the business. He has direct responsibility to his employers. That responsibility is to conduct the business in accordance with their desires, which generally will be to make as much money as possible while conforming to the basic rules of the society, both those embodied in law and those embodied in ethical custom.[11]

Thus, corporations must stick to trying to make money, consistently with law and custom. Indeed, it is more legitimate for the government to make rules that serve public interest than for corporations to make these decisions. In this way, corporations could be left to do what they do best, that is creating wealth.[12]

---

[7] Hansmann & Kraakman, *supra* note 5, at 442.

[8] *Id.*

[9] I don't use this term lightly. As Edmans says, 'to declare that you reject the Friedman doctrine has become almost a requirement for acceptance into polite society'. Alex Edmans, *What Stakeholder Capitalism Can Learn from Milton Friedman*, PROMARKET (Sep. 10, 2020), https://promarket.org/2020/09/10/what-stakeholder-capitalism-can-learn-from-milton-friedman/.

[10] MILTON FRIEDMAN, *The Social Responsibility of Business Is to Increase Its Profits*, NEW YORK TIMES MAGAZINE (Sep. 13, 1970), http://query.nytimes.com/mem/archivefree/pdf?res=9E05E0DA153CE531A15750C1A96F9C946190D6CF.

[11] Milton Friedman, CAPITALISM AND FREEDOM 133–34 (University of Chicago Press 1962).

[12] Leo E. Strine, Jr. & Nicholas Walter, *Conservative Collision Course?:The Tension between Conservative Corporate Law Theory and Citizens United*, 100(2) CORNELL L. REV. 358 (2015).

Friedman then went on add[13]:

> ... it may well be in the long-run interest of a corporation that is a major employer in a small community to devote resources to providing amenities to that community or to improving its government. That may make it easier to attract desirable employees, it may reduce the wage bill or lessen losses from pilferage and sabotage or have other worthwhile effects.

Thus, stakeholder interests are not being totally eschewed. In fact, Friedman brings many actions that promote stakeholder interests within the shareholder value maximization fold. So, in many cases, addressing stakeholder needs will in fact benefit the company. Conversely, corporations, by following the goal of wealth maximization, also tend to make other constituencies better off. For one thing, profitable corporations make investors better off and in turn, the investors can spend their wealth on their families and in buying goods and services, thereby increasing demand and the potential for others to get jobs and become wealthier.[14] For another, profitable corporations will also make other constituencies better off along with investors. As a matter of fact, a corporation that does not make customers better off will not be able to generate any revenue. The same goes for employees and suppliers – if they were not increasing their welfare by working for the company or by supplying to the company respectively, they would not be doing so. For example, Apple, one of the most successful companies in the world, serves customers with high quality products; its employees by providing opportunities for them to grow and develop in such a large and prominent company; its suppliers by investing in long-term relationships; and the environment by transitioning to renewable energy.[15] However, Apple, like most companies (and people), is not perfect and has areas where it can improve. Recall (from Chapter 3) how it handled the Garcia-Martinez situation. Soukup also notes that despite the public emphasis of transitioning to renewable energy, Apple's environmental record is complicated.[16] The point is that even companies that do not

---

[13] Incidentally, this part of the article is rarely cited.
[14] Easterbrook & Fischel, *supra* note 5, at 38.
[15] ALEX EDMANS, GROW THE PIE 40 (Cambridge University Press, 2020).
[16] STEPHEN R. SOUKUP, THE DICTATORSHIP OF WOKE CAPITAL 149 (2021).

effectively serve some stakeholder in a certain context produce social value.[17] In fact, much of human progress has been possible because of new inventions, which corporations have been able to produce at affordable prices so that they are available to most of society.

Other arguments in favour of shareholder primacy are that it is better for the board to only be responsible for shareholder interests since it is the shareholders who ultimately have voting rights to appoint directors;[18] and that a director asked to serve more than one master has been 'freed of both and is answerable to neither'.[19] The reasoning behind this argument is that a director who is supposed to serve more than one constituency could serve his/her own interest and be able to justify the action as furthering the interest of some other constituency (stakeholder) and thus remain in compliance with the duties of directors.[20] Further, even a loyal director asked to serve more than one stakeholder might not be able to take any actions since almost every scenario involves prioritizing the interests of different stakeholders.[21]

The case of *Dodge v. Ford Motor Company*[22] became famous for being a judicial precedent in support of the shareholder primacy view. In this case, the Michigan Supreme Court remarked:

> There should be no confusion... A business corporation is organised and carried on primarily for the profit of the stockholders. The powers of the directors are to be employed for that end. The discretion of the directors is to be exercised in the choice of means to attain that end, and does not extend to... other purposes.[23]

---

[17] Bernard S. Sharfman, *A Fuller Sense of Corporate Purpose: A Reply to Martin Lipton's 'on the Purpose of the Corporation*, OXFORD BUSINESS LAW BLOG (June 9, 2020), www .law.ox.ac.uk/business-law-blog/blog/2020/06/fuller-sense-corporate-purpose-reply-martin-liptons-purpose.

[18] STEPHEN M. BAINBRIDGE, THE NEW CORPORATE GOVERNANCE IN THEORY AND PRACTICE 28–30 (Oxford University Press, 2008).

[19] Easterbrook & Fischel, *supra* note 5, at 37–39.

[20] *Id.*

[21] *Id.*

[22] *Dodge* v. *Ford Motor Co.*, 170 N.W. 668 (Mich. 1919).

[23] *Id.*, 684. While this case has been cited often in support of the shareholder primacy view, some scholars have pointed out that this statement was merely dicta and that as far as this issue is concerned, the case should be treated as bad law. See generally Lynn A. Stout, *Why We Should Stop Teaching Dodge v. Ford*, 3(1) VA. L. &BUS. REV., 163–90 (2008). Others disagree. See Stephen M. Bainbridge, *Why We Should Keep Teaching Dodge v. Ford Motor Co.*, CLS BLUE SKY BLOG (Apr. 26, 2022), https://clsbluesky .law.columbia.edu/2022/04/26/why-we-should-keep-teaching-dodge-v-ford-motor-co/.

In reality, this statement from the judge was necessitated by certain self-serving actions of the director (Mr. Henry Ford), which he presented as actions to favour his employees.[24] Still, the above quote is cited to show support for the shareholder primacy model underpinning modern corporate law.

Another theory that has gained prominence in the United States, the contractarian model, which viewed the firm as a nexus of contracts between various actors, also espoused the basic idea that the corporation, through its directors and managers, had to maximise shareholder wealth.[25] Yet, another theory, the director primacy model, as the name suggests, gives primacy to directors and thus says that directors rather than shareholders control the corporations. However, this theory too views the purpose of the corporation as shareholder wealth maximization.[26]

Finally, it is relevant to note that the shareholder value maximization norm currently informs corporate law and even prominent advocates of the stakeholder theory have accepted this.[27] In this context, it seems that advocates of diversity have assumed that the only way to put diversity on the agenda of regulators and the business community is to show that diversity in the corporation results in increased share value. On the other hand, claiming that diversity efforts will help make the corporation fair and create equal opportunities for diverse people seems to suggest that one is stepping outside the core purpose of the corporation. However, when we recall Friedman's statement about corporations supporting employees for the long-term success of the company, it seems odd that diversity advocates have taken such a narrow view of the shareholder value maximization model. As it happens, the model has come to be regarded very narrowly, with a focus on short-term profits. I will return to the need to revive

---

[24] For the colourful backstory of the case, see M. Todd Henderson, *Everything Old Is New Again: Lessons from Dodge v. Ford Motor Company* 1–2 (Univ. of Chi. John M. Olin Law & Econ. 2nd Series, Working Paper No. 373, 2007), www.law.uchicago.edu/ files/files/373 .pdf.

[25] Easterbrook & Fischel, *supra* note 5.

[26] Stephen M. Bainbridge, *Director Primacy: The Means and Ends of Corporate Governance*, 97 NW. U. L. REV. 547 (2002).

[27] See generally Kent Greenfield, *Sticking the Landing: Making the Most of the 'Stakeholder Moment'*, 26 EUR. BUS. L. REV. 147 (2015); David Yosifon, *The Law of Corporate Purpose*, 10 BERKELEY BUS. L. J. 181 (2013).

the long-term focus of shareholder value maximization model, after discussing the conception of the corporation that is at the other end of the spectrum – stakeholderism.

6.1.2 Stakeholder Value or Stakeholderism as the Corporate Purpose

According to stakeholderist models, the corporation has both a social service and a profit-making function.[28] Proponents argue that the 'social service' element is necessary to ensure that corporations do not harm others through a singular focus on profits. Examples of harms they foresee are product defects, environmental harm, and other corporate failures.[29] While proponents of this theory have not fully specified how such a model is to be given effect (since it involves changing the status quo), generally they envisage a 'multifiduciary duty' model for directors, which would require directors to consider the interests of all constituencies.[30] Such a model, however, runs into the 'many masters' problem discussed earlier.

Although shareholder primacy has been the dominant theory informing corporate law, the past few years have seen some developments in terms of incorporating other stakeholders' concerns in board decision-making. John Ruggie, special representative for the United Nations, outlined a human rights framework which lays out human rights-oriented duties of corporations.[31] In the United States, a few cases in the takeover context have talked about interests of non-shareholder constituencies as one of the aspects to be considered

---

[28] William T. Allen, *Our Schizophrenic Conception of the Business Corporation*, 14(2) CARDOZO L. REV. 265 (1992).

[29] KENT GREENFIELD, THE FAILURE OF CORPORATE LAW 127–30 (The University of Chicago Press 2006). The stakeholder model forms the basis for the corporate social responsibility (CSR) movement. Generally, CSR can be defined as the voluntary pursuit by corporations organised for profit of 'social ends where this pursuit conflicts with the presumptive shareholder desire to maximise profit'. Leo E. Strine, Jr. & Nicholas Walter, *Conservative Collision Course?:The Tension between Conservative Corporate Law Theory and Citizens United*, 100(2) CORNELL L. REV. 358 (2015).

[30] David Millon, *New Directions in Corporate Law: Communitarians, Contractarians, and the Crisis in Corporate Law*, 50 WASH. & LEE L. REV. 1373, 1388 (1993).

[31] John Ruggie, *UN Guiding Principles on Business and Human Rights* U.N. Doc. HR/PUB/11/04 (2011).

by the board. For instance, in the often-cited *Unocal v Mesa Petroleum Co.*,[32] the court observed:

> A further aspect is the element of balance. If a defensive measure is to come within the ambit of the business judgment rule, it must be reasonable in relation to the threat posed. This entails an analysis by the directors of the nature of the takeover bid and its effect on the corporate enterprise. Examples of such concerns may include: inadequacy of the price offered, nature and timing of the offer, questions of illegality, the impact on 'constituencies' other than shareholders (i.e., creditors, customers, employees, and perhaps even the community generally)...[33]

More recently, two cases have re-opened the debate over whether corporate law should deviate from the shareholder primacy norm that seemed, thus far, to have been the accepted view. The first of these cases, *Burwell v. Hobby Lobby*[34] was decided by the US Supreme Court in 2014. In this case, the court seemed to deviate from the strict shareholder primacy view and stated:

> While it is certainly true that a central objective of for-profit corporations is to make money, modern corporate law does not require for-profit corporations to pursue profit at the expense of everything else, and many do not do so. For-profit corporations, with ownership approval support a wide variety of charitable causes, and it is not at all uncommon for such corporations to further humanitarian and other altruistic objectives.[35]

The second case that has prompted a debate about whether corporate law might be deviating from the shareholder primacy norm is the *Citizens United*[36] Case. The *Citizens United* case held that a corporation may make unlimited political expenditures.[37] In this case, the court held that corporations had a right to spend money from general treasury funds in support of political candidates. Influential scholars like Professor Greenfield have argued that the decision was a move

---

[32] (1985) 493 A 2d 946.
[33] (1985) 493 A 2d 946, 955.
[34] 134 S. Ct. 2751 (2014).
[35] 134 S. Ct. 2751, 2771 (2014).
[36] *Citizens United* v. *Federal Election Commission*, 558 U.S. 310 (2010).
[37] *Id.*

away from the shareholder primacy model.[38] According to Professor Greenfield, since the court's reasoning for the ruling was that corporations were 'associations of citizens' with rights of free speech who could be active in the public space, it was a small step from there to then ask corporations to act like real citizens with obligations including social obligations.[39]

However, these views have not gained prominence and shareholder primacy still dominates.

6.1.3 The Middle Ground – Long-Term Shareholder Value Maximization

While the above discussion might suggest that shareholder primacy and stakeholder theory are opposing one another, there is in fact an easy way to reconcile the two – by applying a long-term perspective to the shareholder primacy lens. When one thinks of shareholder interests *in the long term*, one is forced to ensure that all relevant stakeholders that contribute to or interact with the corporations are well taken care of. Happy employees are productive employees. Happy customers become repeat customers. The community or society being happy with a company leads to reputational gains for the firm. This is not an original idea. Recall that even Friedman, seen in some circles as the symbol of everything that is wrong with business, endorsed this view. He even said that expending resources on the community in an area where the corporation operates might be in the 'long-run interest' of the corporation.[40] In fact, this view has even been expressed by the legislature in the UK.

The Companies Act, 2006 (UK) introduced a concept called 'enlightened shareholder value', which takes this long-term view.[41] Although the relevant provision is still grounded in the shareholder primacy model, it states that the board has a duty to have regard to

---

[38] Kent Greenfield, *The Ideological Flip over Shareholder Primacy and Corporate Citizenship*, The CLS Blue Sky Blog (Oct. 19, 2015), http://clsbluesky.law.columbia.edu/2015/10/19/the-ideological-flip-over-shareholder-primacy-and-corporate-citizenship/.

[39] *Id.*

[40] Friedman, *supra* note 10.

[41] The Companies Act, 2006 (UK), s 172. S. 172(1), which introduces this concept, is as follows:

the long-term consequences of any decision and to the interests of non-shareholder constituencies like employees, customers, the external community, and even the environment.[42] The UK Code seems to further emphasise that stakeholder interests should be considered when it says that 'a successful company is led by an effective and entrepreneurial board, whose role is to promote the long-term sustainable success of the company, generating value for shareholders and contributing to wider society'.[43] The upshot of all this is that, although boards have been encouraged to consider the *long term* success of the company and the company's contributions to wider society, both section 172 and language in the UK Code did nothing more than state what directors were already empowered to do. Besides, since it is only shareholders that can sue directors for breach of their duties, there is no incentive in terms of potential liability for directors to change their focus unless investors (rather than stakeholders) push them to.

Similarly, while Delaware law (which I use as a proxy for US law here because it is the state where most corporations are incorporated) does not have such an explicit statement of long-term value, there is nothing in the law stopping directors from using this lens while making decisions.[44] Indeed, the Business Roundtable (consisting of CEOs of

---

Duty to promote the success of the company

(1) A director of a company must act in the way he considers, in good faith, would be most likely to promote the success of the company for the benefit of its members as a whole, and in doing so have regard (amongst other matters) to
   (a) the likely consequences of any decision in the long term,
   (b) the interests of the company's employees,
   (c) the need to foster the company's business relationships with suppliers, customers and others,
   (d) the impact of the company's operations on the community and the environment,
   (e) the desirability of the company maintaining a reputation for high standards of business conduct, and
   (f) the need to act fairly as between members of the company.

[42] *Id.*

[43] UK Code 2018, Principle A, www.frc.org.uk/getattachment/88bd8c45-50ea-4841-95b0-d2f4f48069a2/2018-UK-Corporate-Governance-Code-FINAL.pdf. Previous iterations of the UK Code were silent on the matter.

[44] Most board decisions are protected by the business judgement rule that allows for board discretion as long as some procedural criteria are met.

the top US corporations) articulated such a view in a 'statement on the purpose of the corporation' published in 2019.[45] The statement of the CEOs said that 'while each of our individual companies serves its own corporate purpose, we share a fundamental commitment to all of our stakeholders'. It then specified that the signatories of the statement are committed to servicing customers, employees, suppliers, communities, and *long term*[46] shareholder value. Although this statement made waves both in the popular media and in academic circles, it seems that this stakeholder talk has remained just that – talk – and not actually resulted in changes to internal corporate governance guidelines and arrangements.[47] Putting the hypocrisy aside for a minute, the statement itself tells us that the reason for sticking with a narrow shareholder value maximization paradigm is not really about what the law provides. In fact, Brummer and Strine, in an article to be published in 2022, have gone so far as to argue that the duties that directors are subject to already require them to pay attention to issues of diversity.[48]

However, there is a whole corporate governance ecosystem influencing the incentives that corporations are subject to, even beyond the law. This includes institutional investors, proxy advisors, industry bodies and professional associations, stock exchanges, traditional

---

[45] *Business Roundtable Redefines the Purpose of a Corporation to Promote 'An Economy That Serves All Americans'*, BUSINESS ROUNDTABLE (Aug. 19, 2019), www.businessroundtable .org/business-roundtable-redefines-the-purpose-of-a-corporation-to-promote-an-economy-that-serves-all-americans.

[46] Emphasis mine.

[47] Lucian A. Bebchuk & Roberto Tallarita, *Will Corporations Deliver Value to All Stakeholders?*, 75 VAND. L. REV. (Forthcoming May 2022).

[48] Chris Brummer & Leo E. Strine, Jr., *Duty and Diversity*, 75 VAND. L. REV. 1 (Forthcoming 2022). ['The affirmative obligations underpinning the corporate duty of loyalty, along with the discretion afforded to directors and managers in the exercise of their duties and pursuit of the best interests of shareholders and the corporation, have important implications for corporate Diversity policy. First, the corporation is charged with an expectation of lawful conduct – and Delaware corporate law explicitly identifies legal compliance as a core feature of the duty of loyalty. As such, it requires fiduciaries to ensure corporate compliance strategies exist to assure compliance with key civil rights legislation and antidiscrimination mandates that go to the heart of their operations. Fiduciaries are also not excused from ignoring red flags indicating widespread discrimination; should they do so, not only do companies risk liability accompanying such violations, but directors too face possible derivative suits and liability. Second, the business judgment rule affords directors who view Diversity, Equity, and Inclusion as important values with enormous flexibility to advance such goals, and to do so on firm legal footing as a matter of corporate law.']

media, social media, and the political environment.[49] So, it is not corporate law that needs to be reconciled with diversity and other ESG issues, but rather the corporate governance ecosystem in its entirety. Even Dhir, despite being supportive of legal intervention to improve diversity, acknowledges that 'meaningful change will come only by recognizing the limits of law and bringing into the reform agenda a variety of institutions, organizational structures, and sources of ideas'.[50]

Many institutions within the corporate governance ecosystem have been discussed in earlier chapters of this book (particularly Chapters 3 and 4) and as the discussion in those chapters show, many of these institutions are now paying attention to issues like diversity. Directors are incentivised to prioritise the interests of those who provide capital – investors. However, institutional investors have themselves begun to pressure companies on specific issues like diversity, perhaps in response to social and political pressures.[51] In response to such pressure, coupled with media and societal pressure (being channelled through social media), companies have also started using compensation agreements to prevent or help the company address sexual harassment issues. These movements have also pushed companies to engage in a lot of diversity talk, not dissimilar to the stakeholder talk seen in the Business Roundtable statement, which in most cases was not followed up by action. We also saw, in Chapter 3, how firms that became targets of social media activism tend to respond in haste with some action that they think will assuage the protestors at that point in time. All of this indicates that firms are becoming conscious of the reputational costs (which are reflected in stock prices) of diversity and other social problems.[52] Addressing these issues *ex ante* will help avoid *ex post* costs to shareholders.

---

[49] Dorothy Lund & Elizabeth Pollman, *The Corporate Governance Machine*, 121(8) COLUM. L. REV. (2021).

[50] AARON A. DHIR, CHALLENGING BOARDROOM HOMOGENEITY 280 (Cambridge University Press, 2015).

[51] As Bainbridge muses in his article, the signatories to the Business Roundtable statement 'may be seeking to reposition their companies to take advantage of perceived shifts in consumer and labor demand' and may also be 'trying to head off regulation by progressive politicians'. Stephen M. Bainbridge, *Making Sense of the Business Roundtable's Reversal on Corporate Purpose*, 46 J. CORP. L. 285, 316 (2021).

[52] Mary Billings, April Klein & Crystal (Yanting) Shi, *Investors' Response to the #MeToo Movement: Does Corporate Culture Matter?* (NYU STERN SCHOOL OF BUSINESS, Finance Working Paper No. 764/2021, 2021), https://papers.ssrn.com/sol3/papers.cfm?abstract_id=3466326.

The real problem is not that firms are unaware of this, but rather that they are not addressing diversity, and other issues at the intersection of corporations and society, with the right tools. As a general matter, where there are no legal interventions on diversity and other ESG issues, as Petrin and Choudhury note (harkening back to Friedman's words)[53]:

> ...corporations will be able to ascertain the ethical customs that need to inform their baseline standard and guide their corporate actions based on a requirement to respond to views about corporate responsibility obligations advocated by society; that is, the participants in the relevant markets within which it operates and that represent a consensus in that market. For most corporations, this will involve drawing from views of its consumers, future and current employees, and capital market participants.

However, as discussed in Chapter 4, legal and market initiatives seem to be pointing firms in the wrong direction as far as the diversity issue is concerned. Further, the social media-powered push from stakeholders also seems to focus on numbers rather than systems, as seen in Chapter 3. On the other hand, attention to employee voices, even if they are not the ones amplified by social media, seems to suggest that it is important to focus on the systemic and/or cultural issues that seem to be holding diverse candidates back. Thus, various institutions in the corporate governance ecosystem need to change direction and focus on long-term shareholder value. Additionally, it is also necessary for corporations to take a long-term view and aim to address diversity issues in a manner that brings sustained change and employee satisfaction, rather than immediate plaudits from social media activism. This may mean that corporations forego reputational gains, or even suffer reputational losses, both of which may affect immediate share prices, in the interests of long-term positive impact that will eventually translate into both reputational and financial gains.

Further, in this paradigm of long-term shareholder value maximization, one need not rely on the business case at all. Promoting employee well-being (including the well-being of diverse employees)

---

[53] Martin Petrin & Barnali Choudhury, Corporate Purpose and Short-Termism, in *Comparative Corporate Governance* 22 (Edward Elgar Publishing, 2021).

through good corporate culture, hiring diverse boards and executives to ensure that meritorious candidates who do not fit the usual mould are not overlooked, introducing mechanisms that identify patterns of discrimination, and then rectifying it in the interest of fairness in the corporation, even if it means getting rid of a superstar employee, are all valid means of promoting long-term shareholder value. For instance, a firm that tolerates discrimination and other misconduct from superstar employees might benefit in the present from retaining the superstar employee but will lose out on nurturing a talented pipeline because good employees will vote against bad culture with their feet, that is by simply quitting the company to join competitors that provide a better work culture. Thus, this paradigm can avoid the clash of narrow shareholder value-centric business case for diversity and the stakeholderist arguments about corporations needing to be responsible citizens and eschewing shareholder value.

But one may ask why we should even be considering shareholder value in the long term. Why not just rethink the corporate purpose? Why not validate stakeholderist arguments that the corporation must serve all its stakeholders? Apart from the very real many masters problem, there is a simple and important reason to prioritise shareholder value maximization – shareholder returns and profits are important for the survival and growth of the company. Unless a company is financially healthy, it will not be around to serve stakeholders.[54] Not only this, the more profits there are, the more pie there is to distribute to shareholders and other stakeholders. As Edmans says in his book, we need to think in terms of growing the pie so that there is more for everyone, rather than having a pie-splitting mentality.[55]

---

[54] This assertion is so obvious that it does not need a reference source, but it is so often forgotten that it is useful to point to academics and practitioners who do make this point. See, e.g., Stephen Beer, *ESG Must Learn from the Tech Bubble – Returns Matter*, FINANCIAL TIMES (Aug. 17, 2021), www.ft.com/content/81e04951-b91b-4f40-9253-ebf1bcea18ea. ['History provides many examples of managements focusing on something other than sustainable investment returns, such as the value of their stock options and executive pay, empire building, or political influence. These stories do not usually end well for investors; if shareholder returns are downplayed too far, investors are ill served. Unless a business is sustainable financially it will not be around to exercise responsibility. The prize is found in integrating financial and ESG objectives.']

[55] See generally ALEX EDMANS, GROW THE PIE: HOW GREAT COMPANIES DELIVER BOTH PURPOSE AND PROFIT (Cambridge University Press, 2020).

I should add here that long-term shareholder value should not be seen a model where stakeholders are simply a means to an end. Instead, we should understand that true long-term shareholder value vision can only be realised when stakeholders are seen as partners and sources of ideas.[56] Recall the example of Amazon seeking ideas from its employees, and the example of SpaceX employees being inspired by the mission of the company. In these cases, employees become part of the company's journey.

In reality, both shareholder value maximization and stakeholderism, when construed narrowly, are too extreme to lead us to productive solutions on diversity and other issues where the intersection of corporations and society is brought into sharp focus. Not only this, but the fact that the two extreme models of the purpose of the corporation have no meeting ground has meant that although the stated rationales for board diversity laws and market initiatives in most countries start out as equality and fairness arguments, they eventually morph into the business case because that seems the only way to 'sell' it to companies. In turn, companies have begun to engage in double-speak where they outwardly support these measures and also the business case, while their actions do not reflect any of this.

To solve this issue of double-speak, I would argue that in addition to ensuring that all institutions of the corporate governance ecosystem embracing long-term shareholder value maximization as the corporate purpose, they should also embrace the spirit of open discussion of ideas. For diversity and other ESG issues that are controversial, frank and open discussion from all quarters is the need of the hour. Amongst other things, this openness to different ideas will allow corporate leaders to state their view without fearing extreme backlash. It naturally follows from this that different views should be tolerated, and, even if people make some wrong-headed comments, they should not be demonised (or 'cancelled' to use the trending terms of the day) so long as this is part of a learning process. Besides, a so-called wrong comment may contain the seeds of an innovative solution to diversity issues. In other words, the marketplace of ideas on diversity will

---

[56] This is the substance of what Edmans proposes although he calls it 'pie-growing' mentality rather than long-term orientation. *Id.*, at 213.

suffer because of the uneasiness people feel while talking about diversity issues. As this book has pointed out, the diversity jigsaw is missing many pieces and we need a robust marketplace of ideas to find and add them on to the jigsaw so as to be able to understand the issue fully. This book has found and added some missing piece of the puzzle, but there will be many more and the corporate governance ecosystem should be open to them.

6.2 TOWARDS COMPASSIONATE AND EMPATHETIC CORPORATE GOVERNANCE

One may ask why the board and the CEO would forego financial and reputational gains in the near term to further the long-term interests of the corporation and, in turn, shareholders and other stakeholders. Indeed, this is a valid question. Even if they see the logic of this paradigm of corporate governance, and even if compensation arrangements are tweaked to incentivise long-term value creation, would the CEO, the directors, and C-suite members be willing to face short-term reputational risks by not supporting the cosmetic diversity fixes that social media and other activists seem to call for? The answer to this question is that, as long as there is a genuine commitment to diversity and, more generally, employee well-being, positive information about a firm's culture will eventually percolate out of the firm. It can also be broadcast by the firm itself. To add credibility, firms may seek out third-party certifications on work culture, as Algolia did by commissioning 'Great Place to Work' to survey its employees.[57] A CEO and the directors of a company may eventually become known for the excellent culture that they have fostered. A good example of this is Indra Nooyi, who is credited with introducing 'performance with purpose', which had corporate culture as one of its primary goals.[58] Further, the company will be able to retain talented employees, including diverse ones, and reap the benefits of valuing employee contributions (as we

---

[57] See Chapter 5.
[58] Nooyi herself refers to the 'performance with purpose pivot' as her opus. See Nooyi, 203. For more detail on this, see *Indra K. Nooyi on Performance with Purpose*, BCG (Jan. 14, 2010), www.bcg.com/publications/2010/indra-nooyi-performance-purpose.

saw in the case of Amazon where the idea of Amazon Prime initially came from an employee). If regulators walk back from the current trend of quotas and aspirational quotas (as discussed in Chapter 4) and instead encourage qualitative reporting, companies will be able to showcase innovative firm-specific measures at their firm. These disclosures can be cross-checked by taking note of employee surveys and ratings coming through Glassdoor and even social media channels (so long as the reports are coming from real verifiable employees or former employees of the company).

The next question then is how the board and CEO and other executives can give effect to a paradigm of corporate governance that considers long-term shareholder value. To an extent, the pandemic, and consequent lockdowns, has already directed corporations along this path. As seen in Chapter 5, many measures to help employees, including diverse employees, have already been introduced. But how can the focus on employee well-being and other stakeholder issues be sustained outside of a crisis like the pandemic? Villiers has called for a more compassionate corporate governance model, which, according to her, can be achieved by a retreat from short-termism and by ensuring that there is less distance between the company leadership and employees.[59] In other words, the board and management should listen to employee concerns and ideas through various channels. She also explains that compassion includes: practicing stewardship, listening, empathising, healing, exercising commitment to the growth of people, and building community.[60] She specifically highlights the role of corporate culture in helping leadership build bridges with various stakeholders.[61] The fact that younger millennials and Gen Zers are pushing against hierarchy and instead look for ethical leadership also calls for company strategy, and CEO and other executive behaviour, to embody compassion for others.[62] Although Villiers' proposal already includes empathy, I think the term needs to be emphasised

---

[59] Charlotte Villiers, *Boardroom Culture: An Argument for Compassionate Leadership*, 30(2) Eur. Bus. L. Rev. 253, 262 (2019).

[60] *Id.*, 278. Drawing from Kae Reynolds, *Servant-Leadership – A Feminist Perspective*, 10 IJSL 35–63, 49 (2015).

[61] *Id.*, at 263–65.

[62] *Id.*

more and so I would call for a corporate governance model that under-scores compassion and empathy.[63] I highlight empathy because even directors and executives who are not diverse have the means of learn-ing about the specific problems faced by diverse employees and then working to address them. Of course, this paradigm is meant to also address issues other than diversity (for example, employee issues other than diversity, environmental harms that cause negative effects to communities, etc.), because compassion and empathy are values that can help leadership understand and solve problems of various stake-holders, irrespective of how different their situation is from that of the company leadership. For example, Elon Musk, reflecting on how issues with employees at an earlier company that he founded (Zip2) could have been handled better, said that since the employees don't have all the information that management has, 'you have to put your-self in a position where you say, "Well, how would this sound to them, knowing what they know?"'.[64]

In a way, the pandemic might have exposed company leaders to some problems that were also faced by their employees. For exam-ple, the spread of COVID-19 impacted all classes of people (albeit at different degrees[65]), especially before vaccines were developed. This helped both employees and executives relate to one another, thus resulting in policies that allowed employees leave to care for a family member who was sick. For instance, as Leena Nair, the CEO of Unilever, recounted, she had received news that her mother had been hospitalized due to COVID-19 just before she had to conduct a virtual townhall for employees. So, she 'was forced to be vulnerable with the thousands of colleagues on the call, informing them of the situation and that I wasn't feeling my best'. After finishing the call,

---

[63] The Editorial Board, *Turbulence ahead: New Leaders Required*, FINANCIAL TIMES (Dec. 27, 2021), www.ft.com/content/88b89565-1de9-4579-bb39-b1ee2502acb7. ['The crisis of 2020–21 boosted compassion, communication, and collaboration – once derided as "soft" skills – to the top of the list of leadership traits.']

[64] ASHLEY VANCE, ELON MUSK: HOW THE BILLIONAIRE CEO OF SPACEX AND TESLA IS SHAPING OUR FUTURE 73 (Penguin Random House, 2015).

[65] Middle-aged professionals who could work from home and maintain a semblance of their usual social life on zoom did not suffer in the same ways as the service workers who lost their jobs, the essential workers who were exposed to the risk of infection, and the young people who are more dependent on in-person socialising.

Nair took time off from work to be with her mother in India who eventually passed away.[66]

While being subject to the same personal issues might help company leadership lead with compassion, leaders showing vulnerability in some situations will also help employees relate to them. Interestingly, Nair reflects on how she had believed in sharing challenges with her employees, but never shared personal challenges relating to childcare or other challenges faced at home, perhaps because male colleagues might question her ability to perform at work if she did. These reflections bring to light the 'ideal employee' (discussed earlier in the book) who is supposed to have all their time for work and not have any other issues at home which may require their attention. However, she shared her grief about her mother's passing, Nair notes that she 'realized the most effective way for leaders to bring a sense of purpose, service, compassion, and empathy into the workplace is to be transparent about the challenges in their own lives'.[67] This is a powerful message for leaders – not just women leaders – because the workforce is changing and is one where women, diverse candidates, and even men, will have challenges beyond work which they are not shy to share on social media. Leaders who are able to share their own unique troubles signal that they are willing to redefine the 'ideal worker'. This will encourage employees to voice their concerns without worrying that they will be perceived as incompetent, which in turn means that the company will have the necessary information to enhance employee well-being and retain talent.

However, for compassion and empathy to be sustained beyond the pandemic, and for the stakeholder focus to be better informed and planned for the long term, more investment into understanding the needs of employees and other stakeholders will be required. Specifically for diversity, figuring out the root causes of the problem within the firm and then finding innovating ways (that embody compassion and empathy) will be the way to genuine progress.

---

[66] Leena Nair, *The Soft Stuff Is the Hard Stuff: Leaders Must Show Vulnerability in Uncertain Times*, FORTUNE (Dec. 5, 2021), https://fortune.com/2021/12/05/leaders-must-show-vulnerability-in-uncertain-times-hr-leadership-pandemic-grief-workplace-leena-nair-unilever/

[67] *Id.*

6.3 CORPORATIONS ARE PART OF THE SOLUTION

It is not enough to call for long-term shareholder value as the purpose of the corporation and compassionate and empathetic corporate governance to give effect to it. It is also important for the general public (through social media and otherwise), traditional media, academics and other commentators, regulators, and governments should exercise caution in pushing the 'all corporations are evil' rhetoric. While it is important to hold bad actors to account, a narrative that creates a no-win situation for corporations is bound to result in perverse incentives. Corporate leadership will do the bare minimum to avoid social media backlash, or to stave off regulation, mostly in the form of statements, like what we saw in the wake of #MeToo and BLM without any corresponding actions. Similarly, they will respond to quotas and aspirational quotas (via disclosure requirements) by simply hiring token directors – I use this term to refer to how they are treated by the board rather than their actual qualifications – who are not given important committee roles. In other words, painting corporations as the villains simply pushes them to engage in woke-washing.

Instead, if we recognise that corporations have been responsible for significant innovations that have propelled human progress – the most recent example of this being the quick invention and production of vaccines that combat COVID-19 – we will be able to recognise that corporations might also be able to make social justice innovations both internally and externally where it is relevant to their area of expertise. Incorporating this recognition into policy discussion on diversity and other ESG issues will help bring genuine buy-in from corporations on these issues. As this book has shown, even though the concerns about diversity in the corporation are valid, current solutions that are pushing corporations to the corner are not taking us towards sustained change. Corporations are aware of the need to respond to diversity issues but are being pushed towards woke-washing by various forces. It is time to change the narrative and seek to solve the problem of corporate diversity by giving corporations the agency to find the right solutions for their specific contexts. The same goes for other ESG issues. These innovative firm-specific solutions can help corporations stand out from their peers in social issues. An example of such innovation comes from Lego which is working to make eco-friendly bricks made from recycled plastic bottles.[68] Rather than making commitments and statements on environmental issues, it has sought to contribute by integrating the environmental concerns into its operations and that has resulted in innovation that helps it stand out from its peers. Chapters 3 and 5 provide some ways in which companies can address diversity issues, which would be more effective than simply making commitments about diversity.

6.4 SUMMATION

To tie up the ideas in this chapter, corporate law and the underlying theories that inform it already allow corporate leadership to follow a long-term shareholder value maximization model. In turn, this model allows directors and executives to address issues of diversity (and other ESG issues). However, the entire corporate governance machine should work to allow for this. As this book has shown, various cogs in the corporate governance ecosystem have already begun to echo support for diversity and other societal issues. The problem really lies with the direction that the solutions are pushing corporations towards. It is therefore necessary for all the cogs in the corporate governance machine to actively seek to enrich the marketplace of ideas on how diversity and other issues at the intersection of corporations and society can be addressed.

---

[68] Tom Espiner, *Lego Plans to Sell Bricks from Recycled Bottles in Two Years*, BBC NEWS (June 23, 2021), www.bbc.com/news/business-57575991.

CONCLUSION

Diversity advocates usually list two main goals for corporations needing to be diversified – to bring equality and fairness within the workplace and to bring greater business efficiency. The way I would explain the link between diversity and these two goals is as follows. The logic for the former is that positions of power in corporations should be accessible by meritorious people irrespective of their race, gender, or other characteristic, and the logic for the latter is that businesses will be able to harness the best talent when they get rid of the barriers faced by diverse candidates. There are also arguments about women and other diverse candidates bringing different perspectives to the board or to discussions at other levels of the corporations, but as I explain in Chapter 1, demographic diversity does not necessarily guarantee viewpoint diversity. In fact, this is one of the points that is often missing from many conversations about diversity in the corporation. This is why Chapter 1 set out to define diversity and explain the significance of different types of diversity at various levels of the corporation and clearly flesh out the links between what we mean by diversity and the goals of the diversity project.

Having got the definition of diversity that really is the centrepiece of the corporate diversity jigsaw set up in Chapter 1, the book then discussed diversity in the board and management levels in Chapter 2. The position of the CDO has become increasingly popular in recent times, and I want to reiterate here what I have said in Chapter 2 about this – merely appointing a CDO will not solve diversity issues unless the CDO is given authority and resources to effect change. Not only this, the CEO, board, and top management should be invested in the cultural changes that will need to be brought about (as discussed in Chapter 5) to ensure that there is genuine commitment to diversity. An article in the Financial Times from February 2022 reported that a family law firm had created a position called 'fertility officer'.[1] The position is apparently meant to 'help staff feel more comfortable with talking about planning for a family, pregnancy and fertility problems'.[2] While it is indeed a positive step for organizations to be thinking about issues around planning a family, the same Financial Times article rightly also notes that 'all the champions and policies in the world will fail if the culture is hostile…'.[3] I agree that corporate culture is a vital piece of the corporate diversity jigsaw and have discussed this a little in Chapter 3 and in more detail in Chapter 5. The COVID-19 pandemic and consequent 'work from home' policies have contributed significantly to changing some aspects of corporate culture. For instance, since it became obvious that work could indeed be performed from home (in many types of jobs), and when both men and women of the workplace were working remotely, perhaps it will be easier for companies to see that employees (particularly women) who have childcare responsibilities should be able to avail of flexible work options and still get the job done. Corporate culture is broader than work flexibility and includes a range of issues, as detailed in Chapter 5. A company can be truly diverse only when its culture enables all its employees to thrive. At the board level, a culture that allows all directors to contribute effectively is important. Without such a culture, even if directors bring diverse perspectives to the table, the company will be unable to benefit from these perspectives. Chapter 5 also touches upon the role of recruitment agencies and their role in incentivising cultural change in corporations.

A relatively new phenomenon that is an important piece of the corporate diversity jigsaw is social movements that are leveraging the power of social media to push for social change in corporations. Chapter 3 unpacks the impact of #MeToo and BLM on diversity in corporations and argues that both corporations and stakeholders

---

[1] Emma Jacobs, *Is Fertility a Topic for the Workplace?*, Financial Times (Feb. 22, 2022), www.ft.com/content/9aff3f16-c962-4aad-8c1e-123a852c5ca1.

[2] *Id.*

[3] *Id.*

should be focusing on sustained improvements rather than short-term fixes. This is just the dawn of activism on social media. There will be a lot more in future and the issues identified in the chapter will be relevant not only to diversity but also to other social issues that become the subject of social media activism.

At a policy level, this book, and specifically Chapter 4, has argued that laws that mandating a certain number of diverse candidates on company boards are ineffective and that disclosure laws that focus on numerical targets are also result in more costs than benefits. Instead, the focus should be on incentivising firm-specific innovations in the diversity space. In fact, just as I was finishing work on this book, a County Superior Court in Los Angles, California, provided summary judgment, upholding a challenge to the California board diversity quota law, discussed in Chapter 4.[4] Although the focus of this book is not on the constitutional issues vis-à-vis diversity quota laws in a specific jurisdiction, the decision opens with some sage advice that is pertinent here[5]:

> When faced with a problem, the immediate temptation is to employ the most obvious and direct solution. In most cases, it isn't even fair to call this impulse a 'temptation'. It's just a normal and sound approach to life. But sometimes there are constraints which call for additional care. This is one of those times.

In my opinion, the 'constraints' against a diversity quota law are not only constitutional but, as this book has argued in Chapter 4, are also obvious when a careful cost–benefit analysis of diversity quotas is conducted. The better alternative is firm-specific solutions. Chapter 5, which focuses on culture within the company and at the board and

---

[4] *Crest* v. *Padilla*, LA Super. Ct. Case No. 20STCV37513 (Sept. 30, 2020). The decision states, in relevant part, as follows:

> If demographically homogenous boards are a problem, then heterogenous boards are the immediate and obvious solution. It that doesn't mean the Legislature can skip directly to mandating heterogenous boards. The difficulty is that the Legislature is thinking in group terms. But the California Constitution protects the right of individuals to equal treatment. Before the Legislature may require that members of one group be given certain board seats, it must first try to create neutral conditions under which qualified individuals from any group may succeed. That attempt was not made in this case.

[5] *Id.*

management levels, outlines a number of possible best practices and solutions that companies might adopt, to the extent that it suits them.

Ultimately, as set out in Chapter 6, all the actors and institutions in the corporate governance ecosystem will need to make efforts to ensure that diverse people are supported within the corporation. This chapter also clarifies that theories of the corporation and of corporate governance that inform current legislation regulating companies in most jurisdictions already allow for companies to address issues like diversity. Yet, a shift in this direction is possible only if the importance of diversity is understood and accepted by the relevant actors and institutions. For this, it will be important for different views and ideas on the issue of diversity in corporations to be welcomed both at a policy level and internally in companies.

Just like diversity legislation and regulations, it is possible that well-meaning firm-specific solutions might turn out to be ineffective. However, unlike legislation and regulations, companies will have the flexibility to assess and rework these solutions as and when needed. Thus, frank and open channels of communication within the organization will be important. At the same time, law and regulations should avoid forcing one size fits all solutions like quotas or quantitative disclosures on companies. If they do, they will discourage companies that are attempting genuine change. Similarly, social media campaigns may present both challenges and opportunities for companies that are truly committed to diversity. Chapter 3 has offered some insights to companies in terms of how those challenges should be navigated, without resorting to short-termism.

Although I have discussed many significant pieces of the corporate diversity jigsaw in this book, there are other relevant issues that future work by myself and others should address. Pay disparity is a challenge that companies should consider and address as part of their efforts. This book has briefly touched on some relevant issues including the fact that diverse candidates may sometimes not be given the same perks and benefits that members of the majority group in any given company receive. Pay disparity is an important issue, and more work on how this is to be resolved is required.

Representations of diverse CEOs and board members who are women or persons from minority groups or both in the popular media is another important issue. For instance, media reports about a new CEO often emphasise the gender[6] and race[7] of a CEO when they are a woman or from a minority group. Even if this attention to demographic aspects is with a view to celebrate the diverse appointment, it can take away from the merit of the candidate in question. This is a relatively under-researched area and almost never focused on in discussions about how diversity within corporations can be improved. Somewhat relatedly, even though media stories and popular culture rarely recognise this, corporations could be a force for the good and, with the right incentives, could provide innovative solutions to diversity and other social issues. This is a point I have already made in various chapters (especially Chapters 3–5) of the book, but the issue of society's view of corporations might be affecting how corporations are regulated is worth studying, both in the context of diversity regulation and beyond.

Technology is changing the way in which corporations operate and the way in which various stakeholders interact with corporations. Chapter 3 has outlined how social movements, powered by social media, have impacted corporations, and some ideas on how corporations can leverage technology to address diversity issues. However, more detailed research on how corporate governance practices can be strengthened by the use of technology will be important not only for addressing diversity issues in the corporation but also for strengthening corporate governance more generally.

On a practical level, there are suggestions and ideas about how to address diversity issues throughout this book. I hope that companies will draw from the ideas presented here to devise solutions to match their specific workforce needs. Many of the issues discussed in this book, the 'pieces of the corporate diversity jigsaw' as I have been calling them, are relevant to all employees to varying degrees and companies that being resolving these issues will be able to attract and retain the best talent.

---

[6] See generally The Rockefeller Foundation, *Does the Media Influence How We Perceive Women in Leadership?*, www.rockefellerfoundation.org/wp-content/uploads/100x25_MediaLanguage_report1.pdf.

[7] For instance, Indra Nooyi recounts how the press tended to use pictures of her in a saree when they ran articles about her taking over as the CEO of PepsiCo. This was despite the fact that she had not worn a saree to work in the past twenty-five years. See INDIRA NOOYI, MY LIFE IN FULL: WORK, FAMILY, AND OUR FUTURE 194 (Hachette, 2021).

INDEX

Footnotes are indicated by n. after the page number.

www.ingramcontent.com/pod-product-compliance
Ingram Content Group UK Ltd.
Pitfield, Milton Keynes, MK11 3LW, UK
UKHW020454010325
455719UK00016B/580